The Perfect Mirror

By

Robert F. McKellar

ISBN: 1-4033-0024-0 (Ebook)
ISBN: 1-4033-0025-9 (Softcover)

Library of Congress Control Number: 2002090248

This book is printed on acid free paper.

Printed in the United States of America
Bloomington, IN

1stBooks - rev. 4/26/02

Dedication

"To Jan. Do not go into that dark, dark night but she did."

PROLOGUE

New Year's Eve, 1959

This story was inspired by events occurring between 1958 and 1964. Some names have been changed to protect the author.

> *"The first prison I ever saw had inscribed on its perimeter wall, 'Cease to Do Evil; Learn to Do Well.' But inasmuch as the inscriptive message was on the outside of the wall, the prisoners could not read it."*

George Bernard Shaw.

News Item. <u>**San Francisco Chronicle**</u>, **January 1, 1959**

Quentin Aide Held In Smuggling Case

Sean Sullivan, 33, a correctional counselor at San Quentin, was arrested yesterday on a charge of smuggling contraband-mace into the prison. The spice has for years been on the prison taboo lists because inmates use it as an intoxicant by mixing it with hot water, tea, or coffee.

"I don't know what the clinical action is, but they get dizzy on it," said Associate Warden Lou Nelson. "It's the same with nutmeg. It's surprising what you can do with mother's spice cabinet."

Sullivan, who lives at 3030 Steiner Street, San Francisco, was followed to a San Rafael grocery store yesterday and later searched when he reported in for his shift at the prison.

Four packets of spice were found in his pockets, and under questioning, he admitted carrying in nasal inhalers on other occasions, Nelson said. Sometimes inhalants are also dissolved in hot water and used as intoxicants.

Sullivan has been under suspicion for four of the eight months he has worked at the prison, according to Marin County District Attorney William O. Weissich.

News Item. <u>**San Francisco Examiner**</u>, **January 1, 1959**

Quentin Smuggling Charged—Counselor Two Inmates Held

A prison counselor was arrested at San Quentin yesterday afternoon for smuggling an intoxicating spice inside the gates. "He had intended to sell it to the very convicts whose problems he was supposed to help solve," said Associate Warden W.D. Achuff.

He is Sean Sullivan, 33, a polio-crippled employee of the California Department of Corrections. He walks with difficulty on two canes and, according to Achuff, is estranged from his wife and burdened with high medical bills.

Sullivan, whose home is in San Francisco at 3030 Steiner Street, was booked at the Marin County Jail in San Rafael on a misdemeanor charge of carrying contraband into the prison.

Achuff said Sullivan had on his person four packages of mace, a fragrant reddish oriental spice. When added to hot water or coffee it becomes an intoxicant.

The associate warden said Sullivan had been suspected of smuggling mace into prison for about a month. Sullivan went about his normal duties yesterday morning. At lunch time he left the prison. Unknown to him, however, he was followed by a prison officer. In San Rafael, Sullivan was seen entering a grocery store where he purchased the four packs of mace.

Sullivan returned to the prison without declaring the contraband at prison check-in. If convicted, Sullivan could face up to a maximum of six months in jail and a $500 fine.

"This could have developed into a big business," an observer remarked. "The prisoners are allowed to buy instant coffee and drink it in their cells with hot water from the taps.

"They could add the mace and get drunk, or at least get a delightful glow."

Sullivan has been a state employee since November 1958. He was transferred to San Quentin last April from the Department of Corrections Medical Facility at Vacaville.

His duties were to interview convicts due to appear before the Adult Authority and to counsel inmates on personal problems.

News Item. <u>San Francisco Chronicle</u>, January 6, 1959

Prison Smuggling Suspect To Plead

San Quentin Prison counselor Sean Sullivan, 33, accused of smuggling mace into prison, is scheduled to plead to the charge in Marin Municipal Court next Tuesday.

Sullivan, who lives in San Francisco, is free on $3,150 bail. He was arraigned in Marin Municipal Court yesterday on two counts, smuggling the mace into prison and possession of mace.

San Quentin officials said mace is contraband at the prison because inmates use the spice as an intoxicant.

CLANG! THE STEEL GATE HAMMERED OPEN. THE ICY confines of a maximum security prison were now a reality, the indifference, the blank stares.

"Now I know why they call it the slammer," I said aloud to no one in particular, the guard's baton poking me ever so slightly in the back and directing me where I should step next. "Oh, my God! What have I done!"

My mind dropped into a haze of utter despair, a wave of helplessness washing away any ability to think clearly. I stood stripped of my humanity, self-dignity, and any form of freedom bestowed on the lowest form of animals. This was the pit of human despair. The climb out of this shithole would take many years.

Another locked gate banged open, its steel heavy configuration causing friction-grinding on the mooring.

"Sorry Sullivan, we have to put you in here." The deputy patted me on the shoulder and gave me a slight nudge with his duty baton.

"Don't hurt me—I'm a human being just like you." Thoughts of John Merek, the elephant man, chased into the public urinals of London, flashed before me in surrealistic color—all of it bleak.

"We're not going to hurt you," the deputy replied.

I stumbled into a large barn-like holding cell. The windows of my soul surveyed a room with two upper and lower bunks. Eight or nine guests of Marin County were huddled in one corner whispering. At least I'll have a place to sleep tonight I thought.

I sat on a bench alone, a study in misery. I pleaded to the heavens. "Dear God. If you will forgive the little jokes I've played on Thee, I will forget this big joke you played on me." Shadows of useless wars continued to escalate my emotions.

An effeminate boy of eighteen approached me. Out of the side of his mouth he asked, "What are in you in for, buddy?"

"Smuggling," I croaked, then waved him away in disgust. "I'm not your buddy." My cellmate slithered back to his friends.

"What's wrong with you guys?" I yelled. "At least I didn't rape anyone. I am not a pedophile." I knew sex beefs were not highly regarded by the brethren.

I scanned the room, perceiving an assortment of street people, the true survivors of society. Gold ear rings, clips on noses and tongues, and a variety of tattoos in various colors of the rainbow adorned their bodies. They had desecrated God's perfection.

No sleep tonight. "You can have the bunk," I muttered to the big guy with a gold ear ring. In my wildest dreams, I had never expected to celebrate New Year's Eve in the Marin County jail.

"You can make your phone call, Sullivan," the deputy announced. Clang! Another gate opened.

"Hello, Ma. How are you?" I said, as if simply passing the time of day.

"Where are you?" she asked. "I've been holding dinner for you."

My voice choked with spasms of incoherent speech. "Sorry. I'm in jail." I sighed.

"You're what!" Her shriek could be heard across the Golden Gate Bridge.

I replied in staccato bursts. "I've been arrested and charged with four felony counts of smuggling contraband into the joint. I don't know what to do. Can you call Tom Reade and ask him about bail? Can you bail me out, please?"

The line went dead. Then a soft, "Okay Sean. I'll call Tom and do what I can."

"I'm so sorry," I murmured, cradling the phone. I struggled for air, experiencing another convulsion. The deputy escorted me to a large office where he gave me forms to complete.

"Take your time," he suggested. I would be spared the holding pen for a few minutes.

The documents were demographics requiring detailed information concerning my life. Where I had lived for the last twenty years, education, family, jobs and a long biography. A matrix requested a short paragraph written with the left hand and then with the right. The thought of fleeing to a country without an extradition treaty appealed to me. I saw it in the movies. An inner voice sighed, "Go to Brazil. Go."

After filling out the forms in slow motion, I was escorted by the deputy back to the zoo with its gargoyle collection of characters. Once again I sat with my back to the wall facing my fellow inmates. To my relief they declined to socialize. Why are they staring at me? I thought. I felt like fresh meat on the Serengeti Plains of Africa.

My eye caught a television set placed high in one corner of the holding cell. Hooray! "Amos an Andy"—my favorite. My mood brightened for a few minutes as I ignored the snake pit.

An hour had passed when the jailer appeared at the gate. The deputy spoke the sweetest sounds ever heard by the criminal mind. "Okay, Sullivan. You made bail."

"So long fella. See ya'," the guy with the gold thing in his nose yelled.

"Oh no you won't," I responded.

I signed more papers in the front office. Deputy Cunningham handed me my belt. Suicide had not occurred to me. "We'll give you a lift back to the joint. I understand your car is in the employee parking lot," he said. The cool night air bathed me in freedom. I wanted to take the next missile to the moon.

The deputy gave me a ride back to the joint and left me at the main gate. Next to a correctional officer stood Derek Neilson, Associate Warden of San Quentin, hands on hips, grinning from ear to ear. "We've been expecting you, Mr. Sullivan," he smirked, seeming like a cobra preparing to strike. "So you made bail. So fast. You must have connections," he said. I knew silence to be the better part of survival.

Another CO appeared out of the darkness. They walked me to my car. One in front. One in back.

I had no plans to make a run for it as my headlights guided me to the outer gate. Neilson ran forward yelling, "Your lights! Your lights!" Banging on the sign posted at the gate with his two-foot baton, he presented a Keystone cop tableau. I almost laughed aloud as "Lights Out" in big bold letters came into view.

The CO smiled knowingly as he waved me through the last gate. I drove in the darkness through the village of San Quentin. Rivulets of perspiration ran down my face until I could hardly see the road. Passing the Marin Rod and Gun Club, I turned on my headlights as I gunned the car to Highway 101.

A few minutes later I inserted the key into the latch of my apartment, turning it half way, hoping Ma wouldn't be home. She sat in a darkened part of the living room. An eerie glow from a single light created flickering shadows on the ceiling. A moth danced a around the light bulb.

I sat on the sofa, suppressing yet another spasm of tears. I looked at my mother and could say only, "I'm sorry." Silence filled the little theater flat. I waited for her reaction.

"What happened?" she asked.

"I'm guilty. Burn the mark of Cain on my forehead." I offered an apology. I felt relieved. Confession is better than a bowel movement.

The expected recriminations did not come. Only the silence of a loving mother who gave birth in pain to a son now living a life of shame. Ma understood the black night of my soul.

When I finally stopped crying she said, "You'd better go to bed. It's getting late. You've had a full day." We never hugged. We are not a demonstrative family. I never touched my mother until the day she died twenty-four years later.

I did not dream the dream of dreams. I could not conjure up Cassie. She did not hold me in her arms. No warm embrace. My nighttime reveries turned instead to recollections of a bosun mate.

Months earlier, I had interviewed a retired Navy man who was in for murdering his wife. He had discovered his beloved sleeping with a friend. Six months of lonely sea duty guided his hand.

We sat in my office at San Quentin. The window offered a panoramic view of San Pablo Bay. In the distance a line of navy destroyers drifted by. I waved towards the flotilla.

"I forgot—today's the beginning of fleet week. They're early this year. It's usually held in October," I said. His gaze fixed on the battle-gray ships churning past. I looked into moist eyes.

"I served in the United State Navy," he said. My client then jumped to attention, giving one last salute to memories passing in review. He lingered far beyond the time I typically allotted prisoners.

Sleep continued to elude me. My thoughts focused on the patients of the California Medical Facility and the inmates of San Quentin. I dredged up recollections of my experiences.

The drug dealer who spoke so eloquently regarding the joys of marijuana and coke; the artist who painted his escape; the truck driver who beat his son to death; the gambler whose wife died in surgery; the naked inmate who read the rules finding freedom; Black Fridays, six executions; conversations with my seducer whose eyes glared, "When will you become a mistake like me?"

The first light of day streaked through the blinds awakening me to a day of depression. The first day of the rest of my life. My mother's voice called out, "Sean. Tom Reade is on the phone." I rubbed the sleep out of my eyes as I reached for the phone.

"Hello."

"Sullivan. I want to see you at in my office at eight thirty a.m. sharp on Monday. Your arraignment is scheduled for ten a.m."

1

"CIGARETTES, WHISKEY AND WILD WILD WOMEN"

THE FIRST WEEK OF MARCH 1956. PORTLAND, Oregon was experiencing another snow fall. Autos, fitted with chains of all kinds, were clanking along through the darkness—those that were moving, that is. Headlights punched eerie holes in the fog as the winds from the Columbia Gorge increased the hazards of driving.

Many people considered the City of Roses a great place to raise a family. Oregonians enjoyed a comfortable lifestyle, allowing the good times to roll-fodder for the nostalgia craze of the coming nineties.

I was the sort of person who, being used to major hardships, expects not-so-major comforts by way of social compensation. Yeah, that's me. You bet. By way of example, it goes something like this: I would accept the rigors of a four berth cabin on the Trans-Siberian railroad from Beijing China to Helsinki, Finland, but from the land of the Eiffel Tower to gay Vienna I'd spend my last ruble on the Orient Express. Is this reasoning a bit lopsided? Maybe. But that's me.

I had just settled into my new "digs" near downtown Portland where I shared a fifth floor apartment with a newly acquired friend. The concept of living with someone else was difficult to get used to, but the reasoning was sound. We both wanted to cut expenses. Phil Downey worked as an apprentice hair dresser and agreed to share the apartment and expenses, including food, rent and sometimes girls. Soon thereafter, however, I realized my mistake when he revealed himself as a party-loving womanizer.

A few nights after we settled in, Downey, restless and bored with TV, suggested a party. Recalling my monk-like existence of the six previous years, I said, "Yeah, let's do it."

The following Saturday night, four young men in a variety of costumes sporting red, green, or blue hair do's, knocked at our door. They were of the opposite persuasion. I had anticipated a bevy of beauties invading our happy home. Socializing with people who flaunted a rainbow of dyed hair boggled my mind.

1

During the festivities of the evening, Downey relieved himself on the steam heater in the presence of my friend, Eve Brown. The next morning I said, "Phil, I think we'd better make other plans. I prefer a more traditional lifestyle."

A few days later, Eve came to my rescue. "Sean, the landlady told me there is a vacancy on the third floor. It is a small apartment. I don't think you'll be happy with Phil." I agreed.

I moved my things to a furnished three room corner apartment on the third floor overlooking a park. The living room was adorned with torn curtains and a Murphy bed at one end. An old divan completed the dated early Salvation Army decor.

Fading water colors depicting sailing ships and seascapes hung on each wall. My prized possessions, two hand carved Javanese heads made of jetta wood from the Dutch East Indies, sat on an all purpose table. They gazed out the windows as silent sentinels of something, maybe nothing.

I had recently finished a two and half year tenure as a hospital counselor at the Eastern Oregon Tuberculosis Hospital in The Dalles, Oregon. When the institution converted to a psychiatric facility, I proved unequal to the necessary adjustment. The hospital now required a masters' degree in psychiatric social work. Too lazy to pursue graduate work, I resigned my job and moved to Portland. I soon found a position as a counselor in the Portland Office of Vocational Rehabilitation.

In March of 1956, Frank Jennings, a former classmate at the University of Portland, threw a surprise birthday party for me at my apartment. There I met Miss Cassie Buzbie of Boise, Idaho.

She stood beside her cousin in a crisp blue blouse over stonewashed jeans. Auburn-haired with round white shoulders, like in the Renaissance paintings, she had the look of an eighteenth century beauty. She had a full face graced with high cheekbones and blue eyes framed with dark lashes and brows. Her expression was one of chronic trust.

A happy person, Cassie radiated joy throughout the room each time she laughed—a trait that soon captured my heart. She seemed ill at ease standing alone by the door. Everybody seemed to know everybody at the no-host affair. Despite my low self esteem, I threw caution to the wind and introduced myself.

"Hello," I croaked. "My name is Sean Sullivan. What's yours?"

"Hi, I'm Cassie Buzbie," she offered her hand.

"May I get you something to drink?" I suggested, shaking her hand briefly.

"Thank you," Cassie replied. "How about a beer?"

"Yes, of course." I tried to balance myself as I poured a beer into the only high stem champagne glass we had.

"They tell me it's your birthday. Happy birthday. Nice party," she bubbled.

"Thank you. Last week I mentioned to Jennings that I was turning thirty today. This affair took me by complete surprise. I had contemplated going to a movie tonight."

"What do you do?" Cassie asked. A shadowy smile wrinkled her features.

"I'm a vocational rehabilitation counselor for the State of Oregon," I announced.

"But what do you do?" she repeated.

I elaborated. "After graduation from the University of Portland in 1949, I taught English and social studies for a year in Spray, Oregon." As an aside I added, "Somebody poisoned Fritze, our bird-dog…Then I found a job with the county welfare office in Grants Pass, Oregon. Now, I interview physically and mentally handicapped people who apply for the Disability Freeze under the new Social Security laws."

Cassie, always the good listener, invited more of my verbal meandering with her eyes.

I went on. "This week I interviewed a client who was lifting heavy furniture up a steep flight of stairs with his son. Orthopedic specialists documented the man's alleged bad back. He received his first Social Security Disability check several months later."

"Sounds interesting," Cassie said. "I'm a first year student at Boise State College. Spring vacation came early this year, so I'm visiting my cousin Thelma."

"What courses are you taking?" I asked.

"I'm interested in art and drama," she answered.

I nodded. "Me too. I enjoy the arts, especially the stage. I try go to as many events as I can afford. I've seen Iturbe, Hoffman, Heifitz, Don Cossack choir, Templeton and others in concert." Boy, if that doesn't impress her nothing will, I thought.

"I won several awards in the Scholastic Art contests and had a small part in a play last summer at the college," she countered. A lull appeared in the conversation. Cassie appeared to be losing interest in me when Thelma joined us.

Her cousin quickly deduced my attraction to Cassie. Thelma felt a deep sense of responsibility to her young cousin. Cassie would return to Boise soon and then her cousin could breathe a sigh of relief.

Thelma discussed her family at some length. Her people were the salt of the earth—mostly farmers, truck drivers and small storekeepers. Self-sufficiency was a way of life. Steve Harris, Thelma's husband, drove a truck on long hauls across the country. He didn't come home for days at a time.

"I see you people have introduced yourselves to each other." Jenkins appeared out of nowhere. A tall athletic fellow with an outgoing personality, he fancied himself the occasional matchmaker. He took pleasure in the relationship he perceived blossoming between me and Cassie.

"Yes, we have," I replied

"Sean and I went to college together," Jenkins said. Thelma rejoined us with a vodka Collins in hand. "We had some good times at PU as we called it in those days. Fight, fight, purple and white," Jenkins continued. A rah-rah college boy at heart, he postured in a cheerleader stance. Alcohol dictated the humor of the evening.

"Would you care for another drink, Thelma?" I asked.

"Yes. I'll get it." She turned and headed towards the bar, then did a one-eighty and headed back. "We're going home Cassandra," she called out. Thelma started to grab Cassie by the arm.

"It's only ten o clock," I protested. I wanted companionship. My first marriage had ended in the summer of 1950. Since June had refused to divorce me, I went through the proceedings in October of 1952.

"Yes, stay awhile. The night is young and you are so beautiful," Jenkins added. Taking Thelma by the hand, he danced her around the room. Although not susceptible to Thelma's charms, Jenkins wanted to give me more time with Cassie. He had noticed our frequent eye contact.

"I'll be glad to take Cassie home, Thelma. I have tire chains on the car. I've driven in snow storms worse than this," I said.

"Absolutely not! Cassie is going home with me," she declared with a grimace. Teeth clenched, she grabbed Cassie's arm and half dragged her to the door. Looking back at me, Thelma said, "Thank you for an interesting evening. Perhaps we can get together some other time."

"Yes. Maybe we can," I sighed.

"See you, Sean," Cassie winked. The girls disappeared through the door.

"So long, ladies! Until we meet again," Jenkins hollered after our guests. He became Cyrano de Bergerac posturing a slight bow. A drink or two released his inhibitions. He turned to me. "Hey, Sean, what do you think of her?" He bubbled, "She's your type."

"Nice girl," I replied. "I like her. Damn! I didn't get her phone number. I sure would like a date."

"I bet you would, you old dog," Jenkins said. He whirled toward the bar muttering aloud, "All right men. This is your captain speaking."

The next morning Cassie phoned me. "Would you like to go to a movie some night?" I asked.

"Sure, if I'm not baby sitting. I'm going back to Boise next week. The spring semester starts soon."

"There is a great movie at the Paramount this weekend. It's been nominated best movie of the year," I persisted.

"I don't know, maybe. I'll check with Thelma. Call me tomorrow."

"Okay. See you." I started to cradle the phone. "What's your phone number?" I yelled.

The next morning soft lapis blue crept through the living room window shades. I would not have chosen to be anywhere else on earth. Of all the women in the world, Cassie was the one who would make me happy. I phoned her several days later.

"Why don't you come over here tonight?" she asked. "You can help me watch the kids."

"Oh, I'm not good with children." I could not disguise my feelings. "Maybe some other time," I added.

"Now, Sean, you'll like them. They go to bed early," she cajoled. Cassie percolated like a tea pot beginning to whistle. "Come over about six.."

"Okay." Putting down the phone, an old cowboy ditty came to mind. To the world in general and no one in particular I sang, "Cigarettes And Whiskey And Wild Wild Women, They'll Drive you Crazy, They'll Drive you Insane."

That night Cassie opened the front door. I saw two small children playing in the living room. "This is Chris and this is DeDe," she said in introduction. In a stage whisper she continued, "Her real name is Darlene but she likes to be called DeDe."

"Hi, kids." I tried the friendly approach.

The little boy took one look at me and spit out, "You walk funny."

"Chris!" Cassie yelled. Her face flushed a beet red.

"Oh, don't worry Cassie. Children's remarks don't bother me. I only resent the stupid things said to me by adults." I wanted to put her at ease. Squatting down, I looked straight at Chris. "I have a birth defect in my lower spine," I explained.

He turned and walked towards his sister. I knew I could not satisfy his curiosity. Cassie and I exchanged a few pleasantries.

"I wanna play cards," Chris yelled.

"Quiet, Chris. Maybe Sean doesn't want to play cards," Cassie countered.

"I don't care, I wanna play cards," he demanded.

"Me too," DeDe added.

Spending my first date with Cassie playing cards with a nine year old boy and his eleven year old sister was not my idea of "Some Enchanted Evening."

"I'm sorry, Sean." Cassie appeared to be ill at ease.

"Oh, that's okay," I sighed. I anticipated a long night. Much to my everlasting joy, a thorough search of the house failed to produce a deck of cards.

"Where are they, you guys?" Cassie demanded.

"In the back yard. I think the goat ate them," Chris volunteered.

"Chris forgot to bring them in the house," DeDe tattled. Sibling rivalry took over and the two wrestled for a few minutes.

"Let's play Monopoly," Cassie suggested.

"I'll get the board," Chris yelled. He ran to a cabinet. Oh boy, how am I going to survive the evening? I mused to myself.

"Do you like Monopoly?" Cassie queried.

"Sure," I said. I hoped my face was expressionless. A card table materialized. The fixings for a game of Monopoly appeared out of nowhere. All eyes were on Cassie as she counted the play money. Chris and DeDe tallied their allotment. Never trust an adult.

"I'm first," shrilled Chris.

"I wanna be first," whined DeDe in response.

"Come on now. You guys are making a bad impression on Sean," pleaded Cassie.

"Who cares?" Chris responded. He made a face. I stuck my tongue out at him.

The evening crawled by minute by agonizingly slow minute. I tried to appear happy. Teaching young people in a school room environment is different from playing games with children, I noted. The possibility of a midnight kiss followed by a lasting friendship spurred me to greater efforts. Much to my surprise, DeDe and Chris eventually began to accept me. Before the evening ended I had earned the honorary title of "Uncle Sean."

I wanted to yell, "I'm not your uncle!" Instead, I announced, "Oh my. It's almost nine o'clock." I made a big show of looking at my watch. "Time to go to bed, kids. Chris, you first in the bathtub." My patience was rewarded.

"I don't wanna go to bed," whined Chris.

"Me too," echoed DeDe.

The usual childish arguments ate ten minutes off the clock. A few minutes later Cassie stood in the doorway declaring, "They're in bed at last." She sat down next to me on the divan. "How have you been? I enjoyed your birthday party the other night. Tell me more about yourself." She moved closer to me.

After a few minutes of casual conversation the front door blew open. Thelma staggered into the living room. Cassie jumped to her feet smoothing the folds of her skirt. "I didn't expect you home this early."

"Obviously." Thelma sneered as she approached us, her speech slurred with alcohol. She pushed me aside and sprawled on the sofa between Cassie and I.

"Well, I guess I'd better be going home." I said, extricating myself from the sofa. The gig is up for tonight, I thought.

"It's early, Sean. Why don't you stay awhile. Have some more coffee." Cassie sparkled enthusiasm.

"No thanks." I started to leave. "I really should be going." I could not hide my disappointment.

"It's snowing hard outside," Thelma mumbled, ignoring Cassie's gestures to me.

"I'll call you again if you don't mind," I said.

"Sure," Cassie escorted me to the door. Thelma stared at my retreating form. No good night kiss. No hug. I squeezed Cassie's hand as I disappeared into a mist of snow.

2

"GOODBYE TO THE PAST"

THE PHONE RANG THE NEXT NIGHT AS I WAS throwing the remains of a pasty-tasting TV dinner into the garbage can. "Hi, Gloria. How are you?" We were just friends, but I had other ideas.

"I'm fine. What's new with you?" she asked. "Are you doing anything?"

"Nothing much. Just sitting here." I told her my latest joke.

Gloria ignored my attempts at humor. "Eve told me you met a girl at your birthday party. Sorry I couldn't come, but I had a date," she said.

"Yeah, I know…How about I buy you a cup of coffee at at Mannings after work tomorrow? Your company is bound to be more entertaining than the tube."

I had met Gloria soon after she graduated from high school in Bend, Oregon. She then moved to Portland where she found work at the Meier & Frank department store. She worked with Eve Brown and Lillian Karczynski in the advertising department. In those days we knew Lillian as Pete.

George Champion, a friend from high school days, had introduced me to Eve Brown when I was hospitalized years ago. I thought she was his girl and therefore not fair game.

The phone rang again. Wow, I'm sure getting popular, I thought. "Hi, Eve. What's new?. Why don't you come down to my place and we'll catch up on the gossip."

"Okay. I'm on my way," she said.

"Sorry you missed the party. Gloria didn't show either. She had a date. It turned out to be an interesting evening," I said when she arrived.

"I'm sorry I missed it too. Phil tells me you met a girl. What's her name?"

"Cassie. I helped her baby-sit Thelma's kids last night. Thelma's husband is a truck driver so he's away three or four days at a time. I get the impression Thelma likes to party," I said.

"Why not? I enjoy having fun," she said somewhat defensively.

"But she's married," I said, revealing my sense of morality.

"Well, I don't know the lady but everybody gets lonely sometimes," Eve countered.

"Yeah, I know." I glanced at the Javanese heads in the living room. They glowered in return. I changed the subject. "Sorry I don't have any dessert to offer," I apologized.

"That's all right, Sean. Let's go to the living room," she replied. Balancing a coffee cup in one hand, I followed her. I turned the heads as I sat in the nearest chair. I repeated the sad tale of Koos Bossilaar, my mother's second husband.

"Ma asked me pick up Koos at work after school. His wife in Rotterdam had learned of their marriage and reported him to the U.S. Immigration Service. The lawyer said bigamy. Koos told Ma his wife had been killed in an air raid, or so he had been informed by neighbors. Also during the war, his brother and sister were executed by the Germans as spies and buried in the same grave."

I continued, "Ma was happy married to Koos. They loved to dance. You know my father beat my mother from time to time."

"I don't believe your mother likes me," Eve said. "Remember those nights when we sat in front of the fireplace and she would yell from her bedroom, 'Take that girl home!'?"

"Yeah, sorry about that. I don't think she likes any girl I bring home." I blushed. I changed the subject and we used up the afternoon talking about Phil.

Early the next morning, I busied myself with a variety of small household chores. I phoned Cassie and made a date for dinner and a movie that evening. A halo circled the late winter sun when I rang the doorbell at six.

Cassie opened the door with her usual smile. Dressed in a plaid skirt, wool sweater and two-toned loafers, her hair neatly tied with blue ribbons on either side of her face, she personified the little girl look. Behind Cassie stood cousin Thelma and the children.

"Hi, Sean," Thelma said. "Don't keep her out too late. I'm responsible. Be home by eleven."

I turned to DeDe and Chris. "Hi, kids. How are you?"

"We wanna play Monopoly, Uncle Sean," they chorused.

Oh my God. It was 'Uncle Sean' again. "No thanks, kids. Cassie and I are going to the movies tonight," I responded cheerfully.

"We wanna go too," they demanded.

"No, maybe next time," Cassie suggested.

"Yeah, maybe next time," I murmured.

"Remember what I said, Sean," Thelma glowered.

"Don't worry. I'll have her home on time," I assured her. I found a parking space near Louie's Oyster Bar on the waterfront. My favorite restaurant for first dates.

The major-domo greeted us. As luck would have it, he welcomed me by name. "Good Evening, Mr. Sullivan. Party of two?" he inquired graciously.

"Yes, please," I answered.

We were escorted to a small table in a dimly lit alcove. Candles glowed on either side of the wine list. A fresh bouquet of roses added to the ambience of the room. What else would one expect in the "City of Roses"? Cassie winked at me as the host pulled out her chair for her. I summoned a waiter with the snap of my fingers.

"The maitre d' seems to know you," Cassie said. "I like this place. Do you come here often?"

"Oh, now and then. They have great seafood." I played the role of man about town.

A waiter put in an appearance. I ordered for both of us. "The lady will have the Jumbo Shrimp Chinese-style. I would like oysters ala Rockefeller." I recalled that Chablis or light wines accompanied fish dishes. As an afterthought, I added, "And a carafe of Lord and Taylor's California blush."

"I'm sorry, sir. We do not have a California blush in stock at the moment. Perhaps a Chablis or rosé would suffice?" he asked apologetically.

"A Chablis will be fine," I muttered.

During a moment of silence, we overheard the couple at the next table discussing the recent demise of their uncle. The stress of the funeral had proved difficult. The idea of death took my thoughts back to the hospital in The Dalles.

LATE ONE AFTERNOON, MARY COLLINS, THE CHARGE nurse on the third floor, stuck her head in my office. "Sean, Mr. Rankowicz just passed away. Would you please get his things?" His "things" included wood carving materials. My duties at the hospital involved occupational therapy, counseling, entertainment director, patient shopper, librarian, letter writer and general liaison with the outside world.

My office was directly across the hall from a room set aside for terminally ill patients. For two days, I listened to Rankowicz' moans and groans. In the final hours, his speech became unintelligible. Wheezing and coughing failed to communicate his last thoughts and only added to the struggle. He had no family, no friends, and no visitors. The nurses took turns sitting with Rankowicz. I tried to make sense out of the act of dying. I thought dying alone was the ultimate obscenity.

I stepped into the small white room. The essence of antiseptic saturated the last bus stop. The shades were drawn as though it was written that one must die in the dark. I took one look at the bed. Suppressing an obscenity, I ran from the room. "Mary, the body is still here!" I cried.

"So what! You get used to it. Go in and get the stuff. The undertaker won't be here for a few minutes."

I returned to the dark room. Rankowicz, a large man in his early fifties, look small in death. No "elan," no "joie de vivre," no breath of life. The things were on a night stand two feet from the head of the sheet-covered deceased. I almost lost my balance as I tried to tiptoe to the other side of the bed.

Grabbing the boxed set of wood carving tools, I skirted the bed with its silent occupant. Gulping for air, I fell into my office chair muttering the only psalm I could remember—"Yea, though I walk through the shadow of the valley of death." "Why didn't he use a carving knife on himself?" I asked aloud. It would have been quicker.

THE CLATTER OF DINNER PLATES BEING PLACED ceremoniously before us broke into my reveries. "Sean, what are you thinking? Your mind must be miles away." Cassie inched her chair in my direction. "You seem so sad," she observed.

"I'm sorry. I was thinking of death." I wanted to explain my occasional moments of silence. We spoke little as we enjoyed our meals. "We'd better go. The movie starts soon," I suggested. "High Society is rated the best picture of 1956."

An hour later, I delighted in escorting Cassie through the mirrored hall of the theater with its large glass chandeliers sparkling overhead.

The movies were an escape from the realities of life. I took every opportunity to see the "flicks."

"Let's sit there, Sean," Cassie pointed to the lower floor.

"Oh no. The balcony is more comfortable. It has privacy and a better view. Plus I'm farsighted," I said. Taking her hand, I led Cassie up the stairs. We were just seating ourselves as the theater darkened. The gold trimmed curtains parted.

"Loony Tunes" flashed on the screen. "What's up, Folks?" popped up, conveying the image of my favorite cartoon character of the times. "I love cartoons," Cassie squealed. "Don't you?" She squeezed my hand.

"Yeah. Sure."

"No Smoking In The Theater—City Fire Regulations" flashed before us. Next came, "Eat at Joe's corner deli—Families welcome." Then "Harold's Automotive Repair. NW Fifth and Ankeny. All models, all makes" burst onto the silver screen. Finally, "Visit our snack bar conveniently located in the lobby" concluded the run of ads.

Cassie and I cuddled into comfortable positions. I held her hand. "I hope you like the movie," I murmured in her ear as the feature presentation, "High Society" starring Bing Crosby and Grace Kelly, appeared on the big screen.

I tried to impress Cassie with a repartee of well chosen witticisms. Couples seated in front hissed, "Quiet! We want to watch the picture...Lovebirds." I attempted to fade into the woodwork.

The lights went on a couple hours later. "Let's wait until they leave," I suggested. Cassie acquiesced. Experience had taught me that I could avoid the embarrassment of the stares and occasional comments which accompanied my efforts to walk straight if I waited until everyone left the room. Again my thoughts drifted back to the early nineteen thirties.

"WALK STRAIGHT, SEAN. WHY DOESN'T THAT KID walk straight?" my father shouted at my mother.

"I'm trying to walk straight,' I pleaded.

"He can't, Sully. You know he can't," Ma explained.

Most people called my father Sully rather than Leonard, his given name. My father worked for the telephone company. Dad left this world an unhappy man, his dreams of recognition never realized. Navy service in two world wars qualified him for burial in the Willamette

National Cemetery in northeast Portland—free grave site, expensive funeral.

My mother's face was a corrugated monument to the ravages of time. Kathleen Sullivan's premature gray hair accented blue eyes that searched for an answer to a question that could never be answered. Why me?

During the Indian summer of 1925, my parents had discussed my impending arrival.

"The house needs fixing and some paint," my dad observed.

"I don't think we have enough money," Ma commented.

"Yes we do. We have two hundred dollars in the bank," he pointed out.

"That's for the baby. You said you would send me to Wilcox Memorial when the time came. Same as we did for Zack."

"I said the house needs painting!" Red face, bulging arteries, and asthmatic gasps for breath all pointed to my father's oncoming heart problem or temper tantrum. One did not argue with Leonard Brownlee Sullivan.

"Where are you going?" Ma asked.

"To the bank." With the surprising agility of a gazelle he darted toward the door.

On March 1, 1926, I arrived into this vale of tears at a friend's home down the street. A local midwife did the honors. Born with a hole in my lower spine, I was diagnosed with Mylomeningocele, commonly known as spina bifida.

"LET'S GO, SEAN." CASSIE SHOOK MY SHOULDER, breaking into my reverie. I returned to the present. "I'm sorry. I did it again," I said. The scent of her perfume edged me into reality.

When we arrived at her cousin's home, I anticipated my first good night kiss. Perhaps even a life long relationship. I parked the car in front of a neighbor's house. We could see Thelma peeking through the blinds.

"Tell me about yourself, Sean," Cassie prompted.

"You first," I said.

She complied. "Oh gosh, I'm nothing like you. I've been taking classes in art and drama at Boise State Junior College. I live with my mother, stepfather and stepbrother and sister. And many dogs—Collies. My mother sells them. My parents own a gas station on the outskirts of Boise. It's quiet. The people are nice but dull."

"I enjoy the arts—classical music, paintings, sculpture, stage plays," I offered. "How do you like Boise?" I continued.

Instead of answering, Cassie drew closer to me. I seized the opportunity, snaking my arm around her waist and planting a gentle kiss on her forehead. She spoke. "Boise is okay. I suppose I should say it's fine. It's quiet and the people are nice. Everybody knows everybody. It may be the largest town in Idaho but it's still a small town. You can leave your door unlocked and not worry."

Cassie looked and saw the blinds snapping open and shut again. She continued. "But it's not what I had hoped. My father remarried and has two kids. My mother did the same thing. I sometimes wonder if either of them wants me." The confession had been festering for a long time. She had never voiced her feelings to anyone.

Ill at ease, Cassie took a deep breath. "I'm sorry. Is your mother in Portland?" she asked.

"Yes, she lives with my Uncle Max and Aunt Peggy in West Portland. She wants me to live with her but I value my independence too much," I answered.

"Working for the county welfare sounds interesting," she prompted.

"Yeah, well, in my first six months on the job we found four dead people."

"What!" Cassie said. "Dead people?"

"Yes. I usually made field visits alone but on one occasion a caseworker and I found a body. The homes were isolated. Some clients were physically or mentally disabled. I think the worst thing that can happen to you is to die alone."

"That's depressing," she said sadly, wrinkling her small nose.

I began to regale Cassie with another story. Three years before I had arrived at the county welfare office early one morning to find a woman waiting for me. She had been there for some time. It was a cold winter day and I noticed a tractor parked in front of the Welfare office. I was usually the first one at the office.

A cup of coffee and the morning paper, the <u>Oregonian</u>, typically started my engine for the day. The headline that November 12, 1951 read, "Eisenhower wins by comfortable margin."

"Good morning Mrs. Hager. How are you?" I said as I entered the office.

"My husband died last night, about midnight. It took me over two hours to get here on that damn machine," she answered, pointing outside at the tractor. "I forgot to renew my driver's license." The new widow inquired, "What should I do with the body?"

The Hagers had been farmers all their adult life. Their children had left for the big city on reaching adulthood.

"I'm sorry," I murmured. I explained the details of Social Security and county welfare death benefits. Again I offered my condolences. "If I can be of any further help, please let me know."

"That's fine. But what I am going to do with Harry?" Mrs. Hager asked again.

"I'm sorry. I don't understand. I've given you all the information you need." I avoided the word "death" as though it were infectious. I kept bumbling along, trying to impress Mrs. Hager with my sensitivity, guessing she was more comfortable with beer and midwifing farm animals.

"Well, he's stiff as a board," she answered. "We don't have a phone. Harry didn't want to be bothered with new-fangled inventions. I was surprised when he bought the tractor. Old Ned, our horse, dropped dead last week so we can't use him." Her voice trailed away. "I miss him already. Harry, not the horse."

A tear made it's way down the tributaries of her chiseled features. Too many years in the summer sun. Too many winters shoveling manure out of the barn. It finally dawned on me that the body was still in the house. Our conversation had been a mish mash of misunderstanding. "My God! Do you mean he is still in your home?"

My trembling fingers dialed the local undertaker. Digger O'Leary, as he is known throughout the county, was graphic in his discussions of the newly departed. "Hello, Digger. Sean Sullivan at the Welfare office. How's the family?" Mr. O'Leary didn't object to his sobriquet. He wore it like a badge of honor.

"Mrs. Hager is here in my office. Her husband passed away late last night. Can you meet her at their farm?" I asked. Fifteen percent of the dead people in Josephine County went to their final reward courtesy of the County Welfare. I wanted to wash my hands of this business. I didn't object to the accompanying paper work, but I drew the line at visits to the mortuary.

"What time last night?" Digger's voice crackled over the phone.

"About midnight. She doesn't have a phone. It took her over two hours to drive into town by tractor. Can you help?" I begged.

"Midnight! For Christ's sake, do you know how hard it is to embalm a body after six or seven hours? Rigor mortis, old boy. It'll be pretty hard to get the fluid through the arteries. The Welfare doesn't pay my regular fee, ya know."

Attempts to spare the widow's sensitivities were unsuccessful. My whispered conversation with Digger O'Leary was met with a blast. "Speak up, boy! I can't hear you."

"Okay, okay. Forget the details. Just go get the corpus delecti, will you? And wait for Mrs. Hager. Her tractor tops fifteen miles at full throttle." I hoped the weak smile on my face was a saving grace.

"All right. Tell her I'll meet her at the farm," O'Leary surrendered awkwardly. "And how about some directions?" he demanded.

My story telling was something new to Cassie. Her family and circle of college friends didn't talk of death and dying. Their topics of conversation usually included the weather, farm subsidies, pork belly futures, new babies, and which professor was easy.

"Fascinating. You make a sad story funny," Cassie said.

I nodded. "It wasn't funny but the thought of her dead husband in the house all night really got to me. I didn't realize she couldn't phone Digger O'Leary." I looked out the window. "It looks like Thelma is getting upset," I observed.

"You're right. I'd better go in. Brrr, I'm freezing," Cassie shuddered. She started to leave. I gently pulled her to my chest. The firmness of her breasts startled me, releasing dormant sensibilities from hibernation. It was good to hold a women, young though she was. A kiss gracefully tolerated by Cassie ended our first date.

"May I phone you?" I inquired.

"Of course, Sean. You have my phone number."

I managed a quick peck on her cheek before she got out of the car. She disappeared into the house. The blinds snapped shut. Muffled voices drifted through the walls as I drove away into the night.

3

"THE BIRD CAGE"

I crossed paths with Gloria Norton in a nearby shopping mall on a cool Saturday morning. I suggested coffee.

"How did your date with Cassie go?" She peered into my face.

"How did you know?"

"Phil told me the other night."

"I thought you weren't speaking to him."

"I wasn't, but he came by the other evening. He mentioned peeing on your radiator the night of the orgy." Gloria crinkled her nose as though the bouquet of the incident remained. "By the way, do you like his friends? Colored hair do's and all," she queried.

"Not my cup of tea," I announced. I remained eager for her opinion of my first date with Cassie. Early in our relationship, Gloria had suggested that we be friends, not lovers.

"Sullivan! You've got to stop being so sensitive. Things are not as important as you imagine. Make up your own mind and stop worrying. I haven't met her but Phil said she appeared to be a nice girl." With that Gloria exhausted her sermon for the day.

I responded meekly, "You're right. Sorry to have bothered you."

"There you go again, Sean Sullivan." People put down their newspapers and gave us the Portland version of the stink eye. Gloria continued in subdued tones. "You're not bothering me. I like you Sean. We're good friends, remember?"

I put on a good face as I changed the subject. "Mindy phoned this morning. She put my father in Dammish State Hospital. She claims he pulled a gun on her. He did the same thing to my mother years ago. I have to see him after work sometime next week."

"I'm sorry, Sean," Gloria said.

Now and then I would introduce my girl friends to the "old man" as I called him. He usually looked with favor on my relationships, unlike my mother with her negative reactions.

17

"I know my father likes you," I declared to Gloria.. When I introduced them, he couldn't keep his hands off her. The long handshake; the arm around her waist; the smoochy good-bye kiss.

I continued to regard Eve and Gloria as my girls. After a few minutes of chit chat, Gloria and I parted company. Later in the afternoon, I watched a rerun of "Wanted Dead or Alive" on TV. Slouching in what passed for an easy chair, I decided to call Cassie.

"Hi. It's me, Sean. Oh, sorry. Hi, Thelma. May I speak to Cassie please?

"Just a minute," she answered. "Cassie! It's that college boy." I heard a barely audible conversation in the background.

"Hello, Sean. How are you?"

Oh boy, I must have timed this wrong. She sounded unhappy. "The weather's clearing. Would you like to take a drive through the Columbia Gorge next weekend? Multnomah Falls is beautiful this time of year. Or maybe the beach."

"I'm sorry, Sean. I have to baby-sit. Why don't you come over Wednesday night and we can watch TV with the kids."

"I don't know. I'm going to Dammish State Hospital Wednesday after work to see my father. I might be late."

She didn't ask for details. "Then come on over after you leave the hospital. I'll have a light dinner ready when you get here. The kids will be glad to see their 'Uncle Sean'."

"Oh no. Not 'Uncle Sean' again. Okay, I'll see you Wednesday night."

"I'll be here."

Cassie and I needed each other for different reasons. After a few moments of conversational trivia, we began our walk down the garden path which would lead to suicide, murders, executions and my temporary insanity.

Early the following Wednesday morning, I mapped out home visits for the day. I reserved the middle of the week, and sometimes Fridays, for field trips. Vocational rehabilitation counselors working for the 1956 Social Security Disability Freeze program were expected to observe clients in a home environment. I questioned the policy. Was it an attempt to catch the applicants in the act or an honest appraisal?

The day's activities were all located near Wilsonville, Oregon and Dammish State Hospital. I've never visited anyone in an institution before, much less my own father. The trumpets had blown, duty called.

"Good afternoon, Mr. Klenner," I called out as I drove into a farm yard for my last home visit of the day. Mr. Klenner, Disability Freeze applicant, suffered from arthritic knees accompanied by hypertension. 145 over 74. Age 52. I waved to him.

"Hello," Mr. Klenner responded with a smile. He walked toward the car at a full trot before he saw the decal, "State of Oregon—Official Use Only" on a field of green. He then completed his journey with a noticeable limp while holding his kneecaps in feigned pain.

I introduced myself as I sat in the car. "My name is Sean Sullivan. I'm with the Oregon State Vocational Rehabilitation office in Portland. I have your application for the Disability Freeze program." I pulled myself out of the car, put one foot on the grass and fell into the mud. Slipping and sliding on the wet ground, I eventually managed to grab the door handle. I dragged myself up to my full height of five feet-nine inches.

"Sorry," I apologized. "I have a hard time keeping my balance." I couldn't resist playing the "Can you top this?" game. Mr. Klenner and I braced ourselves against the state car.

"I'm having trouble with my knees. I can't stand the pain sometimes. It adds to my high blood pressure." Mr. Kleener groaned. He was more interested in his fate than mine.

"Yes. I understand," I replied.

"Would you like to come up to the house?" he offered. Mr. Klenner clearly wanted to cooperate. It was in his best interests.

A steep incline lead to the steps of a Victorian farm house. I declined the offer. "Oh, no thanks. I'm making field visits. Getting the paperwork together. We'll be submitting your forms soon." I wanted to put him at ease.

"Oh. You don't approve my application? What is your job then?" he asked.

"No, I don't." I gave a short explanation of who does what and when in the Disability Freeze program. Mr. Klenner breathed a sigh of relief.

"Sure you wouldn't like to come up to the house? I've got some nice elderberry wine. My wife made it last year jest before she passed over. I sure do miss her...The kids visit once in while. They live up in Portland."

Oh my God! He's a widow and lonely, I thought. "Sure, Mr. Klenner. But just for a minute."

No hand rail on the steps. We made our way into the living room bumping into each other. Mr. Klenner offered me an easy chair decorated with white hand knitted dollies. He placed a large ceramic jug of wine on the table next to me, filling two small glasses labeled Kraft Cheese.

"Help yourself," Klenner suggested. Then added, "You're sitting in my wife's chair." I shot out of the recliner.

"Oh, it's all right. Sit. Sit." Klenner insisted I remain in the place of honor. "We spent many a happy evening together listening to Amos and Andy on the radio. Raising the kids," he said. "That's her on the mantle," Klenner nodded towards the fireplace.

I looked for a family photograph and saw none. "I don't see her picture," I said. A large copper container adorned the fireplace mantle. Plastic flowers on each side of the container completed the memorial. Mr. Klenner picked up the copper thing and handed it to me.

"She's in here. I like to keep her with me," he said solemnly. My hands, wet with perspiration, gingerly passed the wife back to her husband.

Mr. Klenner spent the next few minutes in a verbal stroll down memory lane as I murmured the appropriate "Uh huh" and "Oh, is that so?" I made motions to leave.

"Visit a spell. What's your hurry?" Klenner entreated.

At thirty years of age, I hadn't plumbed the depths of loneliness. The Seth Thomas clock next to the oak hutch chimed four times. "I have to stop by the hospital to see my father," I explained.

"Oh, I'm sorry. Hope he'll be all right." Klenner rubbed both knee caps.

"Oh, he'll be okay. It's just a matter of time." I excused myself. Mr. Klenner walked me to the car. As I drove off, he bounded up the stairway two steps at a time.

On the way to Dammish State Hospital, I contemplated with trepidation my coming meeting with the old man. As I drove into the hospital parking lot I could see Mindy, my stepmother, standing on the front step nervously taping her foot. As I got out of the car, she growled, "You'd better be prepared. Your father is in a terrible state of mind. He cries a lot. Brace yourself."

"What the hell is he doing in here," I demanded.

"I had him admitted."

"Why?'

"He pulled a gun on me. He wanted to kill me. I had him committed."

"So what? He did the same thing to me and Ma years ago. I was in casts on both legs up to the knee. I couldn't defend her. Zack came in and kicked the gun out of his hand. I think the old man was bluffing."

"He's in the garden. In the back." Mindy muttered incoherent obscenities as I left her standing in the parking lot. My long walk was interrupted by inmates shuffling back and forth with Freudian fixations on their faces. The hospital reeked of the usual odors of germicide.

A lady in a torn bath robe grabbed my arm. "Would you like to see my little Mary?" Drool dripped down her face.

"Sure." Oh my God! What do I do now? I forced a grin.

Her grimy hand gently unwrapped a pink blanket exposing a red, white and blue rag doll. Orange lipstick smeared on a lifeless face made of rough fabric presented distorted features. Tiny arms and legs flopped as the make-believe mother proudly displayed her little daughter.

"What a pretty baby," I said.

"Yes, she is beautiful. And she's all mine." The lady continued to whisper hallucinations to a child that did not exist. I made several attempts to disengage myself, repeating to the mother my belief in the regal beauty of her child. She turned to walk away.

"I must get her to the doctor. She has the sniffles."

"Good idea. I think the doctor's office is down the hall." I pointed in the opposite direction.

A few more steps and I encountered my father. He was seated at a picnic table, head in hands, contemplating a colony of ants in the cracks of the sidewalk. Dad was a tall, slender man with thinning hair, the recipient of a forced retirement from the telephone company. Service in two world wars and thirty-five years for the telephone company were brushed aside for young men with master degrees in communication.

I saw a gaunt old man sharing his sorrow with the ants as he turned at the sound of my footsteps. His stress-filled voice beckoned me to his side. "Oh, Sean, I'm so glad to see you. I'm so sorry. That woman put me in here." My father threw his arms around me for the first time in memory. He pressed his wet face to mine and our tears intermingled, dribbling down both our cheeks.

The old man pulled me to the bench blubbering incoherent thoughts. I almost landed on his lap. The spectacle of a weeping father with a son who had a long memory proved to be quite emotional.

21

I had learned lessons of self discipline at the Shriner's Hospital for Crippled Children in the early thirties. The name of the game is pain. He who cries first is a baby. The taunt, "Baby, baby, Sean is a baby," rings in my ears to this day.

How does one comfort an inconsolable parent? I had tried to reach the old man on different channels all my life but failed. "Aw, come on, Pa. It's not the end of the world."

What I wanted to say was, "You can't pull a gun on Mindy and expect her to do nothing." My recollections of a 38 caliber steel blue nose revolver and my mother clutching me to her bosom flooded back. No time for revenge. A time for healing.

"Can't you get me out of here? You work for the state. You must know somebody, anybody. Please." Fits of crying followed. His shoulders slumped. He buried his wet face deeper into his hands.

"Did you know ants eat each other? Just like people. We're nothing but animals," he finally said. I had never known my father to be philosophical. A talker and manipulator perhaps, but not a philosopher. He sometimes stumbled over his ego but seldom expressed thoughts of great importance.

"I'll do what I can. I'll talk to Mindy. Be patient," I tried to reassure him.

"Oh no! Don't talk to her. That woman put me in here. You must have a connection. You work for the State." He repeated himself. He became more agitated.

"Don't worry," I placed my hand gently on his shoulder, attempting to ease his mind. Six years of counseling experience abandoned me. Working with strangers in a one-on-one relationship is easy compared to this situation, I thought. My subconscious shouted, "I can't even help my own father!"

"I met a nice young lady at my birthday party. She's in town visiting her cousin. Her name is Cassie. I'vee seen her several times," I said.

He ignored me. "The telephone company wants me to retire. I have four more years. They can't make me leave until I am sixty-two. All those young kids with their college degrees. Of course when I go, I'll get half Navy pay." He took a deep breath.

"That's great, Dad. Sounds like you've got it made." I said.

At last he stopped moaning, latching on to his favorite subject: money.

"You still have the property out in Milwaukee. That ought to be worth something," I said.

"How'd you know I owned it.?" he snapped. His face became a question mark. I didn't answer.

The old man placed both hands flat on the bench and gazed into my eyes. He snorted, "It's mine now. I got it in the divorce from your mother and I intend to keep it. Mindy won't get her hands on my property." But she did.

"All right, Pa. It's getting late. It's probably close to your supper time. I should go." I started to leave. He held on to my arm forcing me back to the bench.

"Don't go. The food here hurts my stomach. I tried to explain my special diet but they won't listen." The old man whimpered. "Please sign me out. You can get me out of here. You're my son, aren't you?"

"Yes, but I didn't put you in here. Mindy did. I'll do what I can. I'll come again. Take it easy," I said as I got up from the bench.

"Damn you!" he exploded. The expletive concluded our conversation. The old man jumped up, turned his back to me, and trotted to his room.

"Aw come on, Pa. Calm yourself," I whispered to the wind. I sat a few minutes in meditation. I had many questions but no answers.

As darkness descended, I set out on the long walk to my car. I noticed many of the patients were in the dining room or their individual padded accommodations. I passed several inmates in the hallway. To my relief, they expressed no interest in me. I had enough encounters in the twilight zone.

I stopped at the reception desk. "Hi. My name is Sean Sullivan. My father, Leonard Sullivan, is a patient. I understand his wife had him committed here." The clerk leafed through the filing cabinet. She pulled out a thin folder and refreshed her memory. "Yes, your mother signed the commitment papers." She smiled.

"She's not my mother. Can I sign him out? I'll be responsible." I knew I was heading into deep waters, making the supreme sacrifice.

"I'm sorry. You'll have to talk that over with the hospital administrator. I believe he is at dinner now. He likes to dine with the patients as much as possible...It was a pleasure meeting you." The clerk extended her hand.

Mindy came up behind me. "How is he?" she demanded.

"He's okay. You're right; he cries a lot. I didn't know what to do. It's difficult to see my father so upset."

"He is not the man I married six years ago."

"Come on, Mindy. The old man has a few good qualities. He took the family fishing and camping for many years. We enjoyed those trips. He gave us his name."

"I hate fishing. I get sick."

"Yeah, I know. I saw you laying on the bottom of the boat the last time we fished the Columbia. You looked nauseous. Sorry."

"I won't go fishing with him again."

"He needs companionship. I'll talk to the hospital administrator."

"Oh no you don't! I don't want him out. At least not for awhile. He's crazy." Mindy paced back and forth. "Sean, I'm not signing any release papers just yet," she said.

"Okay, Mindy. Relax. Take it easy," I said. I turned to go. "I'll see you." In the parking lot, I eased into my car then gunned it, tires squealing as I hit fifty in ten seconds. I had no taste for combat.

The events of the day were overwhelming. The disabled farmer who was not disabled. The twitchy step-mother. The weeping father. My inability to cope with the dilemmas of the day left me depressed.

Overjoyed at the prospect of seeing Cassie, I saw the dawn of a new awakening. If I could just relate to her relatives all would be well.

I saw the blinds move as I parked in front of Thelma's house. Cassie came out to the porch, sparkling in a light blue silk blouse complemented by a navy blue pleated skirt. Pink braided yarn tied in bows held strands of auburn hair blowing in the wind. White saddle shoes completed her teenage ensemble. The marble texture of her skin enhanced her Barbie doll features.

"Hello, Sean. How was your day?" Cassie took my hand and lead me into the living room.

"You wouldn't believe. Hi, kids." We sat down on the sofa.

"Hi, Uncle Sean," DeDe and Chris chorused.

"You guys watch 'Gunsmoke'. Uncle Sean and I want to talk," Cassie suggested with surprising success.

"I'm not your uncle," I said under my breath to no one.

"What did you say, Sean?"

"Nothing." I proceeded to unload the events of the day. "I had a busy day. Many of the applicants for the Social Security Disability

Freeze are in better shape than I am," I said. Cassie handed me a cup of coffee.

I continued. "I saw my client climbing a tree when I drove into his farm. He claims to have arthritis and high blood pressure. He keeps his wife's ashes above the fireplace in a copper container. He said he enjoys her company. Later I visited my father at the State Hospital. Mindy committed him. We had an unpleasant conversation. All my father does is look at colonies of ants in the cracks of the sidewalk and cry. I've never seen him weep. I'm exhausted. Then to top off the day, several coo-coo birds stopped me in the hospital. It was the first time I've ever encountered mental patients. One of them thought a rag doll was her baby. God!"

Cassie came to my rescue. She sat close gently holding my hand. I noticed an unrecognizable scent wafting through the room. "What's that smell?" I commanded.

"It's incense. The kids are studying China at school. Their teacher explained how Buddhists burn incense in prayer. The smoke will take your prayers to heaven."

"Maybe my class should have studied Buddha," I said.

Cassie asked, "How do you like my perfume?"

She moved her cheek next to mine. The combination of incense and her scent confounded my senses. I lingered a moment before answering, "Great. It's spicy."

"We went shopping at Newberry's after school. It's cheap perfume." Cassie jumped up to perform a pirouette. "Do you like my new skirt?" A brief ballet twirl revealed bare legs and color print underwear. "Oh, sorry," she said. She covered her face with her hands, peeking at me in mock embarrassment. She fell into my lap.

"I like everything about you, Cassie." A soft kiss on her earlobe underscored my thoughts.

The leprechauns startled us. "What are you doing with Aunt Cassie, Uncle Sean?" DeDe demanded. I jerked away from Carrie and turned back to the TV. None of your damn business, I thought.

"Nothing. Watch TV," Cassie ordered. She stood up to smooth the wrinkles in her skirt. Her hands slowly ran down her short thighs and legs. I fought to maintain my composure.

"I'm sorry your father is ill," Cassie said. "Maybe things will get better. Can you get him out? You're his son."

"I don't know. The receptionist at the hospital suggested I talk with the administrator. The old man pulled a gun on his wife. I'll see him again sometime next week. I guess it's my duty." I wanted to lighten up the dialogue. "What's new with you?" I asked.

"Nothing much," she said. "Gunsmoke" finally ended. The ritual of "we don't wanna go to bed" followed by "let's play cards" was overcome by Cassie's desire to be alone with me. She won the contest.

Emerging from the children's bedroom she said, "They're in for the night, I hope." We settled in for a two and a half hour session of frivolous talk and hand holding. Later I stole a glance at my watch. "It's getting late. Maybe I should go."

"It's only nine o'clock. Stay awhile. Thelma won't be home until late."

"Okay, if you don't mind. A few more minutes." The woes of the day vanished. Until the front door banged open, shattering our solitude.

"Hi, everyone. It's me. I'm home," Thelma proclaimed. "Hello, Sean. You look good." Her speech was slurred. She opened the refrigerator door. "Would you like a beer, Sean?" she asked. "You're too young, Cassie."

"Sure, Thelma. Thanks." I'm not a beer drinker but I was willing to do anything to encourage the cooperation of Cassie's cousin. A few minutes of convivial camaraderie followed and then I bid Cassie good night. No hug. No kiss.

On the way home the fresh night air caused me to burst into song. "Some enchanted evening, you will find a stranger."

4

"CAN SHE BAKE A CHERRY PIE?"

LATE THAT EVENING, I LUXURIATED IN MY vintage bath tub. Peace descended as the hot water vanquished the pain in my legs and back. I studied the specks of flowered wallpaper peeling slowly downwards. A sixty watt bulb dangled from a twelve foot ceiling, captivating a moth or two. The old thirty watt light had bestowed the milieu of a mortuary on a slow night.

My thoughts turned to Cassie as I anticipated the future. Six years had passed since I had enjoyed the companionship of a girl. I sang to myself a popular ditty from the long ago depression days.

"Can she bake a cherry pie, Billy Boy, Billy Boy?
Can she bake a cherry pie, charming Billy?
She can bake a cherry pie
Quick as a cat can blink its eye,
She's a young thing
Who cannot leave her mother."

But she did.

The next morning at the office, Givens said, "Hey, Sullivan, you seem lost in thought." Jason Givens, the other counselor, disturbed my spider web of meditation. Co-workers at the rehab office tended to interrupt my nostalgic binges from time to time.

"Actually, I met a girl. She's here visiting her cousin. I kinda like her."

"Good for you, Sean. I thought you were acting strange of late," he said. Counselors are apt to offer each other advice from time to time. "Tell me more. She sounds interesting."

Gossip time. Givens tended to explore the lives of others, guided by his own value system. A touch of sadism seeped through his persona from time to time. He dreamed reckless schemes in his climb up the career ladder, his eye on the office of the director of vocational rehabilitation.

I hesitated, reluctant to confide my innermost thoughts. Something in Givens' voice, however, gave me an impression of trust. Here was a man who would not fling back statements taken out of context.

"Well, her name is Cassie and she's quite young. I think she's pretty. She's shorter than I, comes about up to my chin. She has dark brown hair and a great smile. She ties her hair with a ribbon on both sides and wears fuzzy sweaters with pleated skirts." I hesitated. "She has an outgoing personality. She seems to be happy all the time, a fun person. Makes me feel good. If anything, she's too bubbly. But, what the heck? It's nice to have a girlfriend in my life. I'm thirty years old, you know." I never referred to my first marriage.

"I know what you mean." Jason Givens quenched his thirst by drinking in my personal affairs. "My wife likes to party. She's a people-oriented person. She relates well to everybody." Givens divulged more than he wanted. He typicallyb played his cards close to the chest.

"I've only dated Cassie three or four times. I took her to see 'High Society' at the Paramount and then helped her baby-sit a couple times. She's staying with a cousin and her two kids. They like to play monopoly a lot. But it's an opportunity to see Cassie." I terminated the conversation by turning to my desk and immersing myself in paper work. I had already said more than I should.

A few days later I picked Cassie up at Thelma's house. We headed for the Columbia Gorge and Multnomah Falls. "Are you really going to quit school and stay in Portland?" I asked.

"Yes, but I'll go back and finish next year. I just want to take a break," she answered. "My mother doesn't have much time for me. She's busy helping Van with the store and gas station. The kids take up a lot of her day. She divorced my father soon after I was born—Sheridan, Wyoming. Then she remarried. My father did the same thing." Cassie gazed into space.

"I'm glad you're staying. I hope Thelma doesn't blame me." I visualized a confrontation. Avoiding Thelma would not solve the problem. "We have several good colleges and universities in Portland. You can always enroll here. You should complete your education," I continued.

"Don't worry, Sean. It's my idea. Give me time to pacify Thelma. She's going to be mad when I tell her our plans. You'd better make yourself scarce for a few days."

I think Thelma saw me through the bars of a cage. Cassie regarded me as a companion. A possible solution to her problem.

"I have to see my father again next week. He's still in the state hospital. Mindy, his wife, won't sign him out. There's not much I can do about it because she's the one who signed his commitment. Sometimes I wish my parents hadn't gotten divorced," I said.

I wanted to share my burdens, real or imaginary, with Cassie. "I'm sorry. I shouldn't bother you with my problems."

"Please, don't apologize. I'm sure you'll figure out something. They can't keep your father in there forever," Cassie said.

She went on. "I was quite young when my parents divorced. Mother remarried several years later and then Johnny and Stephanie arrived in the next year or two. That marriage didn't last either, so now she's living with Van in Boise, Idaho. He's a nice guy and they seem happy." Her face seemed to have acquired a look of infinite sorrow.

"I was relieved when my parents divorced. When I was little, they tried to kill each other. I couldn't rescue my mother because I usually had braces on both legs or casts up to my hips," I said. "Every time I see Ma or the old man they always ask me how the other one is doing. Only my dad won't quiz me if Mindy is in the room."

The day faded into night. A full moon lit the way home. My old 1951 Ford attacked another curve.

"I don't remember my parents or step-parents ever getting physical. Their kids appear to be important to them." Cassie frowned. She gave away much of herself.

"Oh my, I think I took the wrong turn. I haven't been here in a long time," I said. As usual it was peek-a-boo through the blinds when we pulled up in front to the house. Cassie's announcement would surely cause an uproar in the family. She mentioned her mother's indifference to a college education.

"I hope everything goes okay for you, Cassie. I'll be glad to talk to Thelma regarding the educational opportunities here in Portland if you like. It might make things easier for you."

Cassie exercised a charming fascination over me, dismissing personal misgivings concerning the future. "Don't worry, Sean. I'll take care of

Thelma. I'm a big girl now, eighteen, and both my mother and father are busy with their new families. Besides, I like it here. It's a change."

"I'll call you in a few days. Give it some time." I said. Distant barking split the silence of the evening.

"Do you want me to go with you to the hospital?" she asked.

"Oh no, but thanks. I'd better go alone. Seeing my father in a state mental hospital is a new experience. Frankly, I don't know how to handle the situation."

"Sorry I can't invite you in, Sean. I baked a cherry pie," she said.

"Oh, my favorite. Ala mode of course."

"Of course," she laughed. A firm hug. A lingering kiss ended my day.

At the office, Givens caught me cat-napping after lunch. "Sean, you're wandering again," he said. My eyes were riveted to a spider spinning a web on the window sill. The maze of concentric weaving held hostage a fragile ant as yet impervious to his fate.

"It seems like the big guys are always eating the little guys," I said, more to myself than to Givens.

"What did you say,?" he demanded.

"Oh, nothing. I'm not daydreaming. I'm planning my field trips for today and I may visit my father after work. He's in the hospital."

"Sorry, Sean. What's wrong?" The words said one thing but the tone of his remark revealed his true lack of interest.

"He's sick." Dammed if I would explain. Too many times my honest little songs turned me into the victim of the libretto rather than the hero. I lied. "He had his appendix taken out not long ago. The family is upset." Givens grimaced in response, clutching his lower right side.

Stuffing manila files in a much-used attaché case, I began the long walk to the elevator. Contemplating a variety of physical impediments, I started to make my way through a maze of desks, filling cabinets, an A.B. Dick ditto machine, and people. Givens blocked my way.

"Excuse me," I said. He failed to move. "By the way, the appendix is on the left side," I commented. His face twitched as he laughed a high pitched chuckle. A small prize for the morning. To the demand of a wise man there is always a riposte.

I spent the day in the McMinville-Willamina area visiting clients, helping old people to fill out forms, and talking story. After a twenty five mile ride, I arrived at the Dammish State Hospital. My car radio blared the evening news.

Five-thirty in the afternoon. Supper time for patients at Dammish. The evening meal was a high priority for the old man.

My father had worked the four to midnight shift for nineteen years at the telephone company, monitoring the three major radio networks. The companionship of an evening meal was denied him many times during the 1920's and 1930's. The company cafeteria is a poor substitute for a good home cooked meal.

"May I see Mr. Sullivan? I know it's late but I was in the area," I asked the receptionist.

"Well, it is close to dinner time but go ahead. I think he's out in the garden."

"Thank you. I know the way." The scent of tuberose descended upon me, full of delicate associations. The Chinese called it the "smell of moonlight." If moonlight had a sound it would be Beethoven, I thought.

I surveyed the corridor leading to the garden. A few habitues and a medical cart or two. No display of a dead baby.

The old man sat on a bench preoccupied in the study of bees hovering over a rose bush. Startled by the shuffling sounds of my footsteps, he turned to me. He said nothing.

"Hi, Dad. How are you?" I favored my father with a toothy grin accompanied by a firm handshake.

Ignoring my salutation, he pulled me to a clump of flowers and sputtered, "See all those bees circling the rose bushes? They won't hurt you. I've been studying them for hours. What do you think?"

Theme music for a popular Gary Cooper movie flashed across my mental viewing screen. "It's like the windmills of the mind. Never beginning, never ending," I muttered.

"You always were the poet in the family. I guess it's all those books you read before you started school. When did you begin school?" he asked.

"1937, the fifth grade. Don't you remember?" I admonished.

He didn't answer the question. "Let's sit. I have good news," he said. "I think I'm going home next week. Maude and Harry Ravensbrook talked to Mindy. She agreed to sign me out of this place. I've never been in a mental hospital."

The old man clapped his head with both hands. "Oh my God." Tears welled up in his eyes then dribbled down corrugated cheeks. "I'm not a bad guy, Sean. What have I done wrong?

Something in his tone compelled me to hug him. An Irishman's sense of tragedy overtook me as I held my father. The old man shuddered as he composed himself. "Remember all the fishing trips? The camping out? Those were good days, weren't they?" he asked plaintively.

"Yeah, I remember." I wanted to say, "I also remember when you abused Ma as I sat on the floor with a five pound brace on each leg. I remember when you pointed a blue nose 32 at me and Ma as she clasped me to her bosom. The bullet would strike me first. Zack came in and kicked the gun out of your hands." But I didn't say these things.

My father broke away whispering, "How's your mother?"

Surprised I answered, "She's okay. She moved to Northern California and is taking care of a motel near where Zack lives."

"She cooked the best grits with pork chops. Always center cut," he reminisced. "The food here is terrible."

"Yeah, I know."

"I remember. I worked for Western Union in New Orleans before the first World War. I was only sixteen or seventeen. Your grandmother passed away. Several months later my sister died in the flu epidemic of 1916. I delivered telegrams on my bicycle to the whore houses in Storyville before the Navy burned down the district. It was the jazz center of the world. The madams would ask me in for biscuits and honey with grits."

"Sounds like fun—the whore houses, not the grits." I said.

Ignoring my humor, he continued his walk down a street called Memory. "The manager of the Western Union taught me Morse Code. I was on the wire when I was seventeen." The old man suspended his recitation for a moment as he focused on some bees hovering over the flower bed.

"It was a great time for jazz. Your half-brother Bill was born in New Orleans. When I found out Minnie was pregnant, I joined the Navy. They sent me to a communications school at Pensacola Florida."

I knew little of my father's early life. Information concerning the Sullivan side of the family came second hand from my mother.

He broke out of his reverie. "I'm hungry. Sorry, I can't invite you to stay."

"That's okay. It's getting late. I should go home." I said.

"Say hello to your mother." We shook hands. He shuffled towards the dining room.

5

"SONGS MY MOTHER NEVER TAUGHT ME"

I WOULD CONTEMPLATE TODAY'S ENCOUNTERS when I had time. I hesitated at the reception desk. "May I ask the name of your perfume? It has a pleasant scent. I think my girl friend might like it."

She smiled. "It's called Tea Rose. Off hand I don't remember who makes it but I bought it at the cosmetic counter at Meier & Frank," she replied. "I've received several compliments. Thank you."

"My father tells me he might go home next week," I said.

"Yes. Your mother may sign him out. I'm sure he'll be glad to leave. This place can be confining at times."

"She's not my mother!" I exclaimed. She looked startled. "Sorry. Mindy is my father's wife and I don't regard her as my mother or step-mother. It's been difficult to accept my parent's divorce, even though they parted ten years ago."

"I know what you mean. My folks did the same thing a few years ago," she said. The receptionist's body language spoke a gentle hint of commonalty.

"My parents always ask about each other. They both remarried. Every time I visit my father he asks, 'How is your mother?' And Ma does the same. Apparently they still for care each other," I continued.

"So do my mother and father," she said. It hadn't occurred to me other people experienced the same problems. She breathed empathy. I decided to ask her for a date.

"Do you enjoy going to the movies?" A slight hesitation. "Mister Roberts' is playing at the Broadway in Portland. By any chance would you like to go with me.?"

Gently but firmly she replied, "I'm sorry Mr. Sullivan. I'm a married women with a baby girl." The echo of rejection resounded from the mountain tops. The initial trauma left me with faint resources of indignation.

"Excuse me," I said. I left as gracefully as I could while sinking into a quicksand of mortification.

The following Saturday morning I completed my chores in the usual halfhearted way. Dishes washed. Kitchen mopped. Laundry put away. At least my conscience was at ease.

I called Cassie. "Hi, Cassie. This is Sean. Are you busy?" I felt at ease with her.

"Hi, Sean. No, I'm not doing anything. Thelma and Steve took the kids to the park. I think they want to be alone. A neighbor gossiped to Steve regarding the parties and Thelma. I'm here by myself."

"Good. Why don't we take a Sunday drive to the coast? It's a nice day. Or maybe to Jantzen Beach. You'll love the roller coaster. I can pick you up in about forty five minutes." I tried to suppress my eagerness. Bonding with Cassie became much more than a physical need. I could not unscramble my feelings.

"Jantzen Beach sounds fine. Come by in an hour. That'll give me time to get ready."

"Wear jeans. It's kinda chilly out today," I advised.

"Okay. See you soon," Cassie said.

An hour later Cassie Buzbie appeared as the Junior Miss of 1956 in her gray bulky knit sweater. Rolled up jeans, which did nice things for her figure, were complimented by black and white saddle shoes. A pony tail replaced the blue ribbons and braids of last week. "Oh boy," I said to myself.

"Hi. Nice to see you again. Kinda cool," she breezed.

Being in the presence of a girl humanized my attitude. Cassie glided onto the seat next to me. I squeezed her hand. I felt ambivalent to a hello kiss.

"Today should be fun. I'm getting tired of listening to Steve and Thelma fight. He's really upset over her partying—staying out late and not taking care of the kids. And I'm getting tired of baby sitting," she said. Cassie seldom complained. Her self addressed monologue surprised me.

"Sorry about Thelma. But I'm sure you'll have fun today. They have all kinds of rides and amusements at the park—roller coaster, merry go round, house of ghosts and pink cotton candy." I was elated at the prospect of an afternoon with Cassie. It was a wonderful day, but all too soon it came to an end. We drove back to Portland.

"Would you like to stop by my place?" I asked. "We can watch 'The Steve Allen Show,' but I only have a black and white TV."

"Sure, but let's stop somewhere for a bite to eat first."

"Okay, how about Chinatown? It's only a few blocks away." Cassie agreed to my choice of chop suey joints, as they were called in the 50's. The month's budget broke beyond repair.

After we consumed a dinner of assorted delectable delights of the Far East presented on a large lazy susan, Cassie and I drove the short distance to my apartment. To my everlasting delight, she expressed approval of the day's activities and the evening meal in particular. "Wait a minute, the lights." I switched on all the lights in the living room with the idea of putting her at ease.

My experiences with the ladies were limited. One brief marriage to June Petersen followed by two sterile friendships with Eve Brown and Gloria Norton. I glanced at the kitchen clock, "It's almost eleven. Time for Steve Allen." Tuning in the TV and turning off two of the lamps gave my digs an atmosphere of coziness. I joined Cassie on the divan.

Our fits of laughter at the "On The Street" interviews with Louis Nye, Don Knotts and Tom Poston ended in happy tears. "Boy, was that funny," I said. I managed a faltering kiss which was spoiled by a staccato knock on the door.

"Sean. Aren't you going to see who it is?"

"Yeah, I guess so." I got up and jerked open the front door.

"Hi, Phil. What are you doing up this late?" I made a vain attempt at hiding my disgust. He peeked over my head at Cassie sitting on the sofa.

"Oh, you're busy," he said. "I'm having a party at my place tomorrow night. I thought you might like to come. Both of you."

"Oh yeah? Who's coming?" My irritation faded.

"The usual colorful hairdressers and other interesting people. Bad manners, Sullivan. Aren't you going to introduce me to your friend?" Phil ventured two tiny steps forward, his face brimming with curiosity as he peered over my shoulder.

"Sure. Cassie, this is Phil Downey. We were roommates." I continued to block his way. "I'll call you." I said.

"You don't have my phone number," he countered.

"What is it?"

Smiling peevishly, Phil engaged in tight lip silence.

"Well…," I said.   Patience ranked low on the list of my many virtues.

"555-6271," he muttered.

"What? I can't hear you."

"555-6271. Well, I guess I'd better go. Give me a call," he said.

"Sorry. I'll phone you tomorrow."   Gently but firmly I shut the door in Downey's face. Turning to Cassie, I smiled an apology. After the strain of dealing with Phil, I was eager to look at the brighter side of things. We returned to the sofa and Steve Allen.

Cassie suppressed a yawn. "I'm getting sleepy," she said.

"Me too. Let's take a nap," I said. The phrase "let's take a nap" was my call to arms. I had used this ploy with some success over the years in darkened bedrooms and back seats of cars. On one memorable occasion, a sandy beach behind a large rock had served the purpose.

IN THE SUMMER OF 1943, AT THE TENDER AGE OF seventeen, I made the greatest discovery of all time. Sex. Better than the wheel.

After a football game, Marie and I drove to my home in Portland. We were both tired after a long day. "Come on in, Marie. It doesn't look like Ma is home yet." I escorted her into the living room. "It's cold. I'll build a fire. That was some game—yeah Benson! Glad we won the game."

"Where is your mother?" Marie didn't seem uneasy, but the dictates of morality required her to make some inquiry.

"She went to the beach with a friend. Said she'd be back late tonight or early tomorrow," I answered. We sat in front of the fireplace, embers crackling in every direction. Marie, lulled into drowsiness by the flames, folded into my arms. The promise of young love raced through my mind.

"Let's take a nap, Sean," the little kitten from Jacksonville, Florida purred in her melodious southern accent. Syrup over a waffle.

Hand in hand to the bedroom we went. A kiss, an embrace, a surge of affection. I suffered an agony of suspense knowing the excitement of love makes for an easy surrender. Fumbling with zippers and hooks, garments fell to the floor one by one. Then I saw all of her.

Buttons flew in every direction as I ripped off my shirt. Shucking my pants and underwear at the same time, I seized the moment and Marie. Thoughts of Ma rippled through my mind. Is she coming home? What should I do?

Marie began to pull her underwear down over sun tanned legs. Generations of Presbyterian virtues took command. I pinned both her arms down, canceling my admission to paradise. Yanking her lingerie up, I muttered, "I'd better take you home. I think I have some gas stamps." I sold the sizzle not the steak.

Fifty-one years later, in the wee hours of the morning, I call up memories of the almost conquest of Marie McCabe of Jacksonville, Florida. The little nurse's aid with a Southern accent.

IMAGES OF THE LITTLE KITTEN FROM FLORIDA FADED as I jerked the old Murphy bed down from the wall. I gently placed a 45 record on the table phonograph next to the Javanese heads. A Chopin Etude would enhance the mood of the evening. I could have chosen the "Flight of the Bumble Bee" by Rimsky-Korsikoff.

Uncorrupted by evil, Cassie and I lay down in our Garden of Eden, squeaky bed and all. Our adventure began. Love making is basically a mind game for me. I do not have any feeling where it most counts.

Years before a gaggle of neurologists had given me some news. "You're sterile, Mr. Sullivan. I don't know how else to express myself." Dr. Starbuck had set down the chart and gazed compassionately at me. "You will probably never father a child," he intoned.

Looking into his solemn face I asked, "Why?"

"Your sperm count is low. And if, by some miracle, you do father a child, there's a fifty percent chance it will be born with a Mylomeningocele, hydrocephalus, or even an ancephaly," Dr. Starbuck explained.

"I don't understand," I said.

"I'm sorry—born with a hole in the spine, water on the brain, or no brain," he had clarified.

"Sean. Call me Sean. Please." I hadn't believed the doctors.

I came back to Cassie. I engaged in a demonstration of faltering techniques accompanied by half hearted "I love you's." I felt awkward. So did she.

Cassie pulled away from me whispering, "Sean, can I stay here with you?"

"My God! How nice!" I answered.

She did not respond.

Love making was one thing. An affair to remember never occurred to me. "Of course, Cassie." I drew her to my chest. The fondling and love making began again.

38

I discovered sex is the perfect form of exercise. Psychological and biological needs guide me to exhilaration and ejaculation. Our lives became a sleigh ride on the twin slopes of lust and desire, ending in disaster.

6

"THE DREAM CATCHERS"

DAWN TWINKLED THROUGH THE BLINDS IN Apartment 513 early Wednesday morning. The first day of the rest of our lives. I looked at Cassie.

My awkwardness had disappeared. An abundance of happiness quickly scaled the pinnacles of ecstasy. As dream catchers we began a flight of a thousand and one nights on a carpet of airy hopes. I sighed a long remembered quatrain from the "Kasidah" gently into her ear.

"What did you say, Sean?" Completing the journey from sleep to awareness, Cassie sat up stretching her arms.

"Oh nothing. Muttering my favorite verse."

"I prefer painting and stage plays."

"Yes, you mentioned your high school awards in the Scholastic Art contest."

"I have to get my things," she said.

"How can I help? I'll be glad to pick up your belongings," I offered. I knew Thelma would skewer me on the spot.

"Let me handle it, Sean," Cassie suggested.

The alarm went off, clinking like a toy fire bell. Cassie Buzbie and I had discovered as much about each other as two new pupils in the school of love from which everyone else was strangely absent. I had quenched my thirst for a greedily desired object.

Cassie prepared a breakfast of coffee and day-old pastry. "Jeez, Sean. How long have you been a bachelor?" she mumbled, peering into the refrigerator.

"Six years," I shot back. "I've got to get to work. I'll see you later. Make yourself at home. I'll get you a duplicate key." As an afterthought I said, "Stay away from the landlady. She may not approve of our lifestyle."

"HEY, SULLIVAN, YOU LOOK LIKE THE PROVERBIAL Cheshire Cat. How come the smiles?" Givens asked. I wanted to keep my affair with Cassie a secret. His curiosity overtook him.

"Nothing special. Today has been a good day," I responded.

"Come on, Sullivan."

"I finished all my paperwork for this week and caught up on my field visits. Ready for the boss."

"Speaking of the Devil," Givens muttered.

Givens quick-stepped up to the well-dressed man entering the office. Shaking his hand vigorously, he clutched Mr. Kaufman's left shoulder in the classic pose of General MacArthur. Givens and Kaufman had both served in World War II.

"Mr. Kaufman, welcome to our happy little home." Givens physically guided our visitor to his desk.

The boss didn't mince words. "I have something to tell you and Sean. We're closing the Portland office and relocating you both to the Salem office late next month. Budget cuts you know."

Sam Kaufman eased his large frame into my chair. His many achievements included college football. Tall, deeply bronzed, with short cropped hair over azure blue eyes, he commanded an impressive presence. His stolen moments at the club contributed to his still-athletic physique. Mr. Kaufman was also a racquetball enthusiast of league caliber.

"There's something else I want to tell you. Confidentially, Cynthia complained to the Salem office about working conditions here. She said you are racist, bigots. That you treat her unfairly." Kaufman leaned back to await the expected onslaught of denials.

"Not true," Givens said. He responded with something of the shrill acerbity of a sergeant major on a barracks square.

"Well, she claims you guys make her feel uncomfortable." Kaufman looked me in the eye. "What do you say, Sean?" Always the spectator, seldom a participator, I could only disavow the charges.

"Gee! I thought she kinda liked me."

"One day she said 'I got rights'," Givens reported.

I refused to be dragged into a conversation on what I might or might not do or say in any number of circumstances. I didn't think I had any race or color prejudices, even though my father was born and raised in Mississippi. Our family conversations had been permeated with such expressions as "colored folk" and he was a "good nigger."

"I can assure you, sir, that I have not made any offensive remarks or gestures which might be construed as even slightly racial or bigoted,"

Givens announced. He towered above Kaufman, arms folded, expressing defiance.

"Nevertheless, I suggest you people conduct yourselves in a more exemplary manner. Above reproach," Kaufman replied. He paused, turning as Cynthia entered the room. "Oh hello, Cynthia. Didn't see ya. How are you? We were just talking about the move to Salem." The dialogue had become a game of circles.

"You can't expect me to move to Salem. I have kids. Someone has to be responsible," she asserted.

"Let's talk." Kaufman said.

Cynthia Coleas Jefferson marched into a glass enclosed office trailed by Mr. Kaufman. Dissonant sounds pierced the partition. Finger pointing in sync with appropriate facial expressions followed. Kaufman did not seem to be enjoying the responsibilities of an administrator.

Givens stared at Cynthia. A wounded animal confronting his attacker. I remained sharp and sprightly as with the heathen in his blindness. "Hey, Jason, did you know Jackie Robinson was named athlete of the year?" I asked. Givens was aghast at a potential confrontation with a co-worker.

I left the office as quietly as possible and raced home to Apartment 513. "Cassie, where are you? I'm home. It is I, your lover," I proclaimed grandly. The newness of the game left me anticipating the delights of the body. No response. Silence. Heavy breathing from the closet. "Cassie? Are you here? Come out, come out, where ever you are."

"Sean? Is that you?" a small voice whispered. Clutching a short towel to her body, Cassie materialized from inside the closet. "Oh, I'm so glad to see you. Your Uncle Max was here a few minutes ago. I was afraid to let him in the apartment. I had just stepped out of the bath when he knocked on the door. There I was, stark naked."

Cassie caught her breath. "I didn't want to embarrass you. He kept knocking on the door for the longest time." Gathering her emotions, I pressed her close to my chest. The towel dropped to the floor.

"That's okay." I said. "I'll call him. Don't worry. Uncle Max is a good guy." Slowly dialing the numbers, I reflected on what I might say to my favorite uncle. Shall I explain my amorosa and thereby risk condemnation by the family, or assume the mask of innocence.? As I dialed the number, droplets of perspiration webbed my neck and cheeks. The art of misinformation is an acquired talent.

Cassie started to dress. "I have a surprise for you. I'm going to be transferred to the Salem office in a month or so. Care to join me?" I asked. She colored like the ceramic coquette she pretended to be.

"Do you want me to go with you?" she asked.

"I would miss you." I gave a slow smile. "I have a good job. The future is ours." The silence was broken by the one word I yearned to hear.

"Yes."

The Javanese heads, who had long since become the deities of the household, silently chirped to each other in excitement. Cassie placed a large cardboard box, brown with time, on the Salvation Army dresser. "Sean, can I put some of my things in with yours?"

"Sure. Make yourself at home."

The phone jingled. As I reached to answer it, I placed my hand gently on Cassie's shoulder. "Hello? Oh, hi Thelma. How are you?" That was a mistake. Maybe she doesn't realize Cassie moved in with me. Expecting the worse, my fears were soon realized.

"She's underage! I didn't know." I feigned ignorance. "What's the legal age in Oregon?" I made a vain attempt to talk on the edges of a verbal mine field. "Aw, come on, Thelma! Cassie's a big girl. Her parents have their own families. I'll take good care of her. You don't need to worry."

Jerking my hand away from Cassie, I pantomimed defiance. "What?" I continued. "I'm sorry you feel that way, Thelma. Cassie can take care of herself." Thelma continued her harangue.

"I agree. She should finish her education. We have some fine colleges and universities here in the Portland area." I endured an old fashioned tirade for a good five minutes before, in surrender, I handed the phone to Cassie.

Cassie was enraged; her face turned beet red. A muted dialogue followed. I cannot bear conflict. I went into the living room and began a silent dialogue with the divinities of the household. My visitors from Surabaya.

"Yes, Thelma. I understand. I don't think my folks will be too concerned. They have their own families you know. Sorry." Cassie said. The conversation seemed endless. Cassie finally hung up the phone.

Before her tears dried she declared in sorrow, "I'm only eighteen. My cousin told me never to come back to her place if I stay with you.

She's going to call my mother. I don't know what to do. I am not going back to baby sit the rest of my life."

"Don't worry, Cassie. Something will work out. It always does." I remained the optimist.

"Hey, I have an idea," I said. "Let's go to Seattle for the weekend. Next Monday is Memorial day—a three day weekend. We need a change of scenery. I'm getting cabin fever."

"What's cabin fever?" she asked.

"A twelve foot stare in a ten foot room." Flushed with cheerfulness, I bid farewell to sadness and hello to the good times.

The following Saturday morning, I bundled Cassie into my old Ford and drove North across the Vancouver bridge in a torrential rain storm. "It would rain today. I was really looking forward to this weekend."

"Relax, Sean. The weather will clear." Cassie edged closer to me. My spirits soared. The rain lessened as we drove onto highway 99 North. Approaching Kalama, Washington, I talked fishing stories and the good old days.

Cassie broke my trance with, "Sean, you know I'm only eighteen and you've taken me across a state line. Maybe we should turn back."

"Why are you getting legal on me now? You want to go to Seattle with me, don't you? You sound like Thelma." Losing my taste for the love game, I considered alternatives. She calmed my fears by snuggling into my arm. I pulled her closer to me.

"Of course I do, Sean. I've never been to Seattle. It's new to me." Cassie continued her reassuring strokes. The old Pacific Highway took us West of Boeing field. A large sign on the right declared "King County Airport."

I scanned the area for a motel. "It's getting late. We should be looking for a place to stay for the night." I avoided the word motel.

"Oh, Sean, there's a clean looking motel." Cassie pointed to clapboard lighthouse attached to a string of small units. A flashing neon announced "The Dew Drop Inn Motel."

"Too sleazy and cheap looking. It doesn't look safe."

"Come on, Sean. We have to stay some place for the night. It's too late and too far to drive back to Portland. There! The Sixth Avenue Inn. That looks nice."

"Okay." I pulled into the alcove next to the office. Underneath the sign in bold gothic script, a sign read, "Please register here." "Where else would you register?" I questioned out loud. I accepted signs in their literal sense.

Once in a young man's life, he must climb to the top of a greasy pole to experience the first careless rapture of a night of bedroom gymnastics in a motel.

"Yes, Sir. Can I help you?" A gorilla of a man put down his well chewed cigar, placing both palms flat on the counter in a challenging stance. A yellow stained toothy smile snickered across the unshaven balloon of his face.

The office fronted small living quarters. A pinched faced women of graying years sat in an easy chair facing a box like TV. 'The Gale Storm Show' flickered through the darkened room, bouncing shadows off the ceiling.

"Yes. My wife and I would like a room for a night." My falsetto voice barely passed the test. Lies are spoken in silence.

The big bear squinted through rain swept windows. "Is that her sitting in the car?" he bellowed. The scent of cheap whiskey floated into my face.

"Yes." Perspiration formed on my forehead. Burning lava filled my mouth. Breathing became difficult. I began to salivate. My innards dissolved into a mixer of churning acid. I wanted to shout, "Of course it's her, you idiot!"

"Fill out this form," the keeper of the keys to paradise ordered.

Clutching a pen in my right hand I attempted my first pass at registration. Uncontrollable palsy guided my right hand. My efforts looked like Indian petroglyphs carved on stone.

"You forgot the license plate number." The manager's beer belly spilled over the counter. I couldn't have remembered the license plate even if he had a gun in my back. I struggled out the door into a torrential downpour to check the numbers.

Slipping on the wet pavement I fell into a large pothole filled with water. Howling to God in general and to no one in particular, I roared, "Not to worry, Dear Lord. This is my welcoming ritual for Seattle." I returned to the office and wrote in the plate number on the soggy form.

The big man said, "Here you are, son." Tossing room keys to me he winked, "Have fun."

I escorted Cassie to cabin number twelve. Down the path of love into the motel room. "Well, it looks clean," Cassie declared. She ran her hand across the top of a thrift shop dresser. I bounced on the bed signaling Cassie to join me.

"I wonder what's on the telly?" I said.

"You mean you've come all this way just to watch TV?" Her eyes flashed disgust.

"Sorry, I was only kidding." I pulled her to me.

"Let me shower first," she said, pulling away. Taking a pink lacy peignoir from a shopping bag, Cassie floated into the bathroom. "Five minutes," she promised, closing the shower door.

I switched on the TV and dialed in "The Honeymooners." Jackie Gleason doing the Ralph Kramden schtick brought tears of laughter to my eyes as Cassie appeared framed in the doorway. Completely nude, she struck an inviting pose.

"Sean...Me or the TV?" she murmured.

I tripped over the coffee table in my hurry to turn off the tube. Crashing to the floor, I made a futile attempt to regain my composure.

A long remembered evening of delicious sexual delirium tremens followed. Pleasure seeking continued far into the night. Cassie Buzbie and Sean Sullivan reached the peak of Mount Orgy.

"You know, Cassie, I can't feel a thing." I said. My spina bifida left me without sensation in an area where it most counted. Complete silence, then we became a whirling dervish in a frenzy of sexual gratification. I had never known such sweet thunder.

She wanted more of me. Cassie surrendered to a session of gyrations which surprised me. In the first torment she loved me. Two years later she loved love.

Dawn lurked through the blinds. Awake, we decided to take a short tour of Seattle before returning to Portland. Two hours later we circled back to the floating bridge and Mercer Island. We turned South on Lake Washington Boulevard and headed back to Portland.

IN THE LATTER PART OF JUNE 1956, WE PACKED UP OUR few belongings and moved to Salem, Oregon. A few days later Cassie joined me for a brown bag lunch at my office. I introduced her to Mr. Kaufman. He expressed curiosity as to our relationship.

Cassie met me at the front door on my return from the first day of work. "How do you like your new office, Sean?"

"It's great. The people are nice. It's a much bigger office than in Portland—two counselors and a full time doctor on staff. He's a nice guy but I think he is an alcoholic. A dermatologist by specialty," I answered. "Say, do you think the landlady knows we aren't married?"

"I don't know. Don't worry. We're not causing any trouble."

"She gave me a funny look when I walked into the apartment," I said. I proceeded to profile my co-workers in some detail, then asked her, "How was your day?"

"I spent most of my time putting things away and talking to the landlady. She's interested in your physical condition."

"Oh God, that's all I need."

"Don't worry. I said you were injured in a car accident. I didn't say anything about your bowels and bladder. People don't understand." She sighed. For the next three years Cassie would find herself in situations explaining or defending me.

I bellowed Shakespeare's, "They jest at scars that never felt a wound." Why not enjoy the face of desire and the mask of a dream? June faded into July 1956. Cassie became important to me.

Jerry Burns and I made up the counseling staff in residence in Salem, Oregon. Dr. Haas, medical consultant, and Mr. Kaufman, the supervisor, were augmented by a covey of clerical people.

The doctor had fallen on hard times thanks to his drinking. Dismissed by clinic partners, he had lost his family and the respect of his friends. He lived a wretched lonely existence.

A shabby three room flat sufficed as his digs. On the occasions when he failed to report for work, a staff member would volunteer to phone or visit his home. We usually found him sprawled over an old moth-eaten easy chair. We felt waking him would be an insult to what little dignity he possessed.

Dr. Haas became the office yarn spinner. In his moments of sobriety, the doctor unfolded tales of student days in gross anatomy; macabre in content, droll in rendition. "Hey you guys. Did I ever tell you of the time we excised a spinal ganglia from a human cadaver?"

"No," we chorused. We anticipated another slice of life.

"A visitor came into the gross anatomy lab. We told him we had excised the backbone of an elephant." Forced chuckles would follow.

"We would put human heads in someone's locker." A tomb-like silence stilled any response.

"I guess it's time for lunch. I'm bagging it today," he said. Dr. Haas bit into a homemade cheese sandwich as though it were his last meal.

Probably the only meal of the day. I mumbled something about skipping lunch as I walked out of the office.

The dog days of August were upon us with a severe heat wave. At a staff meet our supervisor bellowed, "Listen up everybody." Mr. Kaufman waited for our attention. "I'd like you to meet Helen Atwood, our new counselor." Pleasantries were exchanged. Helen soon became "one of the boys," yet still managed to retain her femininity.

Engrossed in my own bit of heaven, I failed to notice anything different in the office. "Psst, Sean, come here," Burns whispered a few days later. He pushed his chair back. We huddled together speaking in loud stage whispers. "Did you know the boss and Helen are having an affair?"

"No. How long?" I asked. My voice penetrated the far reaches of the office.

"Apparently it started when she moved over here from the V.A." Burns offered more tidbits of gossip. Just then Kaufman and Helen Atwood returned from a three martini lunch, noisily interrupting our conversation.

"Hey, Sean. I want to talk to you," Kaufman said. My supervisor wheeled into his office, waving me to a chair. The man was obviously drunk. The conversation rambled. He gradually introduced budget cuts into the dialogue. Justifying the need for such action he announced, "We're going to have to let you go, Sean. I'm sorry."

A crisis is best met with silence. To myself, I said "Don't whine, you idiot." Aloud, I said "I've tried to do a good job."

"Oh no, Sean! It's not your performance. You're a competent counselor, and it's been a pleasure knowing you. It's the damn legislature." A few minutes of grief counseling followed. I left the office with as much dignity as I could muster, paying particular attention to my balance.

"By the way, Sullivan, are you living with that girl?" Fumbling for words he continued, "What's her name?" He slumped into his chair. "Just remember, you can make a mistake without being a mistake."

"Her name is Cassie and we plan to get married," I declared with the finality of a Martin Luther nailing the ninety-ninth thesis to the church door. I had viewed Kaufman as a friend. I staggered to my desk.

"Sullivan, what's the matter? What happened? What did he say?" Jerry Burns nervously inquired.

"I've been fired. Let go. Sacked. Terminated. Budget cuts," I stammered. "I don't know what to do. What will I tell Cassie?"

"That's news to me. I haven't heard anything regarding budget cuts. I think you're the only one they're letting go. I bet he's making a place for Helen at your expense." Burns turned and walked away.

That night, dinner crawled along in silence. "What's wrong, Sean? You haven't eaten anything." Cassie had gained experience in defining my tastes.

"I have some bad news for you. I lost my job today."

"Oh, Sean! I'm so sorry. What happened?" Her voice touched me and a gentle melancholy fell upon me with a strange enchantment.

I screamed a silent scream, followed by a cry of agony, "Oh God!" I became a strong swimmer in a sea of weeds. The words popped out of nowhere. "Cassie, will you marry me? I think we can have a great life together."

7

"HAPPINESS IN THE PRESENT TENSE

THE HEADLINES OF SEPTEMBER AND OCTOBER 1956 read, "Soviets invade Hungary, The British and French invade Egypt."

News Item: "Jackie Gleason, Art Carney, Audrey Meadows and Joyce Randolph finished the last of 'The Honeymooners' thirty-nine episodes. Meadows, whose two brothers were lawyers, obtained a residual contract on all reruns; forever. Gleason secured a generous percentage of rerun profits."

Elvis Presley appeared on the Ed Sullivan Show singing "Don't be Cruel."

John Lardner wrote in Time magazine, "Elvis acts like an outboard motor in love."

The newspapers advertised a two-door Bel Air Chevrolet convertible for $2338.

The bird of sorrow sobbed.

"What are we going to do? Kaufman said I could stay until the end of the month," I said. I felt like Jesus on the cross.

After a few moments of meditation, Cassie's eyes sparkled with an idea. "I know. You can get a job as a teacher or a counselor. You have experiences in welfare, right?"

"Yes, but where are we going to live? I don't have the slightest idea. I don't want to go back to Portland; it's too wet. But we wouldn't be happy in Salem—no friends or family." We each offered a smorgasbord of proposals. Pros and cons of arguments were considered and rejected.

In exasperation I slapped the table. "Let's move to Eureka, California. My mother and brother live nearby. You won't mind living close to my relatives." I didn't wait for an answer. "My mother manages a motel in Klamath and my brother Zack lives in Crescent City. I might be able to get a job with the county welfare."

Cassie remained silent. Hearing no opposition, I took her silence to be a yes vote. She changed the topic to wedding plans. "I would like a church wedding," she said.

"Where? Portland? Salem? Eureka?" And as an afterthought, "Boise, Idaho?" I asked.

"Oh no! Not Boise. I don't think my folks would come to the wedding."

"Remember when we drove by the old Mt. Tabor Methodist church on Stark Street in Portland?. It's my mother's family church. They attended services there for years," I said. She made no comment.

"I think it's across the street from a grade school Ma attended in 1910."

"Sounds interesting, Sean."

"Then let's go to Portland next Saturday and make inquiries."

"Okay."

"My last day at work is on a Friday. How about Saturday, September first, for the wedding?" Our plans became an adventure into the unknown.

"Sounds great! I need to write my cousin Jayne and ask her if she'll be my maid of honor. You'll like her. And tomorrow I'll go shopping at Meier & Frank for my wedding dress."

"I didn't know they had a store here in Salem." I speculated on how much her dress would cost.

"Let's go to bed. It's getting late. I'm tired." Cassie said. We fell into a sleep full of sweet visions of things to come. Nothing happens unless first you dream. A week later I met her cousin.

"Sean, I'd like you to meet Jayne. Jayne, this is my husband-to-be, Sean Sullivan." Jayne extended her hand. I acknowledge her presence with a slight bow.

"Just think, this time next week you'll be a married man." She winked. Jayne Blaine, from Boise, Idaho, a tall willowy blonde, smiled demurely. Thoughts of marrying the wrong cousin flashed through my mind.

"Sean, what do you think of my wedding dress?" Cassie asked. Her question startled me. She held up a gown of deep purple.

"Why not white?" I asked.

She didn't answer. Jayne was probably the only virgin at our wedding. After a few minutes of conversation the wedding party went to lunch.

ON SATURDAY, SEPTEMBER 1, 1956, THE DAY OF THE wedding, rain threatened. The place, Mt. Tabor Methodist Church Portland, Oregon; Charles R. McCorkle presiding. "You may kiss your bride," he commanded solemnly. Then the red headed Irishman offered his congratulations.

I lifted Cassie's nose-length veil. In due time the deed was done. My father demanded many poses for his new hobby—photography. Mindy had diverted his outbursts of temper with a new toy.

My cousin, Duncan MacDonald, served as best man. "Sean, your side of the aisle is quite full. But I don't see Aunt Kathleen anywhere," he whispered.

"I talked to her on the phone last week. She wasn't able to get away from the motel," I replied. I sensed Ma did not approve of the marriage. She had been shocked by my first trek to the alter with June Peterson.

After the wedding June's father had said, "You married half a man." The reference to my birth defect was a flaming arrow to the heart. My thoughts were interrupted by my cousin.

"You said she runs a small motel in Klamath, California," Duncan half questioned, half answered.

"Yes, that's right. It's a popular tourist resort in Northern California. Good fishing." Eager to be with Cassie, I turned away. I turned back, "Thanks for being my best man. I appreciate your time. Excuse me, I have to talk to Cassie."

I moved towards my father. "Hey, Dad. Can I have some copies of the pictures as a memento? I'll send you our new address." I looked at my father.

"You still live in Salem, don't you. Why are you moving? Where are you going? Come here. I want to talk to you." The old man grabbed me by the arm.

At a momentary loss for words I finally stammered, "Yesterday was my last day on the job. Budget cuts. We're moving to Eureka, California. I think I can get a job with the county welfare. Cassie and I are spending the night at the Multnomah Hotel."

My father lectured me loud and clear on the health of the soul. The rewards of honest toil were high on his list of priorities. Heads turned. Eyes narrowed. An unseen thunder of quiet muffled the joyous gathering.

"Tell me, Mr. Sullivan. Is this a 35 mm with telescopic capability? I've always wanted one." Reverend McCorkle inspected the old man's camera.

"Let's go, Cassie. Throw your bouquet to Jayne. I think she wants to get married." As we approached our car Cassie smiled, turned and tossed her wedding bouquet over her head in the direction of her cousin. My father caught the flowers.

Thirty minutes later, Cassie and I hopped, skipped and jumped through the lobby of the Multnomah Hotel in downtown Portland. I fell. Recovering with as much aplomb as possible, we proceeded to the front desk holding hands and giggling.

Uniformed bellboys stood at attention. Chandeliers glittering overhead with leather Ottomans and cushioned settees conveniently placed adding to the European ambience of Portland's finest hotel. The Multnomah. Twenty five dollars for a double, tax included. I caught the eye of the desk clerk.

"We have a reservation. Mr. and Mrs. Sullivan," I announced. How sweet the sound.

The innkeeper drawled, "I'll check, Sir." Slowly rifling through a rolodex, the peacock announced, "Yes, Sir. I believe we have a room for a Mr. & Mrs. Soloman."

"No! No! That's Mr. and Mrs. Sullivan of Salem, Oregon. We just got married. This is our wedding night." I announced to one and all. A demure Cassie presented the required blush.

"Oh, yes, Sir. That's Sullivan with two 'l's.' So sorry. Please fill out this form." The functionary smiled a we shared a secret look. Holding my right hand steady, I did the Seattle motel paux de duex. Nervousness became prickly heat. Every inch of my body needed scratching. An eternity followed before the blessed words were spoken, "Your room key, Sir."

Zigzagging to the elevator, we boarded our magic carpet and smooched our way to the long anticipated promised land. "You don't have to carry me across the threshold, Sean," Cassie said.

"It's okay. Just observing tradition." Gently I put her down on the bed. A few minutes later she retreated to the bathroom.

Cassie donned a pink peignoir, posing in a "tonight is the night" look. She turned and performed a little shimmy. I had never seen a women so beautiful or so happy. Her face was full of trust.

The scent of Jasmine stirred our desires over and over. As the evening grew darker we professed our eternal love. Kind, if not severe, in my love making, I sensed something missing. A strange void unfilled. A change in attitude. A friendship slowly withering.

The final verdict would arrive in the summer of 1959. I had romanced her at leisure and wedded in haste. Seizing fate by the throat, we strangled ourselves in kisses and hugs.

The next morning, after a shouting match, Cassie finally managed to extricate her remaining wardrobe from cousin Thelma. Several "you'll be sorry!" admonitions pierced the snow flakes. I waited in the car at a discreet distance.

A man's white shirt, source unknown, overlapped her rolled up jeans. Penny loafers and a pony tail completed her getup. Cassie had recently read The Portland Oregonian article featuring the fashions of the times.

"Did she give you a bad time? I'm sorry. I should have been with you." On occasion, life became past tense for me.

"Let's go," Cassie said.

On September 2, 1956, we set our compass South for Eureka, California, on a voyage of no return with the firm belief that all our days would be spring-like. Clickity-clacking down Highway 99, the old Ford coughed asthmatically as we towed a U-haul "rent it here-leave it there" trailer filled with Goodwill furniture.

Passing through the farm towns of the Willamette Valley, I opined, "We must look like characters from 'Tobacco Road'." Pulling into the first Shell station on the outskirts of Grants Pass, Oregon, I ordered, "Fill it up, please, and check the oil." Then asked, "Can you suggest a good restaurant hereby?"

The Fraiser boy was beginning to realize that dropping out of high school hadn't been such a good idea. Pumping gas or janitoring had lost its youthful appeal. But how else could he support a girl friend, now wife, pregnant with twin boys?

In a few minutes we found our way to the Cafe Elite, locally known as Tomaine Tommys. "Sean, it's a long way to Eureka. Should we stay here tonight? You must be tired." Cassie expressed concern.

"Oh, I guess I didn't tell you. Tonight we're staying at my mother's motel near Trinidad, California. It's a few miles north of Eureka. I talked to her on the phone the other day while you were shopping." I seldom sought the confidence of anyone, preferring the fait accompli approach to decision making.

"I'll have to change clothes. I can't meet your family looking like this," she said.

"Sure you can. You look good to me."

"Oh, no! I'm not going to meet your mother dressed like this," she insisted.

"Cassie, it's your personality, your character, that's what counts—not what you're wearing," I said. She scurried outside to the car, and yanked a cardboard suitcase out of the trailer. She made her way to the ladies room, the stares of fellow diners following her every step.

Cassie returned to the cafe a few minutes later decked out in a feminine green pinafore with a red-laced bodice. Her hair was festooned with two blue ribbons on either side, topping off the cute little girl look of 1956. Her facial expression said, "God, I hope his mother likes me."

Two and a half hours later kith and kin greeted us at my mother's motel near Trinidad. "Family, I would like you meet Cassie." Grinning like a Cheshire cat, I continued, "Cassie, this is my mother, brother Zack, Uncle Max and Aunt Peggy. Oh, and this is Scottie, the family dog."

Brother Zack accepted Cassie with a bon vivant attitude and a condescending bow of the head. A gallant kiss of her hand brought forth an "ooh" from Cassie. "Tell me, were you drunk the night you married Sean?" Zack laughed.

"I don't understand," Cassie grimaced. Few people understood the sick humor existing between the Brothers Sullivan. "Just kidding, Cassie. Welcome to the family," he smiled.

"Pleased to meet you, Cassie," Ma said. My mother held out her hand. Her tone of voice and body language gave away her true feelings. I had feared she wouldn't approve of this marriage. She didn't.

"Hi, Cassie. How are you?" Uncle Max smiled. His winning ways put her at ease.

"Oh, you look so pretty! What a nice dress," Aunt Peggy hugged her. Chit chat completed, the clan adjourned to the living room for coffee and canapés. A newly made fire crackled under the mantle was decorated with family pictures.

Ma assigned us room nine. Upstairs in the corner over her bedroom. The next morning, after three or four rounds of, "Goodbye! Have a good trip," we continued South to Eureka.

Early in the evening our headlights spotted "The Breakers—Accommodations by the Day, Week, or Month." Located in the middle of Eureka on Fourth Street, the place had seen better days. "It'll only be for a few days. I'm sure we can find something permanent soon," I said reassuringly.

"Sure, Sean. It looks okay to me." Cassie was the good wife.

I registered with gusto, grabbed the room keys, and walked towards the car. No more playing the wimp. No more ceremony of innocence. I spent the next few days looking for a job and enjoying marriage in general.

The manager of the motel referred us to a lady in Arcata, the home of Humboldt State College. A small two bedroom house, badly in need of paint, awaited our inspection at 1337 Sunset Lane. After a brief conversation, the owner agreed to a rent of $75.00 a month.

The landlady, Mrs. Garbarino, had recently secured title to the house in a divorce action. Her fall from grace was completed the following Sunday. The church suggested she practice her religion elsewhere.

"Will you accept our check? It's on a Portland Bank. We haven't had a chance to change our account yet," I said.

Cassie chimed into the conversation. "I think we'll set up an account at Bank of America. Do they have a branch here in Arcata?"

"Yes, they do. It's on Fifth and L Streets."

I miscalculated the amount due the landlady. She studied the paper for an eternity. "I'm sorry Mr. Sullivan. The amount is wrong. You forgot to add in the deposit, which is refundable." Mrs. Garbarino handed the check back to me.

Cassie grabbed the check and wrote in the correct amount. I mouthed, "There goes the savings."

"I'll furnish the paint if you'll do the work," Mrs. Garbarino said. She looked straight at me.

"I like this place. What color for the house?" I said. Cassie envisioned hues of desert sand with borders of lemon yellow.

"You don't think I'm going to paint this house by myself?" I declared.

"Of course not, Sean. You know I love to paint. Anything." I walked around the outside. Maybe it didn't need painting.

"What type of work does you husband do?" Mrs. Garbarino inquired.

"Sean is a teacher-counselor. He taught English and social studies in Oregon. He also worked as a hospital and vocational rehabilitation counselor."

"Humboldt County Welfare is in need of social caseworkers. My ex-husband is a friend of the administrator. I'd be glad to call him," Mrs. Garbarino offered. She paused. "We're still on amicable terms, despite the divorce." Our new landlady turned out to be a fountain of information, making suggestions and giving directions.

"And for lunch I suggest Lazio's at the foot of C Street in Eureka. You do like seafood, Mr. Sullivan?"

"Yes." We headed towards Eureka and a late lunch.

"Sean, you'd better stop at the supermarket on Broadway. I don't think we can afford to eat out."

TIME, A SONG WITHOUT END, SANG A HAPPY TUNE THE Fall of 1956. Cassie painted the house. The county Welfare department hired me.

"Your case load will include General Assistance, Aid to Dependent Needy Children, Old Age Assistance and The Hoopa Valley Indian Reservation. You also will be required to serve as intake worker at least two days a week." Edmund Nix, the deputy administrator, fingered his thin moustache, straightened his Stanford school tie (Cardinal red), and continued a precise description of the job at hand.

"I understand," I said.

"Bye the bye. When you're acting as the intake worker, you will dole out to selected General Assistant clients the correct measurement of surplus items such as rice, lard, sugar and assorted canned food. The proper amounts are posted on the wall in the back room. The client will present you with a chit signed by myself or Betty Higenbothem the administrator."

Nix, the number two man, scrutinized me with arrogance. Earlier in the day he had voiced his opposition of me to the administrator. A clerical person related the conversation to me at a later time.

"But Sullivan's a cripple. How can he do the work? He has to drive up to the Reservation and most of his caseload is in the country—walking up and down stairs."

"As you know, my younger brother Ted, a veteran of World War Two, is in a wheelchair for life. Consider his many accomplishments. And he won the Klamath River Salmon Derby last fall." Mrs. Higenbotham paused in reflection. "By the way, in what service did you perform your duty?"

Mr. Nix averted his eyes. A spot on the ceiling held his attention. Betty Higenbothem, an imposing figure, graying in her forties, summed up her endorsement of me. "I have observed Mr. Sullivan driving around town." Quietly she added, "Besides, I like him. He will be a welcomed addition to the staff. Perhaps even a role model to some of our welfare career clients."

The Indian Summer of September 1956 dissolved into October rains. Cassie finished painting the house. I addressed my new tasks with a vigor motivated by the responsibility of having a wife.

"You sure are taking your new job seriously. Good for you! How do you like the people at the office?" Cassie asked.

"They're good people and I like what I do. But I have to work with dubious clients sometimes. They're poor—many of them really need help." I added, "Several clients received an extra ration of lard and beans this afternoon. Nix is stingy with government surplus."

The following day I set out for morning coffee at the Sheriff's office—a newly acquired habit. I thought the Sheriff a fountain of information, not realizing I gave more than I received. In reality Albert Nicholson's cooperation became more important than tidbits of gossip. The coffee was free.

"Sean, I think some of your clients are hiding their timber resources. One of my sources mentioned a well-known family. You should look into the records." He gave me a name.

I put down my doughnut and coffee mug, emblazoned with gold letters, "Property of Humboldt County- Sheriff's Office." "Excuse me." Scampering out the door, I set sail for the county record's office. A few minutes later I discovered gold in the county clerk's office. "Eureka," I hollered. "Just as I thought."

"Yes, this is Eureka, California. Did you find something?" the county clerk responded. She was a tiny gnome of a lady with a heart bigger than her deformed body. Hazel Carr, born with a humpback, had become the major-domo in county offices by out-performing the competition every day of the week. She had accepted me as a member of the brethren the moment we first made eye contact.

"I sure have. I'll talk to you later. Thank you so much." Pushing the oversize handwritten ledgers in her direction, I rushed out the door. Highway 299 took me to State 96 near the Hoopa Valley Indian Reservation and my target; the Sandoval cabin. I anticipated a hostile situation as I headed North to Arcata in a "State of California - Official Use Only" Ford.

Turning into a driveway, I called out, "Hello, Mr. Sandoval." I stepped out of the car. "I'm Sean Sullivan, your new caseworker." A menagerie of bleating, braying and breeding farm animals joined by a pod of children of various sizes, shapes, and ages descended on me. An emaciated farmer with tobacco juice dripping down his unshaven face grimaced a toothless grin in my direction.

Henry Sandoval, clearly displeased with the turn of events, surveyed me. The fragrance of a nearby coffee pot filled my nostrils. A woman's voice said, "What happened to the other caseworker? She and I got along fine."

A tired looking woman in her forties appeared on the porch. A dirty blanket served as the front door. Holding a frying pan sizzling with greens and fat back, she slowly moved towards me. Her face was plundered by the relentless caress of time. "How do? I'm the misses," she rasped. Several pimply urchins grabbed her hands demanding to play ring around the rosy.

"Pleased to met you, Mrs. Sandoval. I'm Sean Sullivan from the county welfare office." Answering her question I said, "She retired, health reasons. Her family put her in a nursing home up near McKlinlyville, near the ocean. I'm taking her place."

"Well, she was getting long in the tooth. Sorry to see her leave, though." Mrs. Sandoval picked up an empty plate. "Care for some mustard turnips and hog fat? Real good."

The lady of the housed waved a crackling frying pan in my face. Jumping back, I stumbled and lost my footing. I landed in a mud puddle and flayed away at the sky in an attempt to get back on my feet. I clutched the car door in a death grip. After an eternity, I succeeded in raising myself to my full five feet nine. Ma and Pa Sandoval stood smiling rotting teeth at me.

"I've been going over your file. The office of deeds indicates that you hold, in joint tenancy, seventy fives acres of prime timberland. Usable and saleable." I stated, "If this is true, you no longer qualify for Aid to Needy Children or any other public assistance."

"What! How'd you find out? I'll bet it was that midget down at the county offices!" Mrs. Sandoval screamed. Unthinking, I blurted out, "She has been helpful."

"Well, by golly, I demand a hearing!" Mrs. Sandoval, experienced in the ways of welfare, continued her harangue. "We've had hearings before and we've always won. Ya hear?" Pushing the frying pan into my chest, she and the whole entourage shuffled closer to me.

"Now let's stay calm, folks. I'm not out to do you any harm, but you haven't declared all your resources. I'm required by law to hold your next check." I launched into a short dissertation on county and federal requirements for applicants. Something the Sandovals had known for years.

"You sound like them lawyer fellas in Eureka town. We have our rights," Mrs. Sandoval said. The mother hen protected her brood, including her husband, as a lion with cubs. The velocity of the conversation subsided. Retreat seemed to be the better part of something.

"Let me go back to the office, folks, and study the situation," I said. The phrase "our rights" irritated me. I also have rights.

"You better," they demanded over the cacophony of eight kids, assorted farm animals, and the stridency of "Rock Around The Clock" emanating from an unseen radio at ear splitting volume. I slammed the car door, jammed the key into the ignition, and accelerated the engine twice before racing off in a cloud of dust.

At the stroke of six Cassie welcomed me home. She wore a gray high-waisted skirt trimmed with miniature red roses and complimented by a pink satin blouse. Radiant in her refinement, Cassie performed a petite pirouette ending with a warm kiss. "Hi, Sean. How was your day?"

Cassie became a companion in my labors. She shared my little triumphs and tragedies. The floral scented dew of our honeymoon remained as sweet as the first day of September. "Just fair. I had quite a session with my clients." I hesitated to unburden. Exhausted, I fell into my favorite chair.

"The house looks nice. You've almost finished painting." I wanted to complement Cassie on her efforts. Early in the marriage I made an effort to flatter Cassie often.

"Well, what happened? Tell me about your day. You look pale," she continued. Then added, "Did you remember to pick up the hamburger?"

"Oh, God. I forgot. Sorry." The madness at the Sandovals had emptied my mind of such mundane things as picking up the hamburger. "I thought they were going to attack me. I barely got out of there alive." As a postscript I added, "I'll go get the hamburger."

"I planned to have meat loaf tonight…Who did what to you?" she asked.

"I checked the county records on one of my clients, the Sandovals, this morning and discovered they have seventy five acres of prime timber held in joint tenancy. That makes them ineligible for state and county aid. Of course they were upset when I said I was going to stop their checks." I paused for breath. "I thought they were going to do me harm…You said meat loaf?"

"Don't worry, I'll go. But tell me more," Cassie insisted.

"When I returned from Hoopa, Nix said a hearing has been set for next Monday morning at 10.30. I knew they were going to ask for an inquiry but I didn't think it would happen so soon. It usually takes two or three weeks to arrange an investigation, but apparently the Sandovals know Nix or Betty Higenbothem. As far as I'm concerned, they aren't eligible for public assistance. Too many resources disqualify them. Right is right. And wrong is wrong."

There is always something pathetic in the smashing of a moral code of arms. I played by the rules of the game. Why not others?

"Just relax, Sean. I'll be back soon and we'll have a nice dinner. 'The Millionaire' is on Channel Three. In fact, Channel Three is the only TV station in town." Her suggestion pacified me.

"You get used to having only one station," I said. "At least we won't fight over which channel to watch. Besides I like 'The Millionaire'."

Monday morning arrived. I put the paper down as the hearing began promptly at 10.30 a.m. Those present included the hearing officer, John J. McEwen of the State Attorney General's office, Mrs. Higenbothem, County Welfare Administrator, Edmund Nix, Deputy Administrator, Sean Forte Sullivan, social caseworker, Lisa Perkins, stenographer, and petitioners Henry and Olive Sandoval.

During the prehearing chit chat, I studied McEwen. "Let's come to order folks." J.J. McEwen, former tight end of Notre Dame and 1949 Heiseman Trophy winner, banged his gavel one more time. A tailored cut eliminated much of the informality of his blue sport jacket. An eye patch focused attention on his pink Hathaway shirt. Pleated gray flannel slacks and alligator shoes with explosions on the toes completed McEwen's attire. Even in Eureka, the best dressed logging town in Northern California, McEwen looked as inconspicuous as a gorilla in the hen house.

The Sandovals, attired in their best bib and tucker, portrayed a farm couple dressed in the gothic manner of a Grant wood painting, minus the pitchfork.

The county welfare administrator, regal in an emerald green blouse and sapphire skirt, presented an oriental influence. A jeweled metallic brocade placed high on the left shoulder added to the fashion statement. Edging closer to the deputy administrator, Ms. Higenbotham inquired, "New suit, Mr. Nix?"

Fingering his moustache, Nix was an easy look-a-like for Sir Anthony Eden, British Foreign minister of the time. "Oh, yes. I thought I would make an investment in my career." He regretted the remark. His curt voice masked feelings of resentment. Nix surprised himself by adding, "Betty, I can handle this hearing."

Heads turned in unison. "Oh Edmund, I'm just an on-looker." Her hand on his shoulder restored a sense of camaraderie. The administrator, a one time school teacher, loudly proclaimed, "Everybody, just pretend I'm not here."

Tolstoy's famous quote, "Try not to think of an elephant under a street lamp," surfaced in my thoughts.

"Look here, Mister McEwen, let's get started. We have to feed the hogs and the other livestock and it's a long ride home." Already irritated, Sandoval drummed his fingers on the conference table.

"Yes, you're right. Let me first review some of the rules and regulations of several Public Assistance grants." McEwen ticked off, in as many one syllable words he could come up with, the guidelines for Family Assistance and Aid To Needy Children Assistance programs. "The Federal government makes grants to the states to help provide financial assistance, medical care and social services to certain persons in need, including dependent children—"

Sandoval interrupted, "I got eight kids."

Carefully picking lint off of his blue pinstriped suit one piece at a time, Nix admonished, "Yes, we know."

"I'll continue," McEwen pronounced. Quite at home with a football team, he nevertheless seemed ill at ease with the human animal. "And the physically and mentally handicapped. Resources must be valued at $1500.00 or less for an individual or $2500.00 or less for a couple."

"I don't understand." Sandoval's eyes were riveted on me. "Our house, our car and the farm animals?"

"The house you live in and the land under it do not count in the means test. Neither do the farm animals unless you're making a profit—butchering them for sale. What kind of car do you own?" McEwen asked.

"An old Cadillac."

"How old?"

"Don't know."

"It must be older than five years. I'll have Mr. Sullivan do some research."

"What the hell does he know about cars? He's the one started all this. We never had any trouble getting county help before he came to the farm." Sandoval propelled himself out his chair, stood behind me, and slammed the conference table with his fist. The thunderclap surprised everyone at the table.

"Be nice, Mr. Sandoval. Mr. Sullivan is only doing his job. After all, we're dealing with taxpayer money," Ms. Higenbothem said.

The administrator's steady gaze forced Mr. Sandoval back to his chair. He held his wife's hand for moral support. I shot an appreciative glance in Ms. Higenbothem's direction, followed by a look of rebuke to the Sandovals.

"What is it, Mr. Sullivan?" inquired McEwen.

"Nothing, Sir. Sorry."

"Then let us proceed…Mr. Sullivan informed us the county office of deeds and conveyances indicate you own seventy five acres of prime timber land near the Hoopa Valley Indian Reservation. Is this true?"

"Hell, no. We's just po' folks." A Southern dialect, piously adopted, followed by a failed attempt to snap his suspenders, completed the affectation.

"Both Miss Carr, the county clerk, and Mr. Sullivan vouch for the deed recordings and the transfer of land title to you and your wife in joint tenancy, Mr. Sandoval," McEwen persisted. He glanced at me with a hint of reprimand in his face.

Sandoval exploded. "I ain't lyin'! I'm a God-fearin' man. I go to church almost every Sunday." Turning to his wife he appealed, "Don't I?"

"He sure do," chirped Olive Sandoval. She barely survived a boring farm life, experiencing many defeats but few victories. We looked into the old face of a young women who had prematurely reached the age where life's passions had long since disappeared.

"Now, now, Mr. Sandoval. We haven't accused you of falsehoods. We just want to get at the truth. As hearings officer, I will now call each individual to come forward and make their statements."

"Not fair," the Sandovals protested in harmony. "There's four of you and only two of us."

Nix interrupted. "I would like to point out, Sir, that Ms. Perkins, our office stenographer, is here only to take notes of these proceedings. She is not a party to this affair."

I offered, "Let's keep our tempers and try to resolve the situation."

"Good idea, Sean. A touch of equanimity would help matters." The buxom administrator added her presence to the fray.

"May I suggest we ask Hazel Carr to join the hearing? She can verify Mr. Sullivan's report," McEwen said.

"That midget!" Sandoval sneered with screwed up face.

"Mr. Sandoval, please," the administrator admonished.

The hearing officer momentarily hallucinated back to headlines of 1949, "McEwen of Notre Dame Heiseman Trophy Winner." He turned to Nix. "I wish I had never accepted this position. I studied political science at the university, you know. I worked for the governor after retiring from the Detroit Lions. It was a political appointment."

"I know what you mean," Nix responded. I could see Nix smile a touch of comradeship.

Mrs. Higenbotham demanded, "Mr. McEwen, I suggest we adjourn this hearing until next week. I am past arguing."

"Oh no we're not! I'm not flying up here from Sacramento on that old DC3 again. We lost a tire as we landed at Ukiah. Scared the hell out of me." His huge frame slumped forward underscoring his point.

"Then perhaps we could reassemble after lunch. In the meantime, I can ask Ms. Carr to join us," I offered. I wanted to become the peacemaker. The others were astonished.

"Agreed!" McEwen gaveled with relief.

When we gathered for the afternoon session, Hazel Carr, seated between the Sandovals and me, made an attractive addition to the group. She radiated cheerfulness. One could almost forget her gnome-like shell of a body held together by a humpback.

Sandoval pulled his chair closer to his wife, seeking comfort and distance from the humpback.

"This hearing will come to order," McEwen pronounced, to no avail. The participants engaged each other in a clatter of conversation, all except for the Sandovals. Hazel Carr and I huddled together.

"People, please. I have a four o'clock plane to catch." McEwen begged. His pleadings went answered.

Ms. Carr handed a sheave of notarized papers to the hearings officer. I savored a moment of personal triumph. This will save the county $15,000 a year.

"What did you find regarding Henry and Olive Sandoval, Miss Carr?" he asked.

"Mr. Sullivan came to my office to search the county records. After a few minutes he yelled 'Eureka.' I assured him this was Eureka, California." The clerk continued. "I read a notation indicating title to seventy five acres of land near the Hoopa Indian Valley Reservation held jointly by Henry and Olive Sandoval, et al. By the way, 'et. al' means 'and others'."

"Yes, we know, Miss Carr." McEwen squirmed impatiently in his seat. He studied the papers for an eternity. A logging truck roared past, rattling the venetian blinds.

"Mr. Sullivan. Miss Carr. According to these notarized excerpts from the county journal..." The football player and political appointee adjusted his glasses. Slowly mouthing the words, he re-read the several papers before him. "I quote from the Humboldt County Journal Of Deeds and Conveyances, page 386. 'Assignee James and Winifred Sandoval, et al. held in joint tenancy seventy five acres of old growth unimproved land. Parcel account number 032-181-041, plat 021 known as strawberry acres, total assessed valuation at $20,000.' There is a notation that taxes were paid December 1, 1955."

"Total valuation $20,000.00? That doesn't make any sense. It must be worth millions," I said. I leaned over holding my stomach, feigning nausea.

Betty Higenbothem inquired, "Are you ill, Mr. Sullivan?"

McEwen addressed my outburst. "Mr. Sullivan. The property isn't worth much unless it's improved, a structure is built, or the timber sold. Assuming you could find a logging company to harvest old growth."

Unheard by the others, Hazel Carr sighed to me, "Sean, it doesn't matter. Henry and Olive Sandoval don't own the property. His brother and sister-in-law bought the timber. We lost."

Early that evening, I slumped in my favorite easy chair. Swirling a iced scotch and soda in one hand, I placed Tchaikovsky's 1812 Overture on the old Zenith phonograph. The ode to the defeat of Napoleon soon thundered throughout the house.

Fantasy took over. Standing on my feet I ripped the air with my right arm, impressively conducting Toscanini's NBC symphony. My imaginary baton skewered the bass section. "More basso profundo, you fools! Do you not know this is a man's monument to his stupidity?"

"Sean! Turn that down!" Cassie shrieked. "Dinner's ready. We're having deep fried shrimp on rice with marinated cucumber salad." The buzz word "shrimp" brought me back to reality. I turned down the volume then dropped into my chair.

"How did the hearing go?" Cassie asked. Her winsome demure lessened the defeat of the day.

"Don't ask."

"Come on, Sean. It can't have been that bad. Tell me about the hearing. Maybe I can help."

"I don't want to unload on you. It's unfair."

"Well, then, what do you think of my new outfit? I finally finished unpacking and found this skirt at the bottom of the box. According to Teen Magazine, this is the latest fashion." Cassie waltzed around the room lifting her full circled poodle skirt. It had an appliqued cutout near the hemline of a furry-tailed puppy with rhinestones eyes and collar. Her pirouettes revealed several white petticoats under the skirt. A white shirt, small neckerchief, and saddle shoes with bobby sox completed the ensemble.

"You look great. I haven't ever seen you dressed this way." I slowly mellowed as the evening meal progressed. Cassie engaged me in gossip of her day.

"Sean, did you see this notice in today's newspaper?" she asked.

"No. I haven't had time to read the paper. It's been a bad day," I grumbled.

"Well, it says there's a vacancy in the state vocational rehabilitation office. The counselor, Lloyd Astin, is transferring to San Francisco. Would you be interested in the job? Do you qualify?"

"Yes, I would be, and I'm sure I meet the requirements. I'll bet it pays more too. I'll check it out tomorrow. Thanks." Reeling from the day's disappointment, I caught Cassie's life preserver and swam to another island of illusion.

As an afterthought Cassie declared, "Mrs. Garbarino phoned. She wants to sell the house. We have to move in thirty days."

8

"DANCING AT THE CLAIRMONT

"MR. ASTIN WILL SEE YOU NOW," THE SECRETARY announced. Florence Ash surveyed me with x-ray vision as she led the way into a small office facing Fourth Street in Eureka on a stormy November day in 1956. She sensed I might be the new counselor.

A women in her fifties, divorced, apparently without friends or family, Mrs. Ash took solace in the bottle. A slight nervous twitch appeared near her right eye when she drank too much. She was a small leathery person, with the air of one who has been compelled to work with people of whom she did not wholly approve. She thought she had influence over Astin and office policy—who gets what and what happens to whom.

"Mr. Astin. My name is Sean Sullivan." We shook hands.

"I understand you're transferring to San Francisco," I said. A balding man, my height, strolled towards me with a slight limp. Astin offered a me chair. I liked him.

"Well, Sean, why don't you tell me something about yourself," he began. "Oh, would you like a cup of coffee?"

"Yes, thank you. Sugar. No cream."

Sticking his head out the door, he yelled, "Florence, may we have some coffee?"

Slamming her pencil to the desk, she bleated, "I just threw the grounds out. You'll have to wait."

"That's okay. And sugar also."

"We don't have any and I can't shop now. Too much work. I have to get these letters out today."

"I only dictated two letters," Astin said, then retreated. "Okay, okay. But we would like a cup of coffee, please." He turned to me and whispered, "Sorry, Sean. But she may become your problem."

A fifteen minute get acquainted session followed. I related to Astin with ease. We exchanged counselor experiences.

"You'll be expected to offer a variety of vocational rehabilitation services," he said. He took a deep breath and continued, "Those will include performing intake services to determine eligibility, physical restoration, securing on-the-job training opportunities, acting as liaison with state and county offices, administering and interpreting tests, and serving on various community committees." He turned to look out the window.

"Some of the testing such as the MMPI, the Minnesota Multiphasic Personality Inventory, must be given by a clinical psychologist. Dr. Collins at Humboldt State College will help you out. You'll like him. He's a nice guy."

"Sounds great," I said with enthusiasm.

"You will also be invited to give talks or briefings to various groups in the community interested in vocational rehab. Don't pass up the opportunity to spread the good word," Astin admonished. "Getting the physically and mentally handicapped back to work is good business. They pay taxes," he said.

"Yes, I know. Vocational rehabilitation helped me complete my A.B. degree at the University of Portland. My counselor was a classmate of my mother's in the eighth grade, 1915."

"You're just the guy for this job. But I've got to warn you—Florence is a problem. She likes to run the office," he explained unnecessarily.

"Oh, I'm sure we can work something out." I knew I had the job.

"One other thing," Astin frowned. "You missed the date for the California state counselor exam so if the powers that be accept you, it will be as a temporary hire. The state exam is given once a year. You need to take it and if you pass, then you'll be placed on probation for one year. After successfully completing the probation year, then you'll be offered permanent status."

"I understand."

"Good. I think you'll be happy here. I'll call John Todd, the supervisor of the San Francisco office, this afternoon." He handed me some paperwork. "Complete this application and bring it back tomorrow afternoon. We should know in a few days if they're going to hire you."

"Wonderful. I thank you very much. See you tomorrow," I said. I got up to leave.

"Wait. Why don't we get some lunch? Do you like seafood? Fresh oysters, crab, clams, salmon in season. There's a great fish market on Third and E St. Lazlo."

"I love seafood," I replied. We indulged ourselves in a leisurely lunch consisting of the local version of bouillabaisse. Astin and I became counselors-in-arms and lifelong friends.

That night I beamed confidently at the dinner table. "I think I got the job, Cassie" I announced.

"That's wonderful! From what you've told me, it sounds like the kind of work you enjoy." She threw her arms around me and kissed me.

"I think Lloyd will be a great help. He's the counselor I'll be replacing. He's a real nice guy and I feel comfortable with him."

"Oh, Sean, you seem so happy!"

"I am, but there is one problem. The secretary, Ada Ash. She appears to run the office."

"I'm sure you can deal with her." As an afterthought, she added, "Be patient, Sean."

"I have to be honest. I find it difficult sometimes to be tolerant with people in general. The physically and mentally handicapped in particular."

Cassie interrupted. "Oh, I forgot to tell you. I found a place in Eureka, in the middle of town. An old two story building with two bedrooms, a living room, breakfast nook, kitchen and bath." On a note of triumph, she continued, "It's only seventy fives dollars a month, plus utilities. Mrs. Garbarino took me over this morning. Her friend is the manager. We can have a flat on the first floor so you don't have to climb stairs."

"It sounds good. How about lunch tomorrow and we'll take a look?" We moved into our new home the following weekend. I negotiated a six month lease.

A week later Astin phoned. "Congratulations, you're hired!"

Lloyd was generous with his time. He explained job orientation, introduced me to agency heads and community leaders, and walked me through all the paperwork.. The social programs of the day held great promise and potential. We really believed in caring for people.

"You know, I had polio in my younger days. I've done some hospital time," he confided.

"I know what you mean. By the time I was eight years old, I already had five reconstructive orthopedic surgeries at the Shriner's Hospital for

Crippled Children in Portland. I didn't go to school until I was eleven. Boy, what a shock!"

"What do you mean by shock?" Astin interrupted.

"Well, I spent so much time alone the first eleven years of my life that just walking into a classroom traumatized me. I didn't know how to relate to my peers. Some of the kids made fun of my frequent trips to the bathroom. I didn't want to stand up at the urinals and empty the bag so I usually went into the booth." I pulled up my pant leg, displaying the urinal on my right leg.

Few people listened to me as Astin did. I reminisced. "One time, in a public toilet, I couldn't find a vacant water closet so I stood, pulled out the bag and emptied it into the urinal. A drunk next to me yelled, 'What the hell is that thing?' I saw him again, shaking a tambourine in a Salvation Army Band, singing 'Bringing In The Sheaves' with great zeal," I said.

Astin looked me in the eye. "You know, I have a theory. I think it's easier to survive being disabled from birth rather than becoming disabled later in life. I have great empathy for people injured in accidents. I've worked with several clients who suffered the loss of a limb due to a sawmill or logging accident. They have a tough time adjusting to a lifestyle assigned by other people."

I agreed. "I didn't even know I was handicapped until Ma bought my first suit. When I caught sight of myself walking towards the full length mirror, I thought, 'My God, that's me! Is that how I walk?'"

Astin frowned. "Sounds like you suffer from low self esteem. You know, if you don't like yourself, nobody else will," he said.

Our conversation turned to the agenda at hand. "Staff meeting in San Francisco on Monday, December 31, at 9 a.m.," Astin announced. "It'll give us an excuse to go to San Francisco for a long weekend. Bring your wife. You'll be given an airline credit card or you can drive to staff meetings in San Francisco. Keep a record of your expenses and the state will eventually reimburse you." He added, "But they won't pay your wife's expenses."

"That's no problem. San Francisco sounds great," I said.

Astin explained the monthly staff meeting. "Basically, it's an opportunity to meet the staff members, all ten of them. Many are assigned to the Bay Area. Only you and the guy in Redding are located up north and he reports to Sacramento."

71

"Sounds interesting." A new start. A new home. New friends. The future held promise.

"Mr. Todd, our district supervisor, is a real pioneer in this business. He's quite a talker. His wife passed on several years ago and he lives in a large home in Pacific Heights all by himself. He'll retire next spring and Janet Pensky is set to take his place." I figured the change in supervisors wouldn't affect me as I would be alone in the Eureka office, except for Ada Ash.

Later that evening, Cassie made coffee as she put the finishing touches on supper. I relayed the day's happenings. "I have to attend staff meetings in San Francisco every month. The next one is Friday, December 28, on a four-day weekend. Astin is going to introduce me to the staff. Would you like to come?"

"Oh boy, would I!" she exclaimed. Then, pouting, she continued. "But I don't have anything to wear. And can we afford to go?"

"Sure. The State will pay my air fare and hotel, or we can go by car and they'll reimburse me for mileage. The boss said I could have Thursday the 27th off so we can drive down. That way you can go with me and it won't cost anything extra."

"Do you think the old car will make it to the big city?"

"We can try." We lived in a glass of optimism. Never half empty as the pessimists would say.

THURSDAY, DECEMBER 27, 1956. THE DAY DAWNED cold. Our bubble gum romance continued as the old Ford wheezed south on Highway 101, heading to San Francisco in the early morning mist.

Our long weekend began with dodging a few logging trucks on the road. Cassie busied herself with Herb Caen's guidebook "Baghdad By The Bay." She marked all the best restaurants in San Francisco.

Lloyd Astin's directions lead us to the old Gotham Hotel on McAllister street near the Civic Center. The rates were $8 per night. I wanted to impress my bride on our first visit to Hong Kong East. "Oh, that's okay, Sean. We're going to have a good time this weekend no matter what. Let's unpack and get ready for tomorrow. I'm looking forward to San Francisco," she said. That night we began our love affair with our own Portofino By The Bay.

Friday, December 28, 1956.

The next morning Astin introduced me to the office staff. Everyone gathered in the office. Standing with a fixed grin on my face, I'm sure I would have done an Orangutan proud. After a few minutes of, "Oh, is that so? Yes, my wife is with me. No, we don't have any children," I excused myself and retreated to Astin's new office. Breathing a sigh of relief, I fell into his chair.

Chuck Belknap, the assistant administrator, charged into the office. He was inclined to look severe and brooding until he laughed. Partially deaf from birth, he drove a car with oversize rear view mirrors which presented quite a spectacle on the streets of San Francisco. Belknap could perceive, predict, and prognosticate with amazing accuracy, the rehabilitative potential of any client based on a variety of inventories. I made use of his talents during my time at the Eureka office.

"Sullivan, how much testing experience have you had?" he bellowed.

"I taught English and social studies from 1949 to 1950 in Spray, Oregon. I gave the usual secondary tests, school and college ability tests, Sequential Tests of Educational Progress, and Tests of Academic Progress, as well as classroom testing for academic progress in English and social studies," I explained. Boy, I thought, that ought to impress him!

"Nothing else?" he asked. The staff knew Belknap to be all bluster and bluff.

I continued. "Well, from 1951 to 1953 I was a county social caseworker in Grants Pass, Oregon and later Hillsboro, Oregon. I arranged for the state employment office to administer the GED and the SRA office typing skills. I tried to get people back to work and off the county welfare rolls."

"Good luck," he sneered. To the ceiling he said in frustration, "Why doesn't this state require sufficient testing experience of a counselor so he can function in a competent manner?" Turning back to me, he inquired, "Any other related experience?"

I babbled, "I forgot. I also worked at the Eastern Oregon Tuberculosis Hospital in The Dalles, Oregon, from 1954 to 1956, as a hospital counselor. I contacted the local employment agency to offer the General Educational Development test."

He sighed, "I guess we'll survive your ministrations." He leaned toward me. Quietly he said, "If you need any help, call me."

For Belknap the frustrations of deafness had developed in him a great appreciation for the small comforts of life. The state had installed an amplifier on his phone. Totally submerged in a quiet world of testing, he believed himself to be an important part of the program. He was.

"Anyone for lunch?" Astin broke in. Dr. Hirth, the medical consultant, and Dr. Feldman, staff psychiatrist, joined Astin and me in the office. "I was thinking The Domino Club on Maiden Lane. Sullivan will like the place," Astin said.

"He sure will. But I must beg off lunch—patients, you know," Dr. Hirth, a young man in his early thirties, said.

Dr. Feldman mentally diagnosed me as we chatted. He muttered "Count me out, too. I have to give a seminar at UC med school this afternoon—the delights of transference. Got to prepare my notes." Feldman was well liked for his easy ways. He could be an aging Perry Como in a buttoned down shirt with a matching suit of light gray.

"Well, then I guess it's you and me, Sean. Let's go." Astin said. Twenty minutes later we entered the world of upscale cuisine. The restaurant walls were adorned with paintings of naked women. Snobbish waiters in formal attire, overdressed in white ties, floated hither and yon, pandering to the patrons. After an overlong wait, a server materialized to take our order.

"Boy! I can't wait to tell Cassie about this place. It looks like a bordello...I think," I said.

"Sir, your order?"

I ordered the catch of the day. Astin had lamb chops with mint jelly. "Do you and Cassie have any plans for this evening?" he asked.

"Nothing special."

"Would you like to join Carole and me for dinner and dancing at the Claremont tonight?" he invited.

"That sounds great. We'd be delighted," I answered sincerely.

"Wonderful. We'll meet you in front of the hotel at seven."

At the appointed time, Astin appeared driving an old Chevrolet sedan of unknown vintage. He made the introductions, "Sean and Cassie, meet Carole." We shook hands with a young lady who, in my opinion, resembled Betty Boop of cartoon fame.

The maitre d'hotel at the Claremont mumbled a welcome. "Table for four, Sir?" Seated next to some potted palms, Cassie winked at me as she studied the menu.

After dinner, the band struck up "I am the Great Pretender." The combo of four musicians emulated The Platters in a slow rendition of the top pop song of 1956. The tenor was outstanding.

"Cassie, may I have the pleasure of this dance?" Astin stood up and offered his arm. When she offered hers, he kissed her hand. He looked at me, "Okay with you, Sean?"

I certainly couldn't dance. I replied resentfully, "Sure, she likes to dance. Enjoy." I did my best to engage Carole in scintillating conversation.

"The Great Pretender" faded away as Astin and Cassie returned to the table. I scrambled to pull out Cassie's chair for her but my friend won the race. "Thanks, Cassie. That was my pleasure," Astin said.

"Mine too, Lloyd," she smiled demurely. I chugged my Chivas Regal. The music started again and I sat bolt upright. It was a slow expression of Hernando's Hideaway. To dance is life itself. I can handle a tango, I thought.

"Carole, may I have this dance?" I bussed her hand.

To my surprise, she answered, "Of course, Sean."

I moved into her body on the dance floor. The first few steps were agonizing as I prayed, "Oh God! Please don't let me lose my balance." Firm breasts pushed into my chest. Her gold satin dress rustled as I tried to glide around her.

At last! I am in the real world. Hey, this is fun. All too soon Hernando found his Hideaway. We strolled back to the table hand in hand.

"Thank you so much, Carole. You'll never know," I said.

"My pleasure, Sean." Carole executed a small curtsy.

A Johnny Ray wannabe started to cry his signature song, "Just Walking in the Rain." Cassie stood up and looked at me. "How about me, Sean?" she asked.

Floating through the air on a carpet of euphoria, I could only say, "Sure, why not?" The dance did not go well. I started to stumble but quickly regained my aplomb, finishing without further incident.

We all agreed to meet for breakfast next morning. Thus ended an evening of frolic and frivolity.

Saturday, December 29, 1956.

Astin parked curbside late Saturday morning. Repetitions of "Good morning" and "How are you?" were exchanged. "Let's take my car. We may look old but she can still climb the hills of San Francisco," Astin insisted.

We enjoyed breakfast at the Cliff House followed by the grand tour of San Francisco. Late in the afternoon, Astin suggested a snack at an old Italian bar and grill. The Angelo Restorante Italiano on Union street was the very essence of old Italy.

"You are really going to enjoy this," Astin promised. "This section of town is basically Italian and the people play bocce ball in Washington Square on the courts behind the bar and grill on Broadway."

We found a parking lot and headed for the restaurant. As we seated ourselves by a window, the scratchy sounds of Caruso's original recordings, from an old juke box, filled the room. "This is fantastic," I said. "If we ever move to San Francisco, this is the place for me."

"Let's pick up a sandwich. Then we'll take you back to the hotel. You probably want to rest. Tonight we'll take in Phyllis Diller at The Purple Onion," Astin announced.

Our Arabian Night adventures in Shangri-La were beginning to exercise a charming fascination over Cassie and me. Promptly at seven thirty Astin and Carole appeared to convey us to the Purple Onion. Our drinks had just arrived when drum rolls shattered the hubbub of conversation the room.

The emcee introduced Frank D'rone, whose voice was not unlike Eddie Fisher's. He launched into a spirited rendition of "Singing the Blues." Guy Mitchell would have been proud. The twenty minute gig ended with Dean Martin's "Memories Are Made Of This."

Polite applause followed when D'rone called up Tazzie Hamilton, the Australian warbler. She lead the audience in a syrupy sing-a-long fest.

After a few minutes an aberration called Phyllis Diller, with her wacky rubber faced routine, bounced on stage, fright wig and all. Thirty minutes of belly guffaws and "Fang doesn't understand me" followed. Five children and a divorce catapulted Ms. Diller to fame and later to the Bob Hope Show.

"The good times are a coming," I said. D'rone and Hamilton joined Diller on stage. The song fest ended with, "Okay everybody, one last time—Waltzing Matilda." The audience stood up and held hands, swaying to what some consider Australia's national anthem.

"To my dying day, I shall never forget this evening. Thank you so much Lloyd and Carole." I said.

Cassie added a "Me, too."

The Astins dropped us back at the hotel. "Brunch tomorrow morning at the Black Cat. We'll pick you up at 11:30," Lloyd said.

Sunday, December 30, 1956.

A few minutes before noon we entered a den of iniquity. "Why are there so many guys in here?" I asked. Astin's response was a knowing smile accompanied by an almost inaudible snicker. Cassie looked around.

"Hi. My name is George." A well ornamented doorman stood before us. "Let me find a place for you," he offered.

A tall, slender person, with a wedding ring dangling in his left ear, led us to the back of the barn-like structure. Sawdust on the floor added to it's curious ambiance. With much ado, the major-domo pulled out a table for our group, seating us with our backs to the wall.

Blazingly bedecked in a red aloha shirt with short shorts held up by a length of bicycle chain, our greeter sing-songed, "Today's special is corn beef hash, eggs to order, and cottage fries with blackberry jam. Mother made the jam. He is absolutely wonderful with jams and jellies."

My eyes focused on a tattoo. "Death before Dishonor" was forever etched in red, white and blue on his right arm. He caught my gaze. "Oh, you noticed. I had it done before I jumped ship in Boston last year."

George returned in a few minutes with our brunch selections. The lights dimmed. The Black Cat combo of drums, trumpet, and bass blasted "There's no business like show business."

The emcee did a full three sixty and announced, "Good afternoon, Ladeees and Genteelmen! At great expense, the management is pleased to bring you our version of 'My Fair Lady'."

A behemoth of a former football player bounced onto the small stage. A lyrical tenor, he sang "What's so special about a woman?" from "My Fair Lady."

"Hi there. My name is Ralph." The young man seated next to me shook my hand overlong. We shared a few moments of conversation before my attention turned to a bearded singer lip syncing, "I've Got A lovely Bunch Of Coconuts."

Ralph leaned over to me and said, "His name is Fluffy. He's been neutered." He placed his hand on my thigh.

"Sean, are you alright?" Cassie glared at the trespasser. Yanking my leg away, I finally realized what was going on. I was sitting at ground zero of the original San Francisco Gay Community. "L'amour bleu"— the home of blue love.

"Relax, Sean," Carole advised with a slight grin. "They serve a great breakfast. And the entertainment is fab-u-lous."

I perspired profusely as I wolfed down my meal. The prospect of Sunday morning in this evil empire boggled the mind. An eternity had lapsed when Cassie finally said, "Let's go. It looks like we're all finished eating."

Ralph questioned, "Going so soon, Sean?"

I shoved the table away, jumped up, took two faltering steps, and fell flat on my face.

"Let me help you," Ralph offered, rising from his chair. I wiggled out of his arms and stumbled to the door.

Our foursome gathered outside the door. Astin proposed, "Let's grab a cable car. I'll bet you two have never been on one."

"Sounds great," Cassie said.

Soon one of San Francisco's fabled cable cars clanked into view. Laughing, we jumped aboard the Hyde Street car bound for Aquatic Park. The brakeman entertained us with a jingle-jangle of bells. Winner of the 1955 cable car bell ringing contest, he had the makings of a true artist.

As we rang our way down Hyde Street, a tourist, who seemed to have had one too many, roared in the direction of the conductor, "Where's the Barbary Coast, boy? I hear they have girlie shows on Sunday afternoon."

In his best Oxford accent, the Afro-American bell ringer responded, "Sir, if you will disembark at the next stop, Pacific Street, and then walk down the hill past Columbus Street, you will find a variety of entertainment featuring a cornucopia of cuddly cuties."

"What's a 'corno-co-pua'?"

"A horn of plenty, brother." I swear he said "whore."

The pleasure seeker staggered off the cable car. He was last seen floundering in the direction of San Francisco Bay. The brake man manipulated several steel handles as we rattled down the hill. "We must each find our own salvation," he proclaimed.

We jumped off on Beach Street and walked over to the Buena Vista Grill and Bar. Cassie and I drank Irish Coffee for the first time. The day soon mellowed into late afternoon.

"I suggest we pick up a sandwich at Tommy's Joynt on Van Ness," Astin said. "Then you might want to get back to the hotel and catch a nap. Carole wants to change," he added.

"Tonight, the Bocce Ball. We'll pick you up at 7.30 p.m. sharp. Be ready."

That night we made our way to North Beach. "You'll like it here. The young people on stage are budding opera singers. They welcome the opportunity to perform in public."

A small stage sufficed as a platform for the ensemble. A mixed group of five would-be opera stars balanced themselves on rickety bar stools. Simulated electric gas lights semi-circled the stage. A chandelier hung overhead.

Signaling another era, a record was placed on a turntable. Accompanied by Arturo Toscanini and the NBC Symphony, a young man stood up to entertain the Saturday night crowd.

"What is he singing?" Astin asked.

To our astonishment, Carole expounded, "He's serenading us with 'Che Gelida Manina' from Puccini's La Boheme." She added, "Rudolfo, the singer, takes the hand of Mimi, whom he has just met and is fast falling for. He remarks how small and cold her hands are."

"I forgot to mention that Carole is a novice opera singer," Astin explained.

"Just for a year or two. I had to quit. Family." Carole never mentioned drugs. Years later she would join Cassie in their search for the Eylsian fields. They were successful.

The front door opened. Senior Melody, formally the heroic tenor of the Argentine State Opera Company of Buenos Aries, swaggered in, tossing his cape over his shoulder. The wrinkles on his face deepened and twisted and I realized he was probably smiling.

Gesturing gallantly to all assembled, he threw his serape over a chair with the precision of a magician. His fedora quickly followed. A bejeweled cane flashed in the air. A young lady rushed to serve his favorite wine.

"He comes in every night at this time," Astin said.

Carole explained. "Senior Melody always takes his wine at Bocce Ball. It's a tradition."

Astin added, "I recently read an article about him in the San Francisco Chronicle. He lives in the Columbus Hotel across the street. He'll be eighty-three next week. And, by the way, Melody is his real name. He was born in Northern Italy." As an afterthought Astin concluded on a note of envy, "Obviously the girls adore him."

"I hope he sings." Cassie refilled her glass.

"He will. He's just being coy," Carole assured us.

A young lady stood up and announced, "Ladies and Gentlemen! Senior Melody will honor us with 'Nessun Dorma'!"

"Bravissimo! Bravo!" The audience applauded generously while whistling their approval.

Senior Melody bowed as he whispered in the ear of a young soprano. The old man and the young girl sang their way to the front door. At the conclusion of their performance, Maestro Melody tipped his fedora in the grand style and vanished into the foggy night. A thunderous ovation followed.

We finished our drinks and drove back to the hotel. "Tomorrow, Sausalito, San Francisco, Oakland and Jack London. We'll pick you up at 11:00 in the morning."

Astin waved as Carole shouted, "Good night Sean and Cassie! See you tomorrow."

Monday, December 31, 1956.

"Come on, Sean. I don't think there's any football on today. Let's go to breakfast. I'm hungry and they're going to be here at eleven to pick us up," Cassie said.

Quickly I checked the morning paper. "Okay, okay. I just hate to miss the Rose Bowl game tomorrow, but we'll be on the road back to Eureka. UCLA is playing Michigan State—it should be a great game," I muttered.

"Lloyd and Carole have gone way out of their way to show us the city. I really appreciate their efforts," Cassie said. "Maybe there is a game on late this afternoon or early this evening."

Breakfast at Zims, a chain cafeteria, was spartan. We had a brief discussion on what the day's agenda might be. Astin appeared a few minutes later.

"Hi, Sean, Cassie. You folks ready for Sausalito, Oakland and parts unknown?"

"We sure are," I said.

Carole was bedecked in a skirt of stylized printed flowers on a colored background, complete with a chunky Italian sweater with wide armholes. Her appearance belied her thirty years. "Oh hello, Cassie. How are you?" she said.

"I'm fine."

"It's on to the Golden Gate bridge and Sausalito," Astin smiled.

The fog started to burn off the peaks of bridge towers. Toy like, a miniature San Francisco faded behind us. Sausalito loomed in front.

Known for it's panoramic view of the Bay, it remains to this day a popular bedroom community.

"Beautiful. Some day, Cassie, we'll have a home here on the hill. It sure would be a great place to relax after a hard day at the office," I said. Another impossible dream never realized.

"Sure, Sean." Her voice trailed off into Never Never Land.

"Steam beer everybody?" Astin turned to the left and parked. The patisserie offered beer and sandwiches along with a view of the waterfront.

Gwen, a pony tailed waitress in a green pinafore, took our orders. "Beer, pretzels and sandwiches are the specialties of the house. I recommend the hot pastrami," she said.

"We'll drive through town later, then on to the ferry terminal and Oakland," Astin explained. We enjoyed a pleasant hour people watching and gazing at the sailboats racing by on San Francisco Bay.

"Okay, you guys. Girls in the back seat. Boys in the front," Carole announced.

"Thanks Lloyd. Nice place," Cassie said.

We drove back on the Golden Gate Bridge heading East to the Embarcadero. Thick fog still lingered as the mist dissipated. A mournful whistle of an outbound freighter cleared the way for crab boats.

The siren call of a thousand creases beckoned me to far away exotic ports—Yokohoma, Hong Kong, Singapore. The mythical enchantress of the sea called to me. My eyes followed a ship until it disappeared into the vapors.

"I'll get the tickets." Astin parked in a passenger zone next to the ferry terminal.

"The ferry company is going to shut down next year. Too few passengers. Business has declined ever since 1937 when the Bay Bridge and the Golden Gate Bridge were completed," Carole explained.

A toot of the horn and a rumbling of engines announced our departure. The San Francisco skyline miniaturized. The ocean breezes provided the sensation of being at sea. Impervious to the chatter and clatter, I became Walter Mitty at the wheel of a round-the-horn '49 gold seeker. The city might have been a vision fluttering out of a dream.

Astin, the teller of stories, shattered my trance with tales of old San Francisco. Twenty minutes later the ferry docked in Oakland. We walked the several blocks to the First and Last Chance Saloon.

The stern of an old sailing ship served as a beer hall. Lionized by Jack London, local legend has it that he frequented the establishment in his younger days. "What's he doing with the microphone?" I asked pointing to the bar.

"Wait. You'll find out." Astin said.

"Oh boy. How nice. Don't forget to turn off the faucet." The barkeep, his back to customers, offered advice into a speaker system connected to the bathrooms. The ladies were met with stares and guffaws as they came out of the restroom.

Blushing crimson red, Carole demanded, "What happened? Whose idea was it?"

"Calm down, girls. I should have told you," Astin volunteered. "The owner put a one way microphone in the bathrooms. The bartender uses it to the amusement of all. Many of the patrons come here to people watch. Sorry." We drank our beers in silence.

"It's almost five o'clock. By the time we take the ferry back it'll be getting late," Cassie said.

"Okay, let's go. Tonight—New Year's Eve at Banducci's Hungry I. I'm a great people watcher and the Hungry I is the best place in town. Eight-thirty."

Cassie challenged me in our hotel room. "I didn't think the bathroom business was funny. And I didn't expect him to spend the whole weekend chauffeuring us around San Francisco," she said.

I dashed to the TV, twisting the dial. "Nuts. No game." I sat down in despair. "Oh, I forgot. The Rose Bowl game is tomorrow."

We spent New Year's Eve at the Hungry I. On the bill were Professor Corey and the lady who sang "Where Is Love?" Later we had coffee at Pierre's sidewalk café on Broadway.

The next morning we returned to the Hotel Gotham. Alcoholic hugs and kisses were followed by calls of, "Good night, good night! Thank you!"

Cassie continued with an outgoing spirit. She wore the rose of youth upon her face. Time had not yet had the opportunity to wither her. The little girl from Boise had made her marriage with peace of mind.

After three hours of sleep, we packed, paid our hotel bill, and headed north across the Golden Gate Bridge for Eureka, California.

"Sean."

"Yes."

"I'd like to start at Humboldt State College this spring semester. I want to take art and drama. Spring registration begins Saturday, January 28th."

"Sure, that's a great idea."

"Sean."

"Yes."

"I think I'm pregnant."

9

"THE CONFESSION"

"I'M SORRY, MR. SULLIVAN. THE TESTS SHOW A low sperm count. It's unlikely you will ever father a child." Dr. Haber paused. "And if by some chance you do father a child, there's a 50-50 possibility it will have a Mylomeningocele."

"What's a my-lo-men-go-seal?"

"A spina bifida. You were born with a hole in the lower spine."

"Yes, I know. The doctors told me the same thing years ago. I didn't believe them." I stared out the window at a humming bird twittering round and round a rose bush. "My wife is a wonderful person. I love her but we never discuss children."

Dr. Haber spotted the hummingbird, now joined by his mate. "I hope you aren't in love with love."

I bristled with indignation. "I beg your pardon."

"Did you tell your wife the consequences of your physical condition before you got married?"

"No. I should have explained my situation, but I have this life long fear of rejection. I think she wants children." I neglected to add that Cassie might be pregnant.

"She appears to be an intelligent person. I'll talk to her if you like." Dr. Haber smiled reassuringly.

"No thanks, sir. That won't be necessary," I said.

We were joined by his partner. "What's the problem?" he asked.

"I seldom see a spina bifida," Haber confessed. "Mr. Sullivan would be an interesting patient if I were in neurology or orthopedics." The doctors huddled at the opposite end of the room ignoring me.

"Why?" Raised eyebrows expressed a gentle curiosity.

"My examination indicates that he has at least eight diagnoses or problems."

"Such as?"

"Well, for one, Myelodysplasia."

"I'm not familiar with that term. Let's look it up in the book." They leafed through a medical dictionary. "Ah, here it is." He quoted aloud from the big red book.

Dr. Haber proposed, "Let's check Hinsie and Shatzky's psychiatric dictionary." The partner snaked a large green book off the shelve. Quickly he found a citation, "Myelodysplasia."

In conjunction with the study of the urinary apparatus, Adler read, "inherited inferiorities of gland or organs were conducive to a neurotic condition. That is, they caused a child with some inherited stigma to feel a sense of inferiority in relation to his environment. This feeling of humiliation and inferiority induced by some constitutional or organ defect, produces psychic compensatory and hyper compensatory strivings in the individual."

"In other words, 'the soil syndrome.' Feelings of inadequacy." Dr. Haber leaned back. "No wonder he didn't explain the problem to his wife. In a way, I don't blame him."

Dr. Haber turned back to me as his partner left the examination room. "You're sure you don't want me talk to your wife?"

"I'm sure. This will be my little confession. Thanks for your help, Doctor." We shook hands.

That night Cassie and I sat down to dinner. After dinner, I offered a toast. "Here's to you, Cassie. I had a great time in San Francisco." I lifted my glass of wine. We engage in the traditional clinking of glasses, then adjourned to the living room.

Chopin's Nocturne in E-flat minor, Philadelphia orchestra, Eugene Ormandy conducting, served as mood music. Without warning Cassie demanded, "What did the doctor say?"

I sensed a confrontation. I proceeded to dump my medical history on Cassie, emphasizing the difference between sterility and impotency. Many people thought, incorrectly, that I was unable to perform the sex act. I thought my ability to perform, but without physical sensation, was God's sweet revenge for some unknown wrongs of a previous life.

I ended my tale of woe with "I'm sorry I didn't tell you all this before we got married." The cleansing of my soul lifted me to a new high. I could not have anticipated that what had happened in 1926 would be so casually explained in 1957.

Cassie eased my burden with, "Sean, I accept you as you are, not as I would like you to be." The Nocturne ended. I started to change the record to a well known Vivaldi concerto when Cassie asked the question of all questions.

"Sean, can you feel anything when we make love?"

"No." She hadn't known until that moment that I had no feeling from the waist down.

She changed the subject. "I'm going to enroll in Humboldt State College this week. The spring term offers classes in drama and art."

"Wonderful. Good idea. You should do well." I felt relieved. "Your paintings won scholastic art awards."

I reflected for a moment. "I didn't know you were interested in the stage."

"Oh, I've always enjoyed the theater. I had parts in plays in high school and at Boise State College. It's fun," she said.

"Not to change the subject, but Jan Pensky called today to tell me that Ada Ash and I both have to attend the May staff meeting in San Francisco on the 31st. Something regarding training in new clerical procedures."

"I can't go; I'll be busy with school," Cassie said.

Early the following day I announced, "Ada, Mrs. Pensky called. She wants us both at the May staff meeting. I believe it's Friday, May 31. They want to train you in the new bookkeeping and clerical methods."

"Damn. I had plans. Why does she want me down there for a staff meeting? I'm not on the staff. I'm just a secretary." Ada's pencil shot across the room as her fist hit the desk. "Okay. I'll just have to cancel my plans," she whined. "I don't thank you for this."

"It's not my idea...Be sure to mark your calendar." Reluctant to prolong the encounter, I tried to disappear into my office. I announced, "I have to give a talk before the community planning committee this afternoon and I need to brush up on my facts and figures. Please excuse me."

She refused to let me go. "That other counselor was always out of the office. Said he had to talk to people. Guess he was good at talking." Spasms of irritation creased her face.

I laughed. "Better days ahead, Ada."

The day dragged on in slow motion. I gathered my notes. Proceeding to the City Hall complex, I contemplated my relationship with Cassie.

Later that month, Cassie accompanied me to the April staff meeting in San Francisco. Astin and Carole joined us as we enjoyed the night of nights at the Hungry I. The curtain parted. Ada Moore, a young girl of ebony hues, gowned in red, torched "Where Is Love?" The blue spotlight accented her high cheekbones and penetrating brown eyes.

Astin whispered, "That's real soul music."

"I read in the <u>Chronicle</u> last week that her boyfriend beat the hell out of her. She refused to press charges. Said she loved him. That's him at the piano," Carole added.

Astin and I expressed a machismo attitude. "Maybe she had it coming to her."

Carole took up the gauntlet. "Tell me something, gentlemen. If you beat us what will happen?"

Astin answered, "The cops will regard it as domestic violence and probably not interfere."

"If you attack your neighbor's wife, what will happen?" she persisted.

We answered, "We would be arrested and go to jail."

Cassie said, "We rest our case."

Astin responded, "As far as I'm concerned, women are good for two things. One of them is cooking. Would you like to discuss the other?" The thunder of silenced rolled over the room..

Astin finally broke the quiet with a change of subject. He said, "The next time you two come here, let's go up to Lake Tahoe. You'll love the casinos. They offer food, fame and fortune." Carole winked at me.

"That sounds great!" Cassie squealed. "We're taking a few days off in June after the staff meeting. We plan to go to Boise to visit my folks. They've never met Sean. Maybe we can go by way of Lake Tahoe."

"I'll be down for the May meeting, but probably by myself," I added.

"I don't think so. Don't you have to bring Ada with you? The state rehab is changing it's bookkeeping and clerical methods and she'll need to be trained," Astin grinned.

"Oh God! I forgot about Ada Ash. Oh well, Cassie and I will definitely be here the last part of June."

"You can follow us up the hill. A day or two at the lake, then on to Idaho for you and home for us," Astin said.

THE HUMBOLDT STATE COLLEGE DRAMA DEPARTMENT presented "Play Boy Of The Western World" Friday and Saturday May 3-4, 1957. It featured several student actors of the Humboldt State drama department, including Bob Coppin and Herb McAlister. Cassie shined in a minor role.

I sat in the fourth row sparkling with pride. "That's my wife," I informed my seat mate. "The one in the green skirt, in the back." My neighbor remained unimpressed.

Cassie and I joined a cast party at the director's home after the play. The actors considered me an old man due to my thirty-one years. A face composed of pain added to the persona. I did my best to fit in but found it difficult to relate to the younger generation. After the party, we adjourned to the local bowling alley.

"Sean, I want you to meet Diane Anders, a classmate of mine."

"Hi, Sean. How are you?" Diane asked. She was twenty-eight with brown hair drawn tightly back and braided. She looked finished and mature. One stage of her life had ended with an unfulfilled love affair.

After a drink or two, Diane confided to Cassie the recent loss of her virginity to an unnamed gentlemen. Several days later she shared the information with me. Seven years later I would satisfy my curiosity in Diane's home at Willits, California.

After bowling five or six games, the cast members made their way out into the night.

"Sean, can we take Diane home?"

"Sure."

"Drop me off first. I'm exhausted," Cassie said.

"Okay."

Cassie blew me a good night kiss as I pulled away from our apartment with Diane. I followed directions to her cottage in Fortuna. "That's my place there, on the right. The old clap board cottage. I've rented it for two hundred dollars a month." I parked the car and started to get out to open the door.

"How long have you and Cassie been married, Sean?" she asked.

The question surprised me. "Eight months."

"The honeymoon isn't over," she responded. Tones of bitterness invaded the night air.

I sneaked a glance at my watch. Suppressing an alcoholic belch or two, I engaged Diane in a conversation about our mutual field of expertise—teaching and counseling. Twenty minutes passed. I realized we were compatible.

"Would you like to come in for a cup of coffee?" she offered.

"Oh, no, but thank you. Cassie's probably waiting up for me. Can I take a rain check?"

"Sure, some other time." Diane bussed my forehead as she hugged me a good night. The excitement of her unexpected move proved too much.

I said, "On second thought, I will have that cup of coffee."

"Good. Welcome to my little home." Slim beacons of a full moon pierced the slats of venetian blinds. She turned on the ceiling light, highlighting early Goodwill Industries decor. Used couch. Used lamps. Used coffee table. The lot of a country teacher is a sorry one.

"I'll put the coffee on. Make yourself at home. I'm going to change." She did a quick curtsy followed with a knowing smile. She disappeared into the bedroom, her voice filling the silence with, "I'll be just a minute."

In my mind the war raged on between good and evil. Should I or shouldn't I? Diane reappeared wearing a two-piece blue cotton pajama set with an appliqued pink bunny on each breast and one at another strategic location.

"There, that's better. Now for the coffee, or would you prefer tea?"

"Coffee's fine. With cream, if you have it," I replied. "How's school?" Expectations of a conquest slowly faded into thoughts of what might have been.

"Fine. But it's been hard to concentrate of late." Diane recounted her recent love affair with Gary. She paused for a moment.

I asked, "Why are you telling me all this?"

"I have to talk to someone. My parents were killed in an auto accident near Klamath two years ago. A logging truck hit them."

"I'm sorry."

"I knew Gary was married from the beginning. After six months he said his wife wouldn't divorce him. I don't think he even asked her, but I loved him."

"I'm sorry, Diane, but that's the standard b.s. line. I'm not trying to put you down or make fun of you."

"I know. You're right."

I quoted from Cory, "Bitter news to hear and bitter tears to shed." I put my arm around Dianne as an expression of platonic love. She held my hand for a moment then pushed me away.

"No. Not now."

I expected the standard, "We will always be friends, Sean." Instead, she he began a monologue of remembrances—secluded picnics at

Benbow lake, salmon dinners at Requa, gambling trips to Reno. Precise coordination of their lifestyles had resulted in many a rendezvous.

"My wife accepts the fact I will not attend church," Gary had explained to Diane early in their liaison. "Also, she goes bowling with the 'girls' on Wednesday nights, so I can see you twice a week."
In time, Diane concluded her song of songs.

"Finally I said to him, 'divorce her or we're through.' I haven't seen him since that night."

I changed the subject to the trials and tribulations of teaching. We exchanged classroom experiences and gossiped our frustrations. A pleasant hour followed.

The following Thursday night my secretary and I left for the May staff meeting in San Francisco.

"Stop at the next grocery store," Ada demanded. She went in and returned a short time later clasping a small brown bag to her bosom. "Let's go," she barked. Our journey began with Ada clutching her brown bag in a death grip while wailing a catechism of the wrongs her former husband had committed during fifteen years of an unhappy marriage.

Oh my God! Am I going to have to listen to her all the way to San Francisco? I wondered. I navigated the many twists and turns of the Redwood highway. A few of the bigger trees were within inches of the main road.

"Watch out, for God's sake! You almost hit that redwood!" Ada screeched. She braced one hand on the dashboard as the other grabbed the brown bag.

"Maybe driving at night wasn't such a good idea," I suggested.

"I'm not staying in a hotel longer than necessary. My ex and his family live in San Francisco. I hate the town."

"I've been working all day. I'm exhausted."

"So am I."

I suddenly realized how long the day had been and how tired my body was. My bones ached; my temples throbbed. The car made it to a straight stretch of road.

"Oh good, now I can enjoy the rest of the ride." Ada produced a bottle of Southern Comfort from the package. She chugged an ounce or two of the syrupy sedative.

"Have a sip." To my horror, she offered to share her whiskey. Refusal would label me a poor sport. Acceptance would result in blackmail. Drinking on the job.

"No, thank you," I replied.

"Aw, come on, pal! Be a good sport," she persisted.

"No, thanks. I have to drive and it's still another four or five hours to San Francisco. We should stop somewhere and eat," I suggested.

"Eat! What a party pooper! Who wants to eat?"

Our journey spent itself in rumblings, ramblings, and incoherent ruminations. Softly I muttered to myself, "My God, what do I do now?"

"What? What did you say?"

"Nothing. Just mumbling to myself."

Six hours later, a fugue for foghorns punctuated the night air as we drove over the Golden Gate Bridge heading South. Glancing at her watch, Ada slurred, "Well we made it just in time. Drive straight to the office."

"Let's stop for breakfast," I pleaded. "Zims or Foster has a pretty good cafeteria.."

"Hell, no! Here, have a swig." She held the bottle upside down, shaking it bone dry. "Sorry. Guess I finished it all by myself," she tittered. A grin of accomplishment splashed over the furrows of her face.

I parked on Van Ness near the vocational rehab office. Ada Ash disappeared into the ladies room as soon as we entered the office. I seated myself in the assistant supervisors' office.

"What's the matter, Sean? You look like something a cat wouldn't bother dragging home." Jan Pensky closed her office door. I distrusted private conferences. They usually lead to a dressing down or something else negative. Compliments in public were few.

"It's been a long night. Believe me."

"I said on the phone you could take Thursday off to drive down here. What happened?"

The room became a whorl of shadows. My chronicles surfaced in bits and pieces. Words were formed with great effort.

"She's a bloody alcoholic!" I blurted.

"Who?"

I spewed forth a tale reviling "The Ancient Mariner." A few minutes later I realized I had committed a fatal error. I told the truth.

"I'm going to talk to Mr. Todd, the administrator. You wait in Dr. Feldman's office," Mrs. Pensky ordered. She ran out of her office, leaving me to contemplate my sins as I headed for Dr. Feldman's office. On the way, I ran into Lloyd Astin. For the second time I unfolded my story, this time embellished with moments of pure theater designed to impress him with the depth of my dilemma. I tended to decorate the story from time to time.

"I didn't know what to do. She became so coarse and vulgar." I continued my revelations. "Ada finally dozed off for a few miles, then woke up and started all over again. I think they're going to fire her," I added.

"Uh, oh. Well, good luck, Sean. You did what I couldn't do. I tried for two years to get rid of her. You're a lucky guy." Astin smiled.

"Thanks, pal. But maybe I got rid of myself." I had predicted my own fate by going back to the future. "Florence needs help," I muttered.

A cheerful Dr. Feldman walked by the glass-enclosed office. "Good morning, Sean."

"Good morning. Mrs. Pensky told me to wait in your office," I said. Dr. Feldman stood listening like a child.

Pensky stuck her head in the door and announced, "We've decided to fire her. We cannot have this." Her fixed gaze locked me in a kind of paralysis. "I want to talk to you, Sean—my office in fifteen minutes. I have to call Sacramento."

"Yes, Ma'am."

"You'll have to drive back alone."

"Yes, ma'am."

She scurried out of the office mouthing obscenities. For the third time I narrated my recent experience, this time to Dr. Feldman. I adorned each telling of the tale like adding ornaments to a Christmas tree, until it glittered.

"I usually don't give advice…What I'm going to say is unethical, immoral, and may be illegal, but Sean, my friend, you should have kept your mouth shut!" I had prayed for absolution but received rejection. The doctor bowed me out of his office. Another moral icon shattered before my eyes.

"I was only trying to be honest," I said to the world.

Before Mr. Todd retired in March of 1958, Mrs. Pensky engaged in mortal combat with the competition and won the coveted post of district supervisor. I would enjoy a personal triumph a few years later when she was toppled from the throne, transferred to Oakland (the Siberia of California), and replaced by a more efficient soldier of the realm.

The next evening Cassie asked, "How was your trip, Sean?"

"Don't ask." I recited the events of what I now labeled "Black Thursday." Her lips imprinted a pinkish hue on my forehead. Every telling of the story now condemned me.

"And when we got to the office, I told Mrs. Pensky what had happened and they fired Florence on the spot." Expecting approval for my honesty, I received instead another lesson in morality.

"Oh, Sean. You should have kept your mouth shut," Cassie winced.

Ignoring her expression, I said, "Funny, that's what Dr. Hirth, the staff psychiatrist, told me. But it's immoral to lie." I continued, "I was brought up to tell the truth."

"We all were, Sean." She paused. "Did you know she was going to buy a bottle of whiskey when you stopped at the grocery store?"

"No, but I was suspicious when she returned with a brown bag. Astin said she could put it away. She didn't say a word until we had passed Scotia."

"You should have told her before she got in the car that there would be no drinking."

"Hindsight offers a perfect view," I pointed out.

She changed the subject. "Well, don't worry about it. Let's plan our vacation. When can we leave and where should we go?" The evening quickly spent itself as we poured over plans for the big trip. A few days later we left for Boise, Idaho—a journey of some 400 miles.

"We'd better look for a motel when we get to Stateline. Lloyd said they fill up fast this time of year," Cassie said.

"Oh, didn't I tell you? Carole said the county has nice campgrounds. We can sleep there. That's why I packed the green sleeping bag. We'll save money."

"I wondered why you brought that old thing. Okay, but I bet it's cold at night." She shivered in anticipation.

"Relax, we'll be fine. Let's stop at the county campground, reserve a space, and then meet Carole and Lloyd over at Harvey's." I smiled with confidence. "Everything's under control," I assured her.

We checked in at the El Dorado County campgrounds and rented a space for $5.00. We staked out our claim and left for Harvey's Casino, eagerly anticipating the well publicized "food, fame and fortune." Later in the evening I won $25 on a nickel slot machine.

"Good for you, Sean!" Astin patted me on the back.

"Hooray!" Carole squealed.

Cassie said, "Oh, Sean, how wonderful."

In the wee hours of the morning we located our spot in the county campgrounds. "I forgot to bring a flashlight. Sorry Cassie." My apology fell on deaf ears.

"God! It's cold!" She shivered.

"I'll soon take care of that little problem," I said. We spent the night, our bodies entwined, trying to keep warm. Cassie's predictions concerning the weather came true but she had the good grace not to say anything. At first light we packed and set a course for Boise, Idaho, by way of Reno, Elko Nevada and Twin Falls, Idaho.

Cassie's mother, Velma Vandervort, proved to be quite friendly. The stepfather held out a welcoming hand. "Call me Van. Everybody does. Welcome to the family," the big man said.

Turning to a boy of six and a blondish girl of eight, Cassie said, "Say hi to your Uncle Sean"

Oh God, we're starting the "uncle" business again, I thought. "Hi, kids." They hugged Cassie, showing genuine affection.

"Come see our new games," the girl said. The kids pulled at Cassie's skirts, dragging their half-sister to the bedroom. They pushed and shoved each other in mock battle.

"Meet Grandpa and Grandma," Velma said to me. She added in a whisper, "He's hard of hearing."

Grandpa Helton, a retired farmer, eighty-five years young, stood six feet four. His demeanor resembled that of an aging Clint Eastwood— few words but great meaning. We would sit together at the funeral seven years later.

Grandpa Helton pulled his chair next to mine. He knew he had a good listener in range. Hooking his right hand into his bib overalls, he began a journey down memory lane. The good old days were more comfortable than the cold realities of June 1957.

Cassie returned and sat by my side. Grandpa smiled and began his story telling. "Ma gave birth to nine kids on the farm. Never went to a hospital. She almost dropped Velma in the toilet," he said.

"Pa!" Velma covered her face with mock shame.

"You stop telling stories. Give the man a chance," his wife admonished. Grandma placed her hand gently on Grandpa's leg in a show of affection.

"We've been married fifty-five years come next month," Grandpa announced with pride.

"It's getting close to dinner time. Come on Ma, Cassie, help me." Velma headed towards the kitchen. The three women prepared a classic farm dinner.

Later Cassie and I got ready for bed. "I can't remember when I had a meal like that. Your family is great, and Grandpa is quite a character," I said.

"I agree," she said.

Two days later, we were joined by Uncle Doug Sanders, his wife Jean, and their two children. With the entire family we made up a caravan of three cars on our way to Atlanta, Idaho. We bounced over a washboard mountain road following the middle fork of the Boise River for sixty miles. Uncle Doug led us to a cluster of cabins with a fantastic view of the Sawtooth Wilderness area.

Early the next morning I borrowed some fishing tackle and headed out. Following Uncle Doug's directions, I found myself on a bank above a picture postcard stream. Throwing caution to the gods, I stumbled through thick brush down the steep incline. Landing feet first in the stream, I yelled triumphantly to an unseen audience, "I made it!"

A few minutes later, "I got one!" I spent several minutes playing a cutthroat trout as though it were a six hundred pound Marlin. Yanking the fish in I relished my moment of victory when I heard Cassie's asthmatic wheeze at my side.

"Sean, we have to go back to Boise." She struggled for air. "Uncle Doug cut his foot off with an ax."

"Nuts! Just when the fish were starting to bite," I said. We hurried back to the cabins. Everybody helped repack the three cars and we bounced our way back to Boise at full throttle.

"The fishing was great," I lamented.

"Relax, Sean. We can come back next year. It'll still be there."

I found a place to park at the hospital. The waiting room, painted in hospital blue, served as temporary headquarters for the family. A young man in white finally appeared and explained Uncle Doug's condition. "We were able to sew his foot back on. Good thing somebody had the sense to put it in an ice bag."

Several people chorused, "That was Van."

"The prognosis is good. Mr. Sanders will be in the hospital for a few days."

Pulling Cassie to one side of the room, I said, "Looks like no more fishing. Guess we'd better head home tomorrow."

"Aw, come on, Sean. We still have four days of vacation left. It only takes two days to get back to Eureka," Cassie pleaded.

I hadn't realized her need to be with her family. Relenting, I said, "Well, okay. But I don't want to make a mad rush back to California. It's a long trip."

"You're not thinking of leaving us, are you?" Velma called out.

"Oh no, Ma. We still have a few days left." Cassie's face lit up in surprise at her mother's interest.

The following Saturday we loaded up the car and headed for Eureka and home. Hours later I announced, "We are now in the great state of Nevada.".

"It looks the same as Eastern Oregon," Cassie replied.

We stopped at Winnemucca next the little Horse Saloon & Casino. Our hunger pains were quickly dispelled with cheeseburgers and cokes. Cassie lined up four sevens on a nickel machine.

"We'd better go. We'll get into Eureka late tonight," I said.

Cassie agreed. "Let's take a different way home," she suggested.

"Okay. We'll try the scenic route."

Early the next morning I woke her up. "Yoo-hoo, Cassie, we're home," I said. We pulled in front of our apartment house on G. Street and started to unpack. She rubbed the sleep out of her eyes.

"Sean, have you been seeing Diane Anders?"

10

"A FIELD OF BATTLE

I REMEMBERED LLOYD ASTIN'S ADMONITION ON the subject of marriage. "Sean, repeat after me. The three commandments of marriage are: one - don't ever go to bed mad; two - never argue family, sex, religion or money; and three - never try to get even, especially with a woman."

I had considered those words of wisdom for a moment. "Sometimes I don't understand the opposite sex," I said.

"Don't even try," Astin had said.

Mists of fog enveloped the neighborhood as we completed our unloading. "Let me help you," I offered. I dragged the smaller suitcase into the apartment. I felt guilty about Diane. This was one of those times when absolute truth may not necessarily be a good idea.

"I haven't been seeing Diane. The first night I met her you asked me to take her home. Remember?" The depth of my voice surprised me. I took a combative stance.

"Yes, I remember. That was the night we went bowling," Cassie responded. She relaxed.

"Right," I chimed in victory. "I took her home and she invited me in for coffee. She lives out in the country near Ferndale. I didn't want to hurt her feelings, so I accepted her invitation. After coffee I came home. Nothing happened."

"Have you seen her since then?" Cassie's accusing question hit the mark.

"Yes." I paused, frantically seeking a plausible explanation. "Mrs. Pensky came up on one of her frequent visits to Eureka. We accidentally bumped into Diane at the Eureka Inn and Jan insisted that Diane join us for lunch." Trying to maneuver the conversation to calmer waters, I whispered, "I guess Pensky doesn't trust me. She makes frequent field trips to Eureka."

"Don't change the subject. I'm beginning to know you," Cassie said. She pressed on with her newly found aggression. "Bob tells me he's seen you and Diane several times having lunch at Lazlo's or coffee at the doughnut house."

"Who's Bob?"

"Bob Coppen. He's in my art classes at school. We're going to take a life class together next fall."

"What's' a life class?"

"It's a class where people pose in the nude for life drawings."

"That should be interesting. What are my chances of taking that class? I think I like art." I repressed a giggle.

"Never mind...So, is it true?" she persisted.

"What?" I cupped my ear, feigning deafness.

"You and Diane," she yelled.

"Aw, come on, Cassie! Diane and I see each other at committee meetings. I took her to lunch once. We had coffee another time. Nothing special." Exasperated, I started to walk away from the field of battle.

"Lazlo's is expensive. And what committee meetings?" she demanded.

"Sort of expensive...How did you know about Lazlo's?" I changed course.

Ignoring my question she continued, "Diane teaches in Ferndale. What's she doing in Eureka during school hours?"

"She isn't in town all the time. We're on the same county coordinating committee that meets with the city council once or twice a month. The committee consists of city, county, state and federal people. We're organizing community activities. I think it is a good idea."

Starring Cassie down, I continued. "I've even been asked to give a talk on vocational rehab to the county welfare workers. I consider it an honor."

She continued, "Okay, Sean. We'll talk later. I have to get ready for school." She went into the bedroom.

"I thought school didn't start until sometime in September," I called out.

She stuck her head out the door. "I'm enrolling in several summer classes. Don't worry, it won't cost you much."

"I'm not," I replied.

Ten minutes later Cassie hesitated at the front door. "I'm going to visit some school friends tonight to discuss summer course offerings.

Your dinner is in the oven." Her Elvis Presley "Heartbreak Hotel Pink" lipstick flashed a devilish glow. A new Cassie.

"What are you going to do for transportation?" I asked. "We only have one car and it's falling apart."

"Don't worry, you don't have to chauffeur me. I'm taking the Eureka bus line. And I can always get a ride home with a friend."

"That's what bothers me."

She shut the door quietly as I sat down to consider my options for the evening. After a minute or two of contemplation, I said out loud, "What the hell. I wonder what's on TV tonight? Sure wish we had more than one channel."

JANET PENSKY PHONED THE NEXT MORNING. "YES, Mrs. Pensky. I understand."

Born with a thirty percent loss of hearing in my left ear, I limited my telephone conversations to a few sentences, often asking people to speak slowly. The usual response was, "What's the matter, you deaf or something?" My hearing worsened over the next few years. Too many kids in the school yard at lunch time. Too many hours flying a propeller driven airplane.

Pensky went on, "I can't come up now. Advertise in the local paper for a secretary. Be sure to keep receipts. And remember—ability, not looks."

Her voice crackled over the phone. "We'll go over the list of candidates the next time I'm in Eureka. Don't make any decisions; I'll do that."

I enjoyed interviewing prospective Girl Fridays, taking resumes, playing the role of an administrator. Eureka was my second experience. The first had occurred at the Eastern Oregon Tuberculosis Hospital in 1951.

Dr. Model, the administrator, attended conferences with the hospital business manager and the chief of nurse from time to time. Before they left, he would announce, "Okay, Sean, you're the boss. You're in charge. We should be back early this evening or sometime tomorrow. I notified Dr. Coffen (his real name) and Dr. Wisehart. Good luck." Then I would sit down and hyperventilate, somewhere between hysteria and everyday garden variety panic.

The following two weeks at the Eureka rehab office flew by. For my secretary interviews I divided a yellow legal size note pad into three sections: Y-M-No, for Yes, Maybe, and No. The "Maybe" section filled up fast.

"Have you had any experience as a secretary?"

"Oh, yes"

"Where"

"I worked in the office at Arcata Redwood.

"Can you describe your duties?" My God! This is like pulling teeth, I thought.

"I kept the books and did the payroll."

"Are you married?"

"Yes."

Damn! The interview proceeded for another twenty minutes. It ended with a clammy handshake and a forced smile. Holding the door open I said, "Thank you for coming. Don't call us, we'll call you."

Three weeks later, I drove to the Eureka-Arcata airport at McKinlyville. I opted for the airport restaurant, a local newspaper, a cup of coffee, and a large chocolate bear claw. I watched as a Martin 202 prop plane taxied into place. The ladder in the tail section ejected.

Pensky bounced off Flight 134, attaché case in hand, shouting in my direction, "How many people have you interviewed? Did you ask for resumes?"

Ignoring her lack of manners, I forced a smile. "Good morning, Mrs. Pensky. Welcome to Eureka. Beautiful day isn't it?"

"Never mind that. You know the only reason I haven't been helping you interview is because I've been so busy. I hope you didn't promise anyone a job."

"Oh, no. Not to worry," I replied. My newly acquired devil-may-care attitude failed to make an impression. We huffed and puffed our way to the car.

"I'm sure we can pick out a suitable candidate for the position. I have at least eight work histories at the office," I said. Pretending exhaustion, I continued my pleadings. "I'll sure be glad to have a new secretary. I'm getting tired of holding down the fort by myself."

The wind blew as rain fell in rivulets. "Sorry. I forgot to bring an umbrella. Late summer storm."

"Don't bother dropping me off at the Inn. I'm catching the six o'clock flight back to San Francisco. Let's go right to the office."

Upon our arrival, Pensky made a beeline for my desk. "Sit down, Mr. Sullivan. We'll go over the resumes." I became a client rather than a counselor.

She shuffled through the papers for a few minutes. "No. No. Yes. Maybe. Ah-hah! This is the one," she announced. She ripped a folder from the pile and pushed the papers in my face. "What do you think?"

I declared, "Sure, fine with me. Let's call her."

A quick lunch at the Eureka Inn gave me a respite from the stress of the day. Attempts at small talk with Pensky were in vain. After a silent interval, I ventured to try out my favorite joke, praying she had a sense of humor.

"Not funny, Sullivan. Let's go back to work."

I phoned Barbara Young. Mrs. Young, age 35, mother of two, accepted the secretarial job offer. It was the summer of 1957. She proved to be efficient and compatible.

"She must be desperate, agreeing to come out in this storm. But I want to meet her. I'm not going to make another trip up here," Mrs. Pensky remarked.

"I'm sure you'll like her. She's a pleasant lady," I said reassuringly.

Mrs. Young arrived about an hour later. Introductions completed, Pensky interrogated the new secretary at length. To me this indicated Pensky's lack of experience as an administrator. She seemed ill at ease during her entire performance.

"Sean, do you have any questions for Mrs. Young?" Her eyes signaled me to answer no. I took note of my first name status. In private it was "Mr. Sullivan." In public, "Sean" sufficed.

"No, thanks. I think you've covered everything."

"Good. Mrs. Young, can you start next Monday?" Pensky asked. "Your hours will be nine to five, with forty-five minutes for lunch. You can work out your schedule with Sean."

Mrs. Young agreed and a few minutes of personal chatter followed. In time Mrs. Pensky would develop a friendship with Mrs. Young.

"How many children do you have? What does your husband do?" she asked the new secretary.

"I'm divorced."

"Oh."

Mrs. Pensky gazed out the window at the sheets of rain. The personal conversation over, Mrs. Young got up to leave. She winked at me as she closed the door.

Suddenly Pensky turned to me barking, "Sean, you need to get active in the community. Give talks to local groups. Promote the cause of vocational rehabilitation." She straightened her skirt as she led me out the front door. "Come on, let's go. It's getting late I don't want to miss my plane."

"Yes, Ma'am." So, it's "Sean" again, I mused to myself. Kowtowing, I kept five paces behind her. We raced to the airport, keeping a wary eye out for the sheriff.

"Did you work in the Oregon Vocational Rehabilitation office?" Pensky asked. "I remember something in your file."

"Yes." I recalled with bitterness the so-called "budget cuts."

"Do you know Dave Kaufman and Chuck Feeny?"

"Yes. Mr. Feeny is the state director and Dave Kaufmann was my supervisor in the Portland and Salem office," I answered.

"I recently attended a conference in Salem Oregon. Dave Kaufman was fired for having an affair with another counselor. A Helen somebody," Pensky continued.

"Yeah, that would be Helen Atwood. Mr. Kaufman hired her from the Veteran's Administration."

"They also terminated Chuck Feeny for malfeasance of office. Something about the misuse of funds," she said.

"How sweet it is," I muttered in victory.

"Beg your pardon. What did you say?" Pensky demanded.

"Oh, nothing. Just mumbling to myself."

Pensky boarded her plane. I'm sure malicious delight was easily visible in my countenance. I bid her farewell with a weak wave of my hand. She disappeared into the storm clouds.

"Thank God!"

Later that night I sat in front of the television as the credits rolled for "Richard Diamond, Private Eye" starring David Janssen. "I'm tired. I think I'll go to bed early tonight." Yawning, I stretched my arms. "Believe me, it's been a long day."

"Okay. I'm going to take a bath. I'll join you soon." Cassie responded.

"Oh, I forgot to tell you. Pensky asked me if I wanted to go to the state vocational rehabilitation conference next month. It's in Los Angeles at the Mayflower hotel. I said yes."

Thirty minutes later Cassie asked, "What do you think of my new nightgown?" She modeled a floor length cotton garment blazoned with stylized pink elephants on a field of gray. The delights of the evening continued for some time. I devoured her body until exhaustion overtook our minds.

Recently, our marriage had become a charade of semi-weekly carnal conquests. The bloom of desire had begun to fade. Her body was no longer unexplored territory.

Mentally fulfilled, I still savored the event although unable to experience physical feeling. Of all the punishments God can inflict, a birth defect in the lower spine is true vengeance. For what? I will never know.

The conversation turned to hopes and unfulfilled dreams. Without warning she said, "I need some clothes. I can't go to any more cast parties until I get some new things."

"You know our financial circumstances. I can't afford anything now," I protested.

"You're going to attend the conference in L.A. next month," she countered.

"Yes, but the state is paying for the trip. They'll reimburse me for transportation, room and meals."

"You've been making four hundred dollars a month since last November. Why can't you buy me some new clothes?"

I replied patiently, "You just don't understand the situation. Soon. Soon." Believing the argument over, I stood up to go to the bathroom. Cassie blocked my way.

"Soon? When exactly am I going to get new clothes?" she interposed with the acerbity of a parade ground sergeant major. "I need a dress, a blouse and some under things. Now!" she demanded.

Her yammerings struck the core of my soul. Blind rage took over. A Frankenstein awakened within me. The unthinkable happened.

I slammed my fist into Cassie's chest, knocking her against the wall. She fell to the floor and became silent. Stunned, she covered her face with both arms. Wounded eyes peeked through quivering fingers.

She became a frightened fawn tangled in a gray web woven by two people bent on self destruction. She dare not move for fear of more violence. Cassie Helton Buzbie had sought the best in our marriage but now realized the worst.

Dante's Inferno danced before my eyes. A thousand devils pricked my mind. I tumbled to the floor and clasped her body in a grip of steel.

I moaned through the rivers of tears cascading down my reddened cheeks.

"I'm sorry. I'm so sorry," I whispered, gasping for breath. "Help me. Please, help me." Totally out of control, I recoiled from myself in horror. For a few moments I gaped at my little girl in stunned silence. Unbelieving, unthinking.

Banging my head against the wall until blood seeped through the broken skin, I begged, "Please forgive me. Can you ever forgive me? Oh God, I'm just like my father." The words dribbled out of my mouth. I continued to excoriate the demons who had taken over my soul.

Caught up in the whorl of hysteria, she screeched, "Stop it, Sean!" She rocked me back and forth in her arms in a vain attempt to console the inconsolable. Then she yelled, "Stop, Sean! For God's sake, stop this madness. For our sake, please!"

Our emotions escalated into a frenzy of begging and crying. After an eternity, I halted my verbal self-flagellation only to beat my head with both fists. My life force dripped down a gargoyle face of grotesque dimensions.

Grabbing both my hands, Cassie pleaded, "Sean, we have to talk! Stop it! We can't go on like this."

I insisted on debasing myself. Gasping asthmatically for air, I crawled on my hands and knees to the fireplace. I scattered ashes over my head and cried, "I don't know what to do."

"Sean!" Cassie looked into my dilated pupils. She saw a Phoenix struggling to rise from the depths of despair. My crying jag continued for several more minutes. She held me, softly hushing my cries of mental anguish.

"Okay, okay. I'm sorry," I finally shuddered.

"You don't have to buy me clothes just now," she replied, attempting to reassure me.

Wiping away my tears, I said "I'll buy you clothes. I'll buy you clothes tomorrow. Don't worry. I'll get the money."

We talked until early morning. Finally we mutually agreed to put the incident behind us. The six a.m. alarm buzzed.

"I've got to get ready for work," I said.

"You haven't had any sleep. Look at yourself. Why don't you call in sick?"

"I'm okay. Don't worry." I left for work bedraggled and besotted, burdened with the sins of my ancestors. A few minutes later, hunched against the wind and rain, I shuffled into the office.

"Good morning, Mr. Sullivan." A cheerful Barbara Young, the new secretary, greeted me at the door. "There's a Mr. and Mrs. Monroe waiting to see you." She smiled. "And don't forget, you have a speaking engagement at the welfare office at 11:00 a.m. this morning."

A tall blond women in her late thirties, Mrs. Young soon became my indispensable Girl Friday. Her presence became the bright spot in my professional life. She anticipated my every need while maintaining a professional and well run office. She managed to run her home at the same time.

"Thank you," I said.

I greeted my visitors. "Hi, John. Hi, Mary. What's new?" I even managed a slight grin.

Before me sat my favorite clients—success stories in the making. John Monroe, born with a freakish cleft lip accompanied by scolliosis of the spine, presented a lopsided version of a modern day Humpback of Notre Dame. His wife, Mary, a victim of cerebral palsy with a speech defect, held her husband's hand in an iron grip. Drool trickled down the crevices of her chin.

The Monroes held up their hands at the same time. In each fist was clenched a paycheck. John, the more coherent of the two, announced, "We got our first paychecks and we just wanted to thank you. And ask you to thank Mr. Astin for us, too"

"I sure will. I'll be seeing him at the next staff meeting in San Francisco. I'm so happy for you both." A few minutes of unintelligible chit chat followed. I nodded my head frequently rather than attempt to translate Mrs. Monroe's mumbling. Cerebral Palsy had done it's job.

The Monroe's left the office as Mrs. Young came in with a much needed cup of coffee and a doughnut. "I stopped at the bakery before coming in this morning," she said.

"Thank God. Better than a blood transfusion. You must have figured out my philosophy of life."

"The Monroes seem so happy. Although I couldn't understand a word she said," Mrs. Young commented with a smile.

"Mr. Astin arranged a job for Mr. Monroe in an auto shop," I explained. "John spends all day dunking carburetors in three different solutions. One, two, three. I would be bored to death doing the same thing over and over again."

"So would I. How did they ever place Mrs. Monroe? Her speech is so garbled," Mrs. Young asked.

"That one's my doing," I announced proudly. "I talked to the owner of the Breakers Inn and she agreed to hire Mrs. Monroe to clean rooms." I paused for a sip of coffee. "The only trouble is you can't give her more than one command at a time. If you tell her to make the beds, clean the room, and then take out the garbage, she'll go ballistic. Have a seizure."

"Well, you and your predecessor did a good job with those two. I hope the Monroes are able to keep their jobs for a long time," Mrs. Young grinned.

"So do I!" I held up crossed fingers.

"Well, I've got to get to the Welfare office and give that talk on the benefits of rehabilitation," I said. "The other agencies don't fully understand the services we offer."

Mrs. Young meditated for a moment. "Let's see…We offer physical restoration, testing services, educational counseling, on-the-job training, and what else?"

I elaborated. "Anything to restore a physically or mentally disabled individual to the point where he or she can function in the job market. As far as I'm concerned, the some thirty million handicapped people in this country represent a huge waste of human resources. If they aren't working, they aren't paying taxes."

I drove the few blocks to the welfare office. Former co-workers greeted me warmly.

"Well, Sean, how do you like your new role as PR man for the rehab office? I hear you're traveling around the county giving speeches. I didn't know you were such the eloquent elocutionist." Mrs. Higenbothem smiled at me and slapped me on the back.

Betty Higenbotham, all aglitter in her new emerald green dress bordered in sapphire blue metallic brocade, set the fashion standard for oriental influence in Eureka, circa 1957.

"Shucks, tain't nothin'," I responded.

The informational talk went well. I returned home that night satisfied with my efforts. My first attempt at spreading the good word had been a brief but successful experience as a public speaker.

Early in the evening I asked Cassie, "Would you like to go to a movie tonight? 'Love me Tender' with Elvis Presley is playing. His first picture."

"I'm not in the mood," she replied.

"Well, how about dinner at Lenzi's then? Phyllis Diller is the main attraction," I suggested.

"That might be fun," she agreed. "Remember the Purple Onion in San Francisco? Our first trip to the city." She hesitated a moment. "Okay. I'll go get ready."

"Great," I responded.

Much to my surprise, Cassie didn't have play practice or art work to finish at school that night. Her growing legion of friends occupied much of her free time. That night we sat in the front row at Lenzi's supper club.

"What are you doing, Sean?" Cassie asked.

"Counting," I replied, studying the menu. "Hey look, Cassie. They have sixteen complete dinners in the two dollar class on the menu."

"Yes, I see." she said.

We made our dinner choices and the show began. "And now Ladies and Gentlemen, direct from the Purple Onion in San Francisco, Lenzi's proudly presents Phyllis Diller." The introduction by the former circus ringmaster rang out from unseen speakers.

I whispered into Cassie's ear, "I read in the Humboldt Times that she's the divorced mother of five children and in her forties."

"I thought she was wacky at the Onion. What's she doing in this logging town?" Cassie wondered.

"Getting experience." I hummed "Waltzing Matilda" as Phyllis Diller, comedienne par excellence, bounced onto the small stage. Hair askew and rubber faced, she plunged into her now famous routine.

Her targets included Fang, a former husband, and their five children. Her outlandish costumes topped with a fright wig made the audience dissolve into belly laughs. Forty five minutes went by before the emcee concluded, "Thank you Ladies and Gentlemen. You've been a great audience." Miss Diller retreated from the stage, throwing kisses to all.

"She's a funny woman. Do you think she really has five kids?" I asked.

"Sure. Why not?"

We were interrupted by another announcement. "And now, Ladies and Gentlemen, for your dancing pleasure Lenzi's proudly presents 'The

Woodchopper Five'!" The club combo consisted of a bass, drums, piano, clarinet and saxophone. Outfitted in plaid shirts with dirty jeans fastened by huge red suspenders, the group members looked like they had just returned from the woods.

"Oh, Sean...'Hernando's Hideaway'. Shall we?" Cassie oozed excitement.

"I don't know."

"Please..." Cassie was coquettish by nature and her smile held me hostage.

"Okay, let's give it a try." Hand in hand we set a course for the dance floor.

"Uh-oh. Look who's coming our way," she said.

"Who?" I asked, looking ahead.

"Some of my fellow classmates from school," she explained. Three well dressed young men came into view. I immediately assumed my psychological defenses.

"Hi, guys. How are you?" Cassie smiled.

"Hi, Cassie! You look great...What did you think of Madame Diller?" Trivial conversation continued ad nausium.

"Oh, I'd like you to meet my husband Sean," Cassie finally said. At least she admits I'm her husband, I thought. "Sean, this is Herb McCallister, Bob Coppen, and Wally Singer. The finest thespians to trod the boards."

Herb McAllister, clad in a brown plaid sport jacket with color-coordinated brand name flannel slacks, all wool, puffed on his pipe. I took note of his short stature as we shook hands.

"Hey, nice sport coat," I said in admiration. "I think I saw one just like it on sale at Bistrins."

"You did," McAllister retorted. "Got it on sale."

Bob Coppen, a full-bearded young man of medium height, extended his hand. A high blue colored Elvis Presley shirt made his fashion statement for him. A victim of the latest fad.

"Cassie tells me you work for the state," Coppen commented.

"That's right," I said.

"We've had some interesting conversations over coffee at school. She speaks of you all the time." Coppen placed his hand on Cassie's shoulder. She pulled away.

Wallace Singer, a pudgy six foot four, appropriately attired in a locally advertised $54.88 Grey Kuppenhiemer suit, extended his hand. "Pleased to meet you at long last. Cassie talks a lot about you."

"Oh." I attempted a smile, contemplating what she might have said to her friends. Despite my signals to the contrary, Cassie invited them to join us at our table. The wannabe actors grabbed nearby chairs and sat down to continue school gossip. I toyed with my desert— cheesecake smothered in warm strawberries.

Cassie asked, "Did you guys enjoy Phyllis Diller?"

They chorused, "Yes."

I cut in. "It's getting late, Cassie. We should probably head for home. Tomorrow is going to be a long work day for me and I didn't get much sleep last night."

"Yes, you're right. We should go." We stood up to leave.

"But it's still early, and we haven't caught up on the school gossip," Coppin protested. McAllister held up his hand like a traffic cop.

I suggested, "Maybe we could get together sometime soon. I wonder what's playing next month?"

"One of King Farouk's favorite dancers, Boubouka. She has the agility of a contortionist and the grace of a Zypher. Or so say the ads." Coppen laughed. "It might be fun. I'll give you a call, Cassie," he said.

"I've never seen a belly dancer," I commented.

"Sean."

The waiter finished clearing the table, except for the coffee and dessert.

"Cassie, I ran in to Professor Cutler the other day, the art professor. He said you were going to pose for his life class," Singer said. He twisted his head to wink at me. "Sean, how do you feel about your wife posing in the nude?" he asked.

I jumped up, my legs locked in place by muscle spasms. "Pose in the nude!" I yelled as I fell face forward into the remains of my cheese cake. Cassie pulled me back from the mess on the table. I stared through warm strawberries. Flecks of spittle dripped down my chin.

She held my hands. Her little voice said, "Don't worry, Sean. I'm not going to pose naked."

"Uh, sorry Sean. Didn't mean to upset you. Lots of people pose naked, including some guys I know." Singer laughed.

Cassie got into his face. "You son of a bitch!" she snarled softly. Alarmed at the expletive, the three men got up to leave.

"Pleasure to meet you, Sean," McAllister said, pumping my hand.

"Me too," echoed Bob Coppen.

"Again, Sean, my apologies," Singer bowed his head.

"You surprised me. Let's go Cassie." I grabbed my wife's arm in a vice like grip as I hustled her out of the supper club. Crab-walking through the crowd, I bumped into several people on the way out.

"Hey, watch it, fella!"

"Sorry...Sorry," I muttered as we went. We headed for home.

Driving North on Fifth Street we passed J.D. McDonald, the car dealership. "We could sure use a new car. This one is on its last legs." I slowed. "Look, that English Ford is only $1554. What do you say, Cassie?" I pleaded.

"If you think we should." Cassie accepted the inevitable. We bought the Ford before our next trip to San Francisco.

Five minutes later we walked up the path to our apartment. I flopped into my favorite easy chair while Cassie undressed for her nightly soak in the tub. "Hey, Cassie, you gotta read this!" I yelled.

"What?" she asked.

"Billy, the chimp at Sequoia Park Zoo, thinks people differ from monkeys."

"That's true," she responded. "It's pretty late and you didn't get any sleep last night. We'd better get to bed."

"Listen to this headline: 'Girl drops dead after saying she's glad to be close to the Lord'...Do you think she met him?" I asked.

"Met who?"

"God," I said.

Cassie stood in a black lace shortie with a strategically embroidered red rose emphasizing her cleavage. The light from the bathroom framed a silhouette, delicate and fragile.

SUMMER FADED INTO THE FALLING LEAVES OF Autumn. Cassie devoted much of her time to school and friends while still making every effort to share her life with me. We were often joined by college comrades from the art or drama department.

Winter weekends were devoted to TV football or visiting family. Ma found it difficult to accept Cassie. I became the proverbial pickle in the middle.

Cassie and I braved the winter storms, using the monthly staff meetings as an excuse to make several trips to San Francisco. A fun weekend in the big city included a Friday evening visit to The House

That Jack Built on Broadway, where Antonio and Giovanna sang our favorite arias. Then on to Pierre's Sidewalk cafe for a session with Madame Marie, the graphologist.

"Your handwriting indicates you are extremely sensitive. I see events which are not as important as you imagine them to be. You also show signs of being inconsistent," she said to me.

Madame Marie had a long slender nose, prominent cheekbones, and the eggshell pallor of a Manchu. Her black hair was drawn back and braided.

"I hope you are not planning to get married?" she continued.

Cassie looked into my eyes. She answered for me, "We are married...What does my handwriting show?"

Marie glanced at the sample. "Oh my. Oh my." Gulping for air, her face a masque, the graphologist blanched shades of a cadaver painted by a thousand devils. She turned back to the writing pad, studying the quirks and curls of "The quick brown fox jumped over the fence."

Ashen-faced, she spoke the words slowly. "I see a mirror. You are standing in front of a mirror. A loud noise. No! No!"

"What's wrong?" Cassie asked.

Madame Marie jumped up and said, "I must go. Please, my fee." I handed her a ten dollar bill as she ran away, wiping tears from her face as she went.

"I wonder what she saw in my cards," Cassie mused.

"I guess we'll never know," I answered lightly.

We walked a few blocks to the Hungry I. The major domo seated us as the curtains opened to "Hang Down Your Head Tom Dooley." When we got back to the hotel, I said, "The next time we come to the Bay Area we should stay at the Drake Wiltshire on Stockton. I saw an ad in the Humboldt Times advertising rooms for $6.00 a night."

"That sounds like a good idea. This place is too far from the shopping district and I don't like walking through the tenderloin. So many weird people."

"Okay. We'll give it a try next time."

"I'm going to work backstage on 'The Glass Menagerie' at the college starting Wednesday night. I couldn't get a part in the play but Herb said I could use the experience working as a stage hand."

"I'll bet he did."

"Sean, I'll be home every night to have dinner with you as always. Practice doesn't start until seven p.m. Mondays, Wednesdays, and Fridays. We'll still have time together," she reassured me.

"Okay, but I was hoping you and I could go to the movies. Marlon Brando is playing in 'Sayonara' next week at the Eureka Theater and 'The Bridge on The River Kwai' is coming next month. Maybe we can see it at the next staff meeting in San Francisco. Want to come with me?"

"I'm not going all the way to San Francisco just to see a movie!"

Early Sunday morning, our headlights punched holes in a fog of cotton as we crossed the bridge on our way back to Eureka. A bevy of unseen horns harmonized, warning all mariners of the rocky coasts and shallow shoals.

We arrived home in time for our evening television viewing. Eureka finally acquired a second TV station—KVIQ Channel 6. It was April 1, 1958.

The spring of 1958 arrived and we bought a 1957 English Ford. Cassie voiced no opposition. In return I did not object to her occasional shopping sprees. I admired the results of her latest safari into Daly's and Hornbeck's.

"This should complete your new wardrobe," I said. I wanted an end to her shopping binges but I was in no mood for a battle royale.

"Yes, I think so. The new car and this has put us into debt," she acknowledged.

"Oh, don't worry. I have a good job," I replied with confidence.

"I'm thinking about summer school again. I can pick up a few more credits," she said.

The next day the big storm of the year hit Eureka. "Mr. Sullivan, may we take some pictures? We'd like to interview you on camera for tonight's news." A well dressed man, probably in his fifties, gray at the temples, carrying a 50 mn. Hasselblad camera, poked his head through the protective white plastic sheets covering the doorway. A younger man, burdened by an oversized television cameras on his shoulder, followed.

"Sure. Come in if you can." I carried on my duties as though eighty five mile an hour winds were an every day occurrence. Over a pizza and beer that evening, I described the events of the day to Cassie.

"It's fun being on TV. I wasn't nervous at all. I hope I appeared relaxed. It'll be on tonight at six on Channel Three. I've got to call Ma and tell her."

"Sorry about dinner," Cassie apologized. "I picked up the pizza and beer on the way home from class. Play rehearsal tonight at seven."

We huddled together on the couch. I kissed her on the forehead. The warmth of her body ignited lustful thoughts. Forget it, I said to myself. Not enough time.

"What's wrong, Sean?" she asked.

"Nothing…Oh no! I don't believe this." I stared at the screen.

Cassie squealed with delight at the newscast. "You need a haircut," she said. After the news we dissected my first television performance.

To my surprise, Cassie changed the subject. "I know it's not easy for you to accept my schedule. I realize I'm gone a lot, but I have been doing the household chores and cooking," she said somewhat defensively.

"I know, and I applaud your efforts to earn a degree in the arts. But I don't accept the situation as easily as you do," I said.

Cassie shook her head. "The play will be over in another month and the next one isn't until late spring or early summer. Then we can spend more time together."

I continued to gaze at the screen as "Death Valley Days with Your Host, Ronald Reagen" appeared on the screen.

"I forgot to tell you. I've been invited to attend a state conference for counselors in Los Angeles the last week of April at the Mayflower Hotel. All expenses paid."

I know, Sean. You mentioned it last week. Have a good time," she said. She walked into the kitchen and tossed the beer cans and the remains of the pizza into the garbage.

DURING THE LATE MORNING HOURS OF TUESDAY, April Fools' Day, 1957, the airport shuttle deposited me at the entrance of my hotel in Los Angeles. Over-tipping the driver with a dollar bill, I entered a world of incomparable refinement. It reeked of money.

The Mayflower Hotel, one of the top ten such establishments in Los Angeles, presented a welcoming collage of soft colors, friendly people, and well upholstered overstuffed chairs. A huge chandelier sparkled over marble floors covered with Persian rugs. Exquisite pearl-blue Sung ceramic vases, fake of course, were tastefully displayed throughout the lobby, accompanied by ink paintings depicting knights of old.

The walk through the entrance hall became a journey into a world of transient charms. A many-faceted jewel of a hotel, the Mayflower did not cater to street people. "I should have brought Cassie with me. She would really enjoy this," I said out loud to no one.

I dragged my over-packed cardboard box through the lobby. My right leg collapsed in spasms of pain as I fell forward to the marble floor. Sprawled spread-eagled over my flattened suitcase, I asked a gathering audience and the heavens above, "Why me, God?"

"Are you alright? May we help you?" Several ladies formed an impromptu rescue party.

"No, thank you. Thank you," I said.

"Well. We were only trying to help."

I continued to flop like a fish out of water, unable to regain my balance until the third try. Salvation arrived in the person of Lloyd Astin. Comrade in arms.

"Hi, Sean. How are you doing?" We shook hands.

"Not too well at the moment. Damn thing fell apart," I said, indicating the battered suitcase.

"Let me help you," Astin offered. We headed for the hotel reception desk.

Our approach did not go unnoticed. "Oh my God. I think he's going to register," the assistant manager stage whispered to his superior nodding in our direction.

"Not to worry," the manager replied. "He's probably a welfare client, here for demonstration purposes. The counselor conference, you know."

"Good morning," Astin greeted the assistant manager. "Mr. Sullivan has a reservation. He is representing Northern California for the Department of Vocational Rehabilitation."

Later, the manager said to no one in particular, "Unfortunately, it's not a question of what any of us would like, but of what we have to accept."

Astin guided me to the conference hospitality desk. Printed materials, room assignments, and a large button blaring "HI, MY NAME IS SEAN SULLIVAN" over "Eureka, CA" were handed to me.

During the next three days I was bombarded with, "Oh, you're from Eureka, California" and, "You must be Sean Sullivan." A hand often shot out in false friendliness followed by an energetic, "Put her there, Pal!"

"Let's have brunch." Astin suggested.

"Good idea."

From colonnade steps we descended into a garden restaurant not unlike the tearoom at the Palace Hotel in San Francisco. A greenhouse effect added to it's grandiose milieu. The people who patronized these world class eateries oozed money through every pore.

"I beg your pardon, Sir. We require a tie in the Garden Room." The major domo stared at me. "Perhaps we can loan you one of ours, for a fee," he added.

"Oh God, another Edmund Nix," I muttered.

"What did you say, Sean?" Astin asked.

"A tie for breakfast?" I asked.

"Look around you." The major domo produced the proper apparel.

"Let's eat," I replied. I declined to knot the tie in the proper manner.

The breakfast buffet required a balancing act. Plate in hand, I made quick stabs at the food. The table offered a spread of some twenty-one various delectables.

I looked up and grabbed the table to maintain my equilibrium. A young lady, whose delicate perfections fluttered as petals floating from a flower, glided to our table. Green eyes darted to and from under a suggestion of eyelashes. Imitation pearl teardrop earrings swung back and forth—dewdrops on the blossoms of a cherry tree. Teased fluffy hair intensified her Elizabeth Taylor look and her lips were coated the popular "Hound Dog Orange" in homage to the Elvis Presley fad of the time. A white paisley silk blouse with a beige skirt completed her stunning appearance.

Astin stood up as she offered her hand. He kissed her fingers and said, "Of all people! I was hoping you would attend the conference. How are you, Michele?"

"I'm fine. You look great, Lloyd," she said.

"Michele, I'd like you to meet my friend Sean Sullivan from the Eureka office. Michele, Sean. Michele labors in the L.A. office. Sean took my place up north." She thrust her curled hand upward in the direction of my mouth. I gently kissed it.

"Join us, please. We can catch up with the office gossip," Astin said. Stealing occasional glances I saw a young lady in her late twenties. The talk over the back fence continued for a long fifteen minutes before Astin excused himself.

I pictured her in my arms. A three day affair perhaps. The heart of a tiger beat for its next meal. Glancing down at my right hand, I saw my wedding ring glittering in the darkness.

"Tell me something about yourself, Sean. How long have you been working for rehab?" Michele oozed. She scooted her chair closer.

"Well, there's not much to tell." I encapsulated my life into five minutes. I discovered she appreciated the classical arts. We compared schedules.

"Sounds good," I said. "Cocktails before dinner?"

"Fine."

Soft lights and a darkened room greeted us later in the afternoon. A fireplace, glowing at one end of the room, invited Michele and I to a nearby settee. A fifty foot aquarium served as a bar.

Together we fell into the folds of overstuffed love seat. Her hand grasped mine. A few minutes later, we were loitering over our third drinks.

She mused, "You know, I'm getting a little bit hungry."

"So am I. Let's go to dinner." We stood up to leave. At dinner, I regaled her with stories of my experiences as a hospital counselor. I emphasized the death and dying.

"Poor guy,' she said. "Let's go up to my room." I couldn't believe my ears. And she seemed like such a nice girl. "I have to change."

My voice dropped to its best basso profundo, "Okay."

Room 513 at the Mayflower consisted of a bed, a round table, two chairs, a closet and a bathroom. I headed for the chair next to the window, feeling more titillated than sensual. Michelle comforted me with hugs and kisses. In Shakespeare's time. "She would have made me hungry where she could most satisfy."

"What's wrong? Don't you like me?" She ran her fingers through my hair.

"There's something funny going on here," I said.

"Oh, come come. I'm just doing a job. I've already been paid for my services."

"You mean you're a party girl?" I exclaimed. I couldn't speak the word whore. I was aware of the common practice of providing hostesses to conventions and legislatures.

"Do you want me to leave?" she asked.

My twangs of anticipation turned to thoughts of escape. "No. Stay if you can," I said. I attempted to disguise my feelings by offering her a twenty dollar bill.

"You don't need to do this," she said, pushing my hand away. "I'm sorry to have disappointed you."

"I'm not disappointed, just surprised." I became more and more agitated. The situation was appalling.

"Tell me, why are you in this kind of work? You don't really work for vocational rehab?" I had asked the eternal question: Why are you a prostitute?

"I have to make a living. I have two babies at home."

"But why don't you learn a job skill? There are thousands of different occupations you could consider." Another dumb question.

"Because this one pays big money."

My midnight attempts at career counseling in Room 513 were unsuccessful. After an interval she said, "I've got to go. Sorry."

"So soon," I replied.

She closed the door without a sound. I did my best to avoid Michelle for the remainder of the conference. I saw her often in the lounge, at the bar, and in the lobby. Business was obviously good.

Two days later Astin offered me a ride to the airport. The schoolboy in him had to ask, "So, how did you make out with Michelle? Did you score?"

"You son of a gun," I said. "You knew she was a lady of the night."

"No, I didn't. Honest."

"We should do career counseling on the job."

Astin deposited me in front of the Southwest Airlines terminal at LAX. I boarded an antiquated DC3 bound for Eureka with stops at Monterey, San Francisco, and Ukiah. As we approached Ukiah, the plane lost altitude and the pilot had to jockey the aircraft into its final approach.

I peered out the window. The ground came up with dizzying speed. Our flying machine lurched forward causing the flight attendant to lose her balance. Hands reached out to grab her as she fell to the floor.

"What's going on here?" one passenger hollered. Everyone clutched their seats during the crashing and swaying. Something snapped and rattled.

An elderly man advised, "Stay calm everybody."

A high pitched voice shouted, "A bad landing. Damn bad landing. I want to talk to the driver of this airplane."

I glanced out and saw skid marks and rubber scattered over a wide area of the tarmac.

A flight attendant made an announcement. "Ladies and Gentlemen, Captain Schneider extends his apologies. The rubber tires came off both wheels as we landed. No need to worry." As an after thought, she said, "We can disembark now."

A substitute Martin 202 arrived in due time. We completed the journey to Eureka. Cassie met me at the airport.

"Why are you so late? Did you have a good time?" She put her arm around me.

"Rehab conferences are almost as boring as teacher conventions," I replied.

April became May 1958. Cassie continued with her academics in art and drama. I was making progress in rehabilitating clients in Humboldt and Del Norte counties.

Early one Monday morning, my secretary stuck her head in my office. "Mr. Sullivan, you have a long distance phone call from San Francisco. I think it's Mrs. Pensky, the district supervisor."

11

"THE JACKSON STREET IRREGULARS

I WAS READING THE QUESTION OF THE DAY IN the Humboldt Times. A chimpanzee offered the local reporter his complete disdain for the human race. When the phone rang.

"Hi, Sean. Jan Pensky here. I don't know how to say this so I'll just say it. I'm not recommending you for permanent civil service status."

A tidal wave of shock washed over me.

"Sorry, I don't believe I understand," I said. I didn't want to understand.

"The Department has to let you go, Sean."

I stared at the phone unable to speak. My head roared with the heartbeat of a helicopter. Thud, thud, thud.

"Hello? Sean, are you there?" she asked.

My voice, raw with terror, screamed, "You mean I'm fired?"

"Now, Sean, calm yourself. It's not the end of the world," Pensky said.

"For you it's not. I have bills to pay. We just bought an English Ford for $1600.00. How am I going to tell my wife?" I whined.

"She's a mature girl; she'll handle it" Pensky soothed. "Oh, and some good news. We've enrolled you in a graduate program at San Francisco State College this fall. But we can't offer you financial aid due to budget cuts."

"How am I going to finance graduate school? We just bought a new car." I was getting repetitive.

"You didn't handle that drinking affair with Florence Ash well."

"My God! That was almost two years ago. Why didn't you fire me then if I'm such a inept counselor?"

She countered with, "On his visit to Eureka, Sid Edison said he found many mistakes in your case load."

I shot back, "His purpose in life is to find errors in other people's hard work! My case load has gone from fifty to over one hundred. I've ferreted out every physically and mentally handicap person in Humboldt and Del Norte County. Don't my efforts count for anything?"

"You're upset and there's no point in continuing with this conversation. You will receive formal notice in the mail. Stay until the end of the month. My best to Cassie."

I looked at Mrs. Young, my eyes blinking widely with surprise and disbelief. "I've been fired."

That night, Cassie greeted me at the door. A happy person, she radiated joy when she laughed. A trait that captured my heart.

After two years of marriage, Cassie continued to anticipate children. I had failed to confess, during our brief pre-wedding affair, that I had a low sperm count and was probably sterile. Not impotent as many people thought.

"No play practice tonight, Sean. We can spend a quiet evening at home. I made goulash for dinner." She smiled holding both my hands.

As we sat down to dinner, I pronounced sentence on our marriage.

"I have bad news. I don't know how to say it." I hesitated.

"What's wrong? Aren't you hungry? You always like my goulash."

"Oh, the goulash is fine." I paused and took a deep breath before continuing. "Jan Pensky called this morning. She is not recommending me for permanent civil service status."

"What does 'permanent civil service' mean?" The full impact of my words had not filtered through her mind. I made it clear for her.

"I've been fired, terminated, sacked, disposed."

We devoted the evening to an intense discussion of the days' events. It was a shock for two people who, in the ordinary course of events should have anticipated a bright future, but instead found themselves facing an unknown fate.

"I guess the last eighteen months have been for nothing. I feel like killing myself. All my work, for what?" I lamented, head in hands.

"Cheer up, Sean. Things could be worse," she said optimistically.

"How?" I demanded. "Where are we going to live? I don't think the county welfare office will take me back. I sorta told them to go to hell when I quit to take this counseling job."

"You really should be more diplomatic," she suggested. A little late.

"That's not my strong suit," I said. "We could move back to Portland, but I prefer San Francisco." I didn't suggest Eureka, California.

"I think I'd like San Francisco," she said. "Will I be able to finish the spring term here at the college?"

"Yes. Pensky said I could stay until the end of the month. That was nice of her."

The doorbell rang. "I wonder who it could be this time of night?" Cassie asked. She got up and answered the door.

"Hi, Wally," she said. "Sean, it's Wally Singer," she called back to me.

That's all I need, one of her school buddies, I thought.

"Sorry to drop by so late, Cassie, but I've got great news. The drama department is doing 'Kiss Me Kate' next September and you have a part. It's just a small one though." Wally smiled.

"Wonderful!" Cassie danced around the room, kissed me on the cheek, and fell into my lap. Then her expression suddenly saddened. Glee changed to gloom.

She whispered, "I'm sorry, Wally, but Sean lost his job today. We're moving to San Francisco at the end of next month. I won't be able to take the part." She pulled free from my embrace.

I looked at Wally. "I had no idea this was coming. We bought a 1957 English Ford a few months ago. I think we owe twenty four more payments of $51.67. We financed it on a thirty six month loan. The 'never never plan' as the Brits say." I babbled. Wally offered his condolences.

I moaned, "A curse on all career women. Especially women supervisors."

"Is housing a problem in San Francisco?" Cassie asked.

Wally suggested a Victorian rooming house on Jackson street in Pacific Heights. "Mickey Landucci runs the place. I'll be glad to call her. Remember, this is a communal home with shared kitchen and bathrooms."

"Well, it would give us a chance to get organized. Just temporary, until we get back on our feet," Cassie said hopefully.

"Mickey's place is interesting. I think it's the headquarters for the Pacific Heights beatniks. The place is full of characters."

"We appreciate your help," I said sincerely. I now viewed Wally Singer in a new light. I considered him a friend and confidant.

"I guess I could survive in one room." I added.

The farewell parties were made up of Cassie's college friends and a few neighbors. I found it difficult to pursue relationships of a lasting nature. I gravitated toward Cassie's young college buddies. Adieus were suffered through many times during May of 1958.

"Stay in touch. Don't forget to write. Come back and see us soon. Mi casa es su casa."

I had taken great pleasure in the proclivities of a lifestyle that included an artistic wife, an interesting job and a pleasant home. I found it difficult to break the rhythm.

We gave to friends what we could, mostly furniture and bookcases. I threw away memorabilia of happier days including personal letters, old pictures, lesson plans and old text books. I am not a saver. Cassie rescued many an item from the garbage can during our marriage.

The last goodbye rituals completed, the move to San Francisco began early on a Monday morning in June 1958 as daybreak crisscrossed the Eastern horizon.

"Well, Sean, what do you think awaits us in the big city?" Cassie asked expectantly.

Ever the optimist, I replied, "Strange and wonderful experiences."

I glanced down the road. "Let's get going. It'll be light soon. I don't know the streets of San Francisco all that well but I think we should get there sometime this afternoon."

"That's okay, Sean. I can sleep on the way," she said.

"You always do," I murmured.

"What did you say?" she demanded.

"Nothing,' I replied.

Stuffing the last cardboard box into the back seat, we took a tearful last look at our first home.

"I enjoyed living in Eureka. It's so beautiful—the rivers, the ocean," I said.

"Me, too. And I hate to leave my friends." A single tear cascaded down Cassie's cheek. She brushed it away with a trembling hand.

"Say goodbye, Cassie." My voice quavered as I surveyed the scene with a sinking heart. The bitterness of losing my counseling job in Salem three years before coupled with our present circumstances compounded my feelings of helplessness. One more strike and I would be out.

We drove South on Highway 101 pass the sentinels of the Redwood forest. "They say some of these trees were in existence at the time of Christ. Imagine what stories they could tell," I philosophized.

Cassie turned her face to the window as we drove over the Van Duzen River, past the South fork of the Eel and through Garberville. We made a quick stop at Ukiah for hamburgers and coffee.

Soon the storied towers of the Golden Gate Bridge penetrated the late afternoon fog. The silver gray vapors would soon dissipate. Fog horns blared a San Francisco welcome.

I turned to a Cassie. "You can tell the size of the ship by the tone of it's horn. High notes for little vessels and low notes for the big ones." A right turn on 19th lead us to Jackson Street.

"There it is." We stopped and studied the classic three story Victorian house with a turret on the second floor. Mickey Landucci, a petite woman dressed in jeans and a multi-colored blouse generously embedded with sequins, met us at the door. She escorted Cassie and I into a living room accented with a unique blend of pop art decor and early bohemian accents.

Introductions were made all around. Ginseng tea appeared before us. The faint essence of incense wafted through the multi-colored beaded curtains that divided the living room. A ouija board resided on a nearby hutch. I eyed two pocketbooks on the coffee table—"Your Future In The Stars" next to a hardbound "Is There Life After Death?"

The usual banter between strangers followed. A few minutes later, Mickey took us upstairs for a look see. The front room was $40.00 a month, including use of the community kitchen and bathroom. No drugs, no pot smoking and no late night orgies.

I considered the house rules an affront to my puritan morality. "I don't use drugs. I don't smoke pot," I proclaimed.

Cassie giggled, "No orgies. This sounds like a fun place." We returned to the first floor.

"Oh, do come into my quarters," Mickey invited.

The landlady led us into her living room. We looked for a place to sit. Mickey sat on a broken down divan covered with a yellow flower print bed sheet. She easily assumed the popular cross legged lotus position of the beat generation. Cassie sat next to her. Stiff necked as usual, I stumbled onto a large bean bag chair. Its comfort surprised me.

A large living room, kitchen, bedroom and bathroom occupied the first floor of the Victorian. On the second floor, in the round turret room, lived a young Caucasian woman, age unknown. Seldom seen by the other residents, the young woman rarely spoke to anyone. Rumors abounded.

Oh Long tea was offered. Its bitter taste becomes acceptable after the third or fourth sip. My eye caught an apparition floating by the door in a floor length white robe with a braided rope knotted around the waist.

"Cheery afternoon to one and all," she called out as she disappeared upstairs to her inner sanctum. The round room surrounded in mystery aroused the curiosity of all.

"That's Pauline Rose. Our tenants are characters from a Damon Runyan novel or maybe Jack Kerouac's beat philosophy. I'm not sure which." Mickey proceeded to recite a brief biography of each resident.

Cassie squealed, "Oh goody!"

"My God," I groaned. The beatniks were taking over my Presbyterian culture. I dubbed our new housemates the "Jackson Street Irregulars," a title we eventually all came to use for our little group.

Our new landlady, a small person of Italian ancestry, proved to be the mother confessor to the beat generation. I soon discovered Mickey to be not only a master of crisis management, but also a women of exceptional common sense. Although typically reluctant to confide in strangers, I found myself telling her of my recent experiences.

"The bastards fired me. I thought I did a good job in vocational rehab. My case load went from fifteen to over one hundred in less than two years. My boss, a woman naturally, no offense, took over as district supervisor in March. One of her first acts as the new head honcho was to terminate me. Mr. Dodds, her predecessor, had been nice to me."

"Tell me something of your work experiences, Sean," Mickey urged. She reached for my hand, murmuring soothingly, "I understand."

I began to see 2441 Jackson Street as a safe harbor in a sea of troubles. I recounted the highlights of my resume, failing to mention the budget cuts at Salem, Oregon before Cassie and I got married.

Mickey was more than just a sympathetic ear. She offered salvation. "I have a friend at the County Welfare office. She tells me they're always looking for experienced caseworkers. Would you be interested?" Mickey smiled.

"Oh boy, would I!" My spirits soared.

"See, Sean, I told you things would get better," Cassie beamed.

Mickey turned to her. "And there's a small coffee house on Montgomery Street that needs help. Breakfast and lunch only—seven in the morning until three in the afternoon."

"Oh, wonderful!" Cassie danced a jig of joy.

I sputtered, "My God, we hit pay dirt today! You'll have to get up early in the morning, Cassie."

"I don't mind," she said.

"Good, then it's settled," Mickey declared. "Oh, and before I forget, next Sunday the whole gang is going to take the ferry to Oakland. Would you like to join us?" she asked.

"Oh, yes! Count me and Sean in!" Cassie bubbled. A true party lover, she added, "Maybe Lloyd and Carole would like to join us." She turned to Mickey, asking, "May we bring a couple of friends?"

I gave Mickey some background. "Our friend, Lloyd Astin, transferred to the San Francisco office of vocational rehabilitation when I succeeded him as counselor in Eureka. I had been working for county welfare in Crescent City, California. Carole is his lady friend of the moment."

"Sure, the more the merrier," Mickey said agreeably. "The State is going to shut the ferry down at the end of next month so this may be our last chance to ride history. John Reed began the first ferry from Sausalito in 1826 but the Indians paddled faster than he could. They ran him out of business."

Later that evening the scent of burning joss sticks hung thick in the upstairs community kitchen. We gathered with the Jackson Street Irregulars, as I now labeled them. After dinner Cassie told them about our conversation with Mickey.

"That's Mickey—Florence Nightingale to the beatniks," they chorused.

The following Monday, I met with an administrator of the San Francisco City and County Welfare office and was offered a job. Christine Conforti, the Casework Supervisor of the Western Addition, explained my duties, found me a desk and introduced the "new boy" to my new co-workers.

She was a tall slender woman. The silver highlights in her brunette bouffant revealed the slow rape of time. The realities of social casework had eroded the compassion of youth. The helping professions were the last refuge for the bleeding hearts of the world.

"Your district is made up of public housing units, apartments, and a few individual homes, mostly Victorian. The Western Addition is an older section of San Francisco," she explained.

"Sounds interesting," I said.

"Well, I regret to inform you that yours is the toughest case load in town. You know the game. Maybe you can work your way up to the plums."

"I live on challenge, and rejection," I replied.

"You will be expected to do intake work twice a week, on Wednesdays and Fridays. The intake center is downstairs. Home visits are Mondays, Tuesdays and Thursdays. Catch up with the paper work when you can. Your position has gone unfilled for several months so there's a lot to do. Good luck, Sean." We shook hands.

In June of 1958, the County Welfare office was located at 585 Bush Street in downtown San Francisco. It housed fifty to sixty social caseworkers, supervisors and clerical workers. Thirty desks, placed neatly in rows, formed a square in the center of a huge room.

The bee hive welcomed me every morning at eight a.m. Partitioned glass cubicles at the four corners of the barn-like structure were a refuge for low-level casework supervisors. They were the non-commissioned officers of the profession.

An out pouring of cordiality and curiosity greeted me as I introduced myself.

"Yes, I am married—to Cassie Buzbie of Boise, Idaho. No, we don't have children. It just hasn't happened yet." Dammed if I would discuss a low sperm count with these women. People thought I was impotent. Maybe I should provide written testimonials or videos of my bedroom gymnastics, I thought.

"Right now we're living in a rooming house on Jackson Street. It's very 'beat generation'." There were smiles all around and much nodding of heads. I tried to wrap it up. "Well, nice to meet you, Marie, Evelyn."

Picking up a large white binder marked "Policy," I said, "I guess I'd better read this statement." I proceeded to rudely bury myself in reading office regulations and job benefits. Surveying the second floor office, I knew I would become a worker bee surrounded by queen bees in a busy hive.

That night the setting sun, framed by a halo, descended in the western sky as I climbed the stairs to beatsville.

"How was your day?" Cassie asked. Impatient for an answer, she dragged me up the stairs.

Guided by a yellowish funeral glow, I pushed aside a beaded curtain. "Why so dark?" I asked.

Pauline Rose hovered in front of me. "Surprise, Sean! We're having a candlelight dinner for you and your bride."

"What makes you think we're newlyweds?". Inwardly I cried, "Oh God, no! A pot luck dinner!'

"You don't mind my calling you Sean, do you? I never call people by their family names. It's so much easier to love one another by first names, don't you think? They speak volumes," Pauline said.

'Oh, no. I don't mind." What else could I say? I sniffed the strong, fragrant candles. Over a large kettle of something, we immersed ourselves in the "beat" culture of 1958.

"Isn't this dreamy?" Pauline sighed. "I made the candles in my room." She held both arms up to the heavens as though she expected a sign from God. Nothing happened.

"They light the way to the pure land which exists with the enlightenment of the heart," she said.

"What the hell are you talking about?" I cried.

"Buddha, my teacher, explained the eight worlds, which are Hell, hunger, animality, rapture, learning, realization, Bodhisattva, and Buddha."

"Oh, boy, that sounds like fun. Especially Bo-di-sat-va," I mouthed carefully.

"You of the great unwashed," Pauline sneered. She continued to levitate hither and yon in her white gown, knotted with what appeared to be a hawser taken from a ship.

Miss Rose, from who knows where, prattled on about the philosophy of Buddha liberally laced with the popular beat ideology of the times. People seemed to ignore her. She didn't take offense.

"I'm so hungry I could eat a horse. Oops, I probably shouldn't have said that," I said.

Cassie dipped a ladle into the huge kettle and came up with what appeared to be bouillabaisse. A single dark brown eye floated to the surface and stared at me.

"What is it?" I questioned. I cautiously peered into the depths of the pot.

"It's Jambe de Mouton," Mickey announced grandly.

"What the devil is 'Jambe de Mouton'? It looks like a sheep's head to me. I think I found its eye," I exclaimed.

"It is, and you did," Cassie giggled.

"Let's eat out tonight," I quickly suggested. Cassie grabbed my arm, pulling me down to the chair.

"Now, Sean. We have gelato to go with the Jambe de Mouton. A tortini." Cassie pushed a bowl of green and white ice cream in front of me.

"What's a tortini?" I demanded. I made vomiting sounds.

"Italian ice cream."

I picked at my dinner as a premier danseuse would pirouette through a mine field. It was a meal soon to be forgotten.

Pauline gasped. "Oh, Where are my manners? Let me introduce you to our little coterie. Oh, I just love the French language. Don't you?" She floated back to the table.

I managed a, "Yeah. Great people the French." Cassie kicked me in the shins.

"Ladies first. This is Maggie. All the way from Boston." Pauline repeated, "We never use last names."

Maggie, a blond woman in her early twenties, gently squeezed my hand. Her black stockings and blue jeans were complimented by a print blouse, huge bangle earrings, and high laced boots.

"Would you believe Maggie has a Masters' degree in social work? She labors in a halfway house for parolees. She is doing God's work," Pauline said.

Maggie blushed.

"Next we have Marge, from of all places, San Francisco. A real native of our fair city."

I eyed the tall brunette in an oversized black sweater covering an ankle length skirt. Huge rimmed glasses accented her Miriam-the-librarian appearance.

A squeaky voice barely made it through her pursed lips. "Pleased to meet you," she said.

Usurping Pauline's status as emcee, the larger of the two men in the room boomed, "I'm Richard. Welcome to the Jackson Street Irregulars."

Over six feet tall, Richard had closely cropped hair, worn in the duck tail style. He wore a large gold cross over a lavender sweater and blue jeans. I made an effort not to stare at the ring in his left ear.

Pauline, mesmerized by the sound of her own voice, interrupted, "Last, but certainly not the least, here is Scott."

"Hi. Welcome to Beatsville. Hope you enjoy the place. As you can see, it's full of characters." He extended his hand.

"Now don't get mad, Scott, but I must tell our new friends," Pauline stated. Before he could comment, she announced, "He served our country in that horrible Korean War."

Scott squirmed in his chair, embarrassed. A slight, effeminate man, not very tall, he seldom spoke of the war, accepting the beat way of life as his salvation. He managed to keep body and soul together working as a substitute school teacher.

His speech was often interrupted by an irrepressible giggle, much like a nervous twitch. Later he revealed his age—thirty-one. Two years younger than I.

"Well, Sean, how was your first day on the new job?" Mickey inquired.

"Fine. My new boss is a woman with vast experience in public welfare. She also seems to be a fair minded person." Memories of job losses in Salem and Eureka still hurt. I went on at some length describing my new adventures in the bee hive.

Pauline got up and began circling me Indian fashion. "You have such fine features. When is your birthday? Why do you walk with a limp? I ask these questions in the name of love." I didn't know when she would strike.

I uttered an audible sigh. She wouldn't get out of my face. "March first," I croaked. "I was born this way."

Cassie interrupted, "Sean and I both have a birth defects. I have a congenital rheumatic heart. Look at my hands." Cassie wiggled her fingers in Pauline's face.

Taken by surprise I turned to her and exclaimed, "Why didn't you tell me?" Closely scrutinizing her hand I declared, "My God, you're turning blue!"

She jerked her hand away and changed the subject, "We were busy at the coffee shop this morning. Look at the tips I got for today, Sean."

She opened her purse, spilling out a variety of coins. Counting the day's gratuities became a habit in our crazy quilt lifestyle. Cassie's tips nearly doubled her paid wage at the coffee shop.

I looked for evidence of cyanosis from time to time. She continued to exhibit blue lips and blue fingertips, and occasionally swollen ankles.

"My supervisor said we wouldn't have medical coverage until I complete a one year probation." I frowned. Cassie did not respond.

"We agreed I would start school this fall as planned," I said.

"Oh yes. I want you to get a degree. That would be great," she responded.

"Working for the welfare is temporary. The state rehab has enrolled me in a masters program at San Francisco State College." I continued, "Maybe we should have stayed in Eureka...I'm sorry about your heart, Cassie."

"Don't worry about me, Sean. I'm fine. I've had this problem all my life."

June dissolved into a foggy San Francisco July 1958.

Early one morning Cassie yelled, "Sean, you're going to be late to work!"

"I'm on my way," I said, heading for the stairway.

"The bank called again about the car payment. I think they're going to repossess the Ford," she called back.

"Sorry, Cassie, I don't mean to embarrass you. We're three months behind in payments."

"Peace," she replied. Her fingers formed a "V."

"The beatniks are getting to you," I said.

Forty five minutes later, I lurched my way towards my desk in the great assembly hall of the San Francisco County Welfare office. Row three, desk number 12.

I planned the day's home visits to include four clients. Experience had taught me to allow enough time to locate the house and then find parking for the city car. Much of my home visitations were made up of climbing stairs, copying down wrong addresses, getting lost, and long lunches atop Telegraph hill overlooking the bay.

I enjoyed the noon hour on top of Telegraph hill. It was the perfect spot to daydream of exotic ports of call, as ships sailed in and out of the bay.

My second choice was Union Square near Chinatown. It was located only a short walk from the office. My typical post-lunch siesta consisted of a pleasant snooze, with my face covered by the help wanted ads to protect me from the dive bombing pigeons.

Getting prepared for my home visits that particular day, I pulled the case files from a nearby file cabinet. Case #1 read John Brighton. Caucasian, forty-three years old, married, four children, education-ninth grade, job skills n/a, recipient of public assistance funds August 16 1955 to present, congenital back pain-unable to work-reviewed and verified on an annual basis by Dr. Rosenberg of 450 Sutter Street. Home visit completed June 12, 1958.

The case records further indicated that the rent, Aid to Dependent Children, car insurance, medical insurance, and a dental plan were all paid by County welfare.

I drove to the back alley, hoping for easier access to Brighton's place. I didn't want to walk up the steep flight of stairs to the front entrance. Always vigilant in new surroundings, I picked my way through the clutter and chaos leading to the three story apartment.

I saw a man who looked to be in his fifties huffing and puffing up a steep flight of stairs. He was accompanied by a teenager. Together the two juggled an oversized refrigerator between them. The father was lifting with the boy guiding their burden.

I called out, "Good morning! Are you George Brighton?" I couldn't stop grinning.

"What the hell do you want?" Mr. Brighton screeched as he began to lose his balance.

"My name is Sean Sullivan. I'm your new caseworker." I waved my identification at him.

"Oh God," he wheezed. "Come up here." Father and son gently lowered their burden.

"Would you mind coming down to me? It's hard for me to climb stairs," I said. I brandished my cane in Mr. Brighton's direction, using physical disability as an emotional crutch.

I heard a reluctant, "Okay."

He joined me on the second step. I sat down and leafed through my brief case. "Ah, here it is," I said.

I pulled out a bulging manila file embossed in large letters, "ADC." Underneath in bold print were the words, "Brighton, George H. 1221 McCallister Street, San Francisco."

"It's been almost a year since a caseworker has been here for a home visit. That's why I'm here today," I explained.

"Yeah," he responded dully.

"According to the file you receive Aid To Dependent Children due to a qualifying disability. A bad back, I believe." I stared pointedly at the refrigerator.

"That's right. Dr. Rosenberg will verify I have a bad back. I'm unable to work." Brighton moaned.

"Yes. I can see that."

"Well, I can't work," he repeated. "I would if I could, but...I suppose you're going to stop my check."

"Mr. Brighton, I just observed you and your son lifting a three hundred pound refrigerator up a steep flight of stairs."

A long heavy silence fell over us. The veins in his neck stood out in livid ridges. His eyes bulged in their sockets.

"In answer to your question—Yes, I'm withholding your check until I receive medical verification of a qualifying disability," I stated calmly.

"You son of a bitch!" His voice exploded in frustration. He looked at me as one would manure stained boots.

I quickly got up to take my leave. I had a strong desire to avoid confrontation of any kind, physical blows in particular. My right knee gave way and my arms flailed the air as I fell into a pile of garbage over flowing from the dumpster. My head hit the edge of the dumpster. Through blurred vision I saw Brighton sniff haughtily, looking down on me with his lips curled in disgust.

An eternity passed before the son asked, "Are you okay? Here, let me help you." He worked both arms under me and lifted me to my feet.

Regaining my equilibrium finally, I said, "Thanks." Turning to the father, I summoned all the dignity I could muster. "Mr. Brighton, I suggest you contact your doctor. Good day."

Badly in need of a break, I headed for the infamous Haight-Asbury district of San Francisco, the site of my favorite coffee shop. Many considered this district the headquarters of Jack Kerouac, the sweet prince of the beat generation. He had recently been reviewed in the <u>San Francisco Chronicle</u>. Surveying a row of neatly placed marbled tables, I noticed several budding authors scribbling on dime store tablets.

I signaled a waitress and ordered, "Tall single latte, please." She offered to bring the cup to my table.

The Haight street "Ye Olde Coffee House & Tea Shoppe" became my oasis in a combat zone. I could not adjust to the conflicting morality and incompatible standards of behavior of the times. The waitress, costumed as the downstairs maid in an Agatha Christie mystery, offered solace.

"Bad day?" she asked.

"You wouldn't believe it," I replied.

"I'm sorry." She had the gift of making "I'm sorry" sound as if she grieved for me from the bottom of her heart. Her mere presence was balm, her words solace.

"The next visit will be easier," I said.

"What?" she asked.

"Oh, yeah, I guess I should explain. I am a social caseworker making home visits in this district."

"That's it." The warm hearted waitress flounced out of sight.

Resigned to my fate as a pariah in beatsville, I fished the second file out of my attaché case.

Case #2. Jefferson, Sabbolith Crystal. 1221 Fell Street, San Francisco, age 31, four children, education-seventh grade, job skills n/a., arrested June 16, 1951, San Francisco, attempted murder, suspect attacked live-in companion with a knife, victim suffered wounds in the back and leg, victim declined to sign a complaint, no other witnesses. The last home visit was dated August 10, 1957.

I climbed the stairs to San Francisco's newest public housing project. The project had opened in January 1958 to much fanfare and publicity. Due to budget cuts, there was no elevator. I was greeted by garbage in the hallways, urine-stained walls, half-clothed children racing about playing tag, barking dogs, and screeching cats. Chaos and pandemonium reigned supreme.

I observed a partly kicked in door as I approached No. 316. I knocked. I heard loud shuffling noises, and finally a voice calling out, "Who's dere?"

"Sean Sullivan. I'm your new caseworker. I'm here to make a home visit," I yelled through the battered door.

Five minutes later, the door cracked open a bit. A disheveled woman peaked out at me through the slit. "What do you want?"

"I'm your new caseworker. No one has visited for almost a year."

"Okay," my client muttered. She maintained a death grip on the door.

"I have to ask you some questions," I prompted.

"Alright, come in." She backed away from the door and pulled it open. I cautiously entered.

Mrs. Jefferson pointed to a cluttered couch. She pushed a week's accumulation of toys, beer bottles and cat droppings onto the floor without apology. A multi-colored cockatoo screeched from a cage in the corner. The lady of the house slapped the cage with a rolled up newspaper. "Shut up Gwendolyn."

Taking a notebook out of my brief case, I began the questioning.

"How long have you lived here?"

"Six years."

"Mama, Mama." The incessant begging of a five year old waif, clad only in torn underwear, interrupted my questions. I took a quick look at the child. At least two cigarette burns were evident on her ill-nourished body.

"Jest a minute. I gotta answer the man's questions or we don't eat."

"How many children do you have?" I asked. "The file stated four, but that information is a year old."

"I ain't pregnant."

"I'm not asking if you're pregnant. I'm asking how many children you have," I repeated politely.

"Mama, Mama," the little girl jumped up and down.

"Our records do not name the father of your children," I prompted.

"Fathers," she corrected. She mused, "No wonder. I don't know myself."

"What?" I gulped.

"Jessie, who's your daddy? I forgot. I was drunk that day."

"Oh Mama, you know. It's Frank." The little girl climbed on her mother's lap.

"Frank who?" I asked.

"Who cares?" she asked dully.

"Mama, Mama."

"What?"

"Jerry's smoking pot in the bathroom," the little girl tattled.

"Thought I smelled something sweet," I said.

I continued to mush through a morass of misinformation misspoken by a lady who didn't care about life any more. Exhausted, after repeated interruptions, I finally concluded the interview. I wrote in the case records, "fathers unknown."

My stomach told me it was lunch time. It was a warm day for July and I looked forward to a gargantuan meal followed by a siesta on top of Union Square. I aimed the car for Van Ness Avenue and San Francisco's premier deli, Tommy's Joint, located just a few blocks from Union Square. Pastrami sandwiches and potato salad were a specialty of the house.

I picked up lunch then drove to Union Square and parked to enjoy my meal. After a short nap on the grass, I decided not to complete my scheduled home visits. I opted instead to return to my bee hive of an office. A mountain of paper work awaited me.

Entering the great hall, I fielded the usual volley of "Did you have a nice day? How were your home visits?" with a strained smile.

I sat down at my desk and began tackling the mound of paperwork. Sneaking an occasional peek at the clock on the wall, I couldn't wait until it finally inched its way to five. I was not the first one out of the barn.

Stumbling off bus #31, I walked up the hill to Jackson Street.

"Hi, Sean. How are you doing?" Cassie stood at the top of the stairs.

"I don't feel so good—hard day in the field. Thank God the weekend is here!" I staggered towards our room.

Cassie called out, "Not that way, Sean. Good news—we're next to the kitchen now. I moved our stuff this afternoon."

"Great."

Our new digs, located next to the community kitchen and bathroom, overlooked a large garden of multi-colored flowers tendered by a little old lady. We became silent companions in our occasional eye contact. A wave of the hand sufficed for needless conversation.

With an imaginary drum roll, Cassie announced, "And for dinner tonight…"

I interrupted, "What, a pig's head?"

"Corned beef and cabbage," Cassie smiled. "You look a little peeked. Are you feeling okay, Sean?"

"I'm all right."

I was wrong. I soon pushed aside dinner. Fever and chills took over my body.

"Excuse me. I guess I'm not feeling too well after all. I think I'll lie down a bit." I shivered all the way to the bedroom.

"Wait a minute. I haven't made the bed yet." Cassie dashed into our new quarters. She could sense that something was wrong.

"Jeez," I responded.

Uncontrollable seizures, symptoms of a bladder infection, continued throughout the night and into Saturday morning. My bed clothes were saturated with sweat. Retching followed nausea. I moaned to relieve the grinding pain, pleading an occasional "God help me! Why hast thou forsaken me?" Hallucinations had me on the cross of Cavalry.

"Sean! Should I call a doctor? We don't have medical insurance…" Cassie's ministrations were laced with tenderness. She continued placing cold wash cloths on my forehead.

135

I rasped a faint, "No doctor. I'm okay. Maybe some more tea."

"It's Chinese herbal tea. Pauline brewed it just for you."

A distant voice intoned, "It's Kombucha tea. Some call it 'the divine Tsche.' It was first noted during the Tsin dynasty in 221 B.C. We believe it will cure most ills."

Pauline stood in the doorway. "Oh, you're so sick," she crooned. "We should light some incense or perhaps fragrant candles." She was in my face again.

"I'm not dead yet," I croaked.

"Well, if you're not better by tomorrow morning I'm calling Dr. Hirth," Cassie declared.

The next day, as I faded in and out of consciousness, she announced, "I'm calling Dr. Hirth. Sunday or not."

I struggled a weak, "Okay."

To our relief, Dr. Hirth arrived an hour later. He took one look at me and said, "You're going to the hospital."

"But we don't have any medical insurance," Cassie said.

"That's alright. San Francisco General Hospital will accept you. I'm on the staff. I'll make a phone call."

He returned in a few minutes smiling. "I've arranged everything. Go to Emergency at San Francisco General Hospital on Peterro Street. They'll admit Sean right away."

He took my temperature one more time. "104. You are a very sick young man." I sighed in response.

"I can't drive." Cassie announced.

"Sorry, I can't help you there. I've another patient to visit. Everybody gets sick on Sunday." He started to leave.

Richard poked his head into our room. "I overheard. I can drive you to the hospital in my car," he offered. He leaned over me. "How you doing, fella?" His iron cross hit me in the face.

Wrapped like a mummy in several blankets, I was taken by the Irregulars to a waiting 1949 two door Chevrolet. A missing right fender and a dented trunk attested to Richard's driving ability. Cassie and friends maneuvered me into the back seat. Tires squealed as we began the downhill race to San Francisco General Hospital. After several near misses we arrived at the hospital.

Richard's panic-stricken voice asked, "Where's the Emergency room?" He perspired.

"I don't know. I've never been here before today." Cassie remained calm. "Oh, look, there's a hospital worker. He's dressed in white," she said.

Directions were asked for and received. The car screeched to a stop in front of a large sign proclaiming, "EMERGENCY ONLY - NO PARKING." Cassie jumped out in search of a wheel chair. Mission accomplished, they loaded me into the chair.

"Dr. Hirth phoned. My husband is Sean Sullivan," Cassie explained to the admissions clerk as Richard pushed me into the emergency room.

After the paper work was completed, they took me through a succession of swinging doors and hallways painted ice green to Building E, fifth floor.

The charge nurse blocked our way. "Sorry, we're full. Put him in the examination room." She directed us to a nearby alcove across from the main desk.

My vision blurred; my senses faded. I drifted off into Never Never Land. Ghost-like impressions swirled before me throughout the night. White uniforms rustled in an out. Muffled conversations could be heard echoing in the distance. At 0720 hours, the medication spiked the fever.

"We almost lost you last night, Mr. Sullivan," the lady in white frowned.

Lifting my head, I scanned 180 degrees. An IV needle stuck in my right arm and slithered upwards to a transparent container hooked to a pole. A rubber catheter snaked out between my legs, dripping yellow fluid into a fast filling plastic bag clamped to the bed rail.

A cheerful "Time for your shot, Mr. Sullivan. And how are we on this bright sunny day?" welcomed me to the fifth floor. A middle age LPN with a toothy overbite hovered menacingly above me with a hypodermic needle.

"Jesus, you hit bone!" I could feel the tear dribbling down my cheek.

"Sorry. And have we had a bowel movement?" she asked, holding a medical chart up to her flat chest. If I had told the truth the doctor would have ordered an enema and brought in a fire hose.

"Oh, nuts. No enema for you today." She spoke in grudging tones. "Time for your tempy. Open wide."

Anchored to the bed by all the paraphernalia, I demanded, "Why are those people handcuffed to their beds?"

"Didn't they tell you? This is the San Francisco County jail ward. It had the only available bed. You'll be moved later today." The lady in white yanked the thermometer out of my mouth.

True to their word, my bed was moved to a smaller ward that afternoon.

Visiting hours arrived and so did Cassie. "Hi, Sean. How are you feeling?" She leaned over and planted a moist kiss on my cheek. "Sorry I'm late. I had to transfer twice to get here."

"I'm glad to see you."

A few minutes of silent hand holding were interrupted by a voice ghosting out of hidden speakers. "Visiting hours will end in five minutes. Visiting hours will end in five minutes," the lifeless voice intoned.

"Jeez, you just got here," I complained.

"I'm sorry, Sean. I left when I could. I wanted to see you."

"That's okay. You look good. How's business?"

"Busy."

"Visiting hours are over. Please follow the exit signs," a new voice, shrill, crackled out of nowhere.

Cassie and I enjoyed a lingering kiss.

"Can you come back tonight?" I asked.

"Oh, I don't think so. I have to wash my hair."

"To hell with your damn hair."

"Now, Sean…I'll see you tomorrow."

I rolled over to the right so I wouldn't see Cassie leaving. Later I drifted out of dreams, awakening to a far away voice.

"How are you feeling, Sean?" Dr. Hirth look down at me.

"I'm okay. I'm surprised to see you."

"I checked with the resident. You're getting good care. Don't listen to the rumors about this hospital; they're not true."

"Everyone has been concerned."

We engaged in casual conversation for a minute or two.

"Well, I've got to go. My wife's relatives are coming over for dinner tonight." Dr. Hirth grimaced.

"When can I go home?" I asked.

"I'd say in a day or two. You're probably feeling better already. But you've got to allow time for the IVs to flush out your kidneys and bladder and for the antibiotics to kill the bugs." Dr. Hirth turned to leave. An afterthought made him turn back.

"I guess you're getting accustomed to hypodermic needles," he commented. Half question. Half statement.

"Yeah, I am. The shoot me every four hours. Thanks for dropping by, Doctor."

Early the next morning my eyes followed a beam of light flashing here and there in the room.

"Time for your shot, Mr. Sullivan." The night nurse grinned.

"God Almighty. Is it three a.m. already?" I asked.

"Yep, and you get one every four hours."

"I know, I know," I intoned wearily.

"By the way, I've got good news. You're going to be released Wednesday afternoon."

"Wonderful."

JULY 1958 FADED INTO THE DOG DAYS OF AUGUST. I returned to my work in the bee hive at the public welfare office. Cassie rejoiced in her job, meeting people and cementing fly-by-night friendships. She shined in the presence of headline legal eagles who took their morning respite at the Koffee Kup.

Late one afternoon, Cassie returned home with blue fingers and cyanotic lips. She was gasping for air when she reached the top of the stairs. She acted as though nothing was wrong.

"Guess who was in the Koffee Kup this morning? Ordered cappuccino and a chocolate doughnut." Cassie teased, knowing I hated to play word games.

"Who?"

"Jake 'The Rake' Erlich."

"Who's he?"

"A well-known attorney. He kissed my hand. Very European, you know."

"That's nice."

"He's well dressed but a lousy tipper," she continued. She jerked back. "What are you doing?" I had my hand on her throat.

"Taking your pulse. If I ever finish graduate school, the first thing I'll do is send you to a heart specialist. You can't go on like this much longer."

"I've had a bad heart for twenty years."

A few days later, I jumped off the #31 bus as it slowed near the Stockton tunnel. Regaining my balance, I bought the morning newspaper and walked into 585 Bush. The constant buzz of thirty to forty worker bees filled the room. Turning to the help wanted ads, I spotted an administrator's job in the Marin County Welfare Department.

"Oh, Mr. Sullivan! Yoo Hoo!" It was the "ask the personal questions" lady. I thought she was doing a pretty good imitation of a landing officer on an aircraft carrier.

"Yes," I answered.

"Mr. Brighton is downstairs waiting for you. He hasn't received his check yet," she said. "Boy, is he mad."

Three heads swiveled in my direction. "Naughty, naughty" was written all over their faces. I looked at my twenty-five dollar, on sale at Sears, Timex. Eight thirty a.m.

"I don't think he's been up this early in the last five years," I commented. "His doctor's certification just came in the mail yesterday and I haven't had time to do the paper work yet," I responded.

As I walked into the intake office, Marie, the receptionist, pointed to the number three cubicle.

"Good morning, Mr. Brighton." I flashed my warmest smile. Assuming the friendly approach, I offered my hand. He pulled back, regarding me with cold speculation. Deep blue eyes established dominance over me.

"Where's my check?" he demanded. "Dr. Rosenberg said he verified my disability. I can't work."

"If you have a back problem, how can carry a three hundred pound refrigerator up a flight of stairs?" I couldn't help at least asking. A withering stare was my only answer. Beads of sweat broke out on Brighton's forehead.

"I received the paper work yesterday and will be releasing your check sometime today. You should receive it in a week to ten days," I said.

Brighton gave out a ferocious bellow. "A week or ten days! How am I going to feed my family?" He stood, hands on hips, veins throbbing at his temples as his nostrils flared and his muscles tensed. I expected a physical attack.

A loud POP, POP from out of nowhere shattered our moment of confrontation. Irritated, my client peeked out the door. I couldn't resist joining him in the doorway.

"What's going on here?" I demanded of the office at large. I observed fifteen or twenty people milling about the office as Brighton ran out the front door. Apparently he'd seen something or somebody that made him want to leave in a hurry.

"This place is nothing but mass confusion," I said aloud.

A voice filled with terror yelled, "My God! He has a gun!"

More popping sounds followed. People froze momentarily then broke into a melange of clients, social workers, office personnel and on lookers desperately searching for a safe sanctuary. Some people cowered on the floor or crawled under desks. Others raced out the front door, elbowing each other aside. An old lady lost her balance on the slippery marble. A security guard pushed two ladies to the floor and threw himself spread-eagled on top of them.

The gunman, unshaven in stained overalls, ran past me towards the reception desk. He exhibited a strangely business-like manner. Louder popping sounds resonated throughout the foyer followed by a curious silence. The citizens of San Francisco stood motionless, suspended in time.

The bad guy reached the reception desk then tossed a thirty two caliber handgun to the floor. Paralyzed, I watched it slide towards me and stop at my feet. The shooter simply stood there, arms akimbo, waiting to be arrested.

I stared at the offending weapon, half expecting it to strike me at any moment. My heart raced for a long moment before I could shake free of the fear. Finally, in slow motion, I placed my thumb and forefinger on each side of the hand grip and lifted the weapon chest high for all to see. I imagined myself a Roman gladiator. Gently, I placed death on my desk with the barrel facing in the opposite direction.

The Walter Mitty in me took over as I joined several men in manhandling the criminal to the floor.

An office girl called out, "Evelyn's been shot. She's bleeding all over the place. Someone please help me!" Evelyn Hodges, age 37, was one of our social case workers. Her desk was near mine in the welfare office.

Another clerk cried out, "Oh, my God! Marie's been hit too. Someone, please!" His face was glazed over with shock. In the doorway of an intake office lay our receptionist, Marie Pittock, age 25, of California Street.

"Call the police!" another person screamed.

A young clerk, eye glasses awry, holding back tears, raised her hand for attention. "Call an ambulance," she said. "Evelyn's bleeding to death. We can't stop the flow."

"Put a tourniquet on her."

"We can't. She's hit in the chest."

Eric, a co-worker, labored over Evelyn. Put off by his mannerisms, I usually avoided Eric whenever possible. His high pitched voice and feminine demeanor repulsed me. Concerned, I joined the crowd near our fallen comrade.

"Sean, get me a towel or a handkerchief or something," Eric ordered.

"Here, take my handkerchief. Oh, but it's dirty," I replied.

"That's okay. Anything to stop the bleeding. Has anyone called an ambulance?"

"I did. They should be here any minute."

"None too soon," Eric said. Someone handed him a washcloth. He stuffed it into Evelyn's chest.

A lifetime passed. The police arrived in force, followed by several ambulances. The victims were administered to and taken away. Evelyn would succumb to her gunshot wounds two days later. Marie survived.

Statements were given to the detectives. Employees exchanged the story of their lives. Heroes were named.

"That man saved our lives." The ladies pointed to the security guard who had bodily protected them from possible gunfire.

I finished my recollections a second time for the detectives. They were professional and sympathetic as they quizzed each employee. Finally excused, I returned to my desk on the second floor. I needed sanctuary for my shattered soul. My daydreams were shattered by a barely audible voice.

"You can go home, Sean. We're closing early today." Ms. Conforti placed her hand gently on my back. It was a time for sharing.

"Thanks. I'd like to see my wife," I answered. I began to question my own immortality.

"Are you all right, Sean?" she asked.

"Oh, sure. I'll see you Monday morning bright and early." I paused. "Well, I don't know how 'bright' but I'll be here early." I couldn't think of anything funny to say.

As I walked through the foyer, I stopped briefly to watch the maintenance men struggling to clean the blood off the floor.

"I can't get it off the marble," the big guy said.

"Try some of this acid compound," the skinny one suggested. Pushing a plastic container to his partner, he added, "Be careful; this is powerful stuff. Use your rubber gloves."

I poked my cane at the crimson stains, hoping to rub away the offending testimony to the ghosts of the morning attack. Later that evening, I walked up the hill to the house on Jackson Street. Thick tongued, I said, "Hi, Cassie, Mickey. What's new?"

Mickey, replete in her gypsy outfit with head band, clinking jewelry and all, answered, "We heard the news. It's been on the TV and radio all day."

"I was interviewing a client two offices over from the gunman. What a day!" I said.

Cassie walked over to me and sniffed. "You've been drinking," Cassie said. Her eyes held me in contempt.

"I walked over to the Edinburgh Castle on Geary Street. The bagpipers perform every Friday and Saturday night. What a bar!"

Not to be deterred from the more exciting story, Mickey cut in. "Tell us what happened at the welfare office," she implored. She placed her elbows on the table, head in hands, and waited expectantly.

An aftershock of fear guided my thoughts. Left hand twitching, fingers curling into a fist, I stammered out the story of murder and mayhem.

"May I join you?" Pauline Rose glided into the town hall of Jackson Street.

"Yes, come on in. Sean is telling us about the shooting at the welfare office," Mickey said.

"Oh, I'm not interested in such horrible things," Pauline declared. "Life is a rose, is a rose, is a rose." She started to leave but turned back.

In the manner of the ancient mariner, I held all three ladies with the glittering of my eye. Entranced, they listened like children. We were soon joined by Richard and Scott. I continued my tale now twice told and, in time, reached the end of my journey.

"Cassie, I'm going to quit the welfare office and go to grad school next month. I don't know how we'll survive but today was just too much."

"Sure, Sean," she whispered.

"That reminds me," Mickey said. "A friend of mine is leaving her night job at the UC medical center admissions office. You might be interested."

"Good ol' Mickey…" I started to say.

"Hey, watch the 'old' stuff," she protested with a grin.

"I'm interested. Of course it means going to college in the morning and working nights. We need the money." I gave Cassie a peck on the cheek.

"You think you can handle two jobs?" Richard asked.

"Sure," I replied confidently.

"Don't forget—we're all taking the ferry to Oakland on Sunday," tour leader Mickey called out as she jangled her way out of the kitchen.

COMMANDING THE HORIZON OF PARNASSUS HEIGHTS are the clean, poetic lines of the University of California Medical Center. The large buildings of the renowned medical complex have a pervasive influence on the entire area. The center provides quality medical care for all.

I stepped off the bus. Glancing North, I took in the awesome sweeping view of the Bay, Golden Gate Bridge, the Park, and the Presidio. A magic town by the sea. I pulled myself away and headed for the medical center.

"So, you're Sean Sullivan. Mickey phoned. She said you would be in to see us. Have a seat."

Section Chief Nurse Helen Huckabee, B.S., R.N., age fifty-eight, tight lipped, sitting straight backed, looked me in the eye. She was a small leathery woman with a face etched in sorrow. I saw a no-nonsense woman, neither young nor pretty, clinging to her 1920's sense of morality in the face of 1956's declining code of conduct.

The old girl had never married. Over her family' objections, she had answered the call to arms in May of 1917, serving in a field hospital near Troyes, France during World War One. For her, the war became a mosaic of disfigured bodies making a living sacrifice to the hierarchy of insanity. Helen Huckabee was a tough cookie, although a heart of gold surfaced briefly now and then.

"Your application indicates hospital work."

I replied, "Yes, Ma'am. I worked for two years as a counselor at the Eastern Oregon Tuberculosis Hospital in The Dalles, Oregon."

"I notice you have Polio," she commented matter-of-factly.

"No, Spina Bifida. A birth defect."

"Oh, sorry."

Miss Huckabee sat bolt upright, looking like a dingy and outmoded recruiting poster. "Now for business. Yours is the eleven p.m. to seven a.m. shift. The admissions office is next to the emergency room. Your partner is Ed Novak. If you have any questions, ask him."

"I understand."

"Oh, and here's the key to the elevator. Use it when you need to get to the eleventh floor delivery room, nonstop."

She went on. "It's vital to secure financial statements. I mean everybody. No exceptions," she said.

"Yes Ma'am."

"Also, if all the staff members are busy you may have to remove ID bracelets from patients who have expired. Just clip the bracelets to the admitting forms." She smiled at me.

"You mean dead people?"

A look of disgust was my only answer. Miss Huckabee continued with her recitation of my duties. Thirty minutes later I walked out of the building into the sun. She scared the hell out of me.

12

"DEATH DISROBES US ALL

AT OUR NIGHTLY CAUCUS, ON A WARM SEPTEMBER evening I entertained the Jackson Street Irregulars with my latest adventures.

"My new boss is one of those resolute, strong-jawed, hammer and tongs Florence Nightingales. And I have met many a nurse in my time," I said.

"She sounds like a character," Cassie encouraged.

"She is. But I got the job. I start next Monday night I register at San Francisco State College tomorrow morning."

"Are you sure you can handle grad school and working at night? You won't get much sleep," Mickey said.

"Well, I'm going to give it a good shot. After all, a masters degree in rehabilitation would be an 'Open Sesame' for me. I remain optimistic."

Two weeks later I found myself in a classroom at San Francisco State College, trying to pay attention to Professor Orkizewski's nasal drone. The 10:00 a.m. class in ED Ep. 609, Tests and Inventories, anesthetized me. I made an attempt to look interested in a subject reeking of mathematical formulas and obscure terminology. I blotted my face with a damp handkerchief from time to time to trying to stay awake.

"Tell the class, Mr. Sullivan—What is the difference between mean, medium and mode as it relates to the wonderful world of testing?" Great. The one chapter I didn't finish.

"Come, come, Mr. Sullivan. We're waiting." I kept panic at bay by reciting what I could remember. Apparently it wasn't enough.

"Class—Did anybody understand what Mr. Sullivan said?" Orkizewski's grandiose gestures caused all faces to turn to me. Silence reigned.

"Yes, well, I thought not...You're on tomorrow, Sullivan. We eagerly await your presentation." As an afterthought he asked, "And what have you prepared for our edification?"

I boomed, "A survey on suicide with a testing device predicting the incidence of self destruction among the various socio-economic strata in a multi-cultural San Francisco society."

The professor gagged on an unseen particle of food or something. A barely perceptible voice murmured, "Sounds interesting." The bell rang, saving me from any further assault.

I looked forward to my next class, the 11:00 a.m. Ed. Ep. 497, Learning Disabilities. After class, my professor, Artimus Johnson, Ph.D., joined me in the school cafeteria for lunch. He was a rare bird, Johnson—a compassionate man who listened and cared.

"Have you had experience with learning disabilities?" he asked.

"Yes, Sir—my life. I didn't enter school until I was almost eleven years old. Too many trips to the Shriner's Hospital."

"Hmm," a puff of smoke floated upward. Professor Johnson assumed the classic FDR pose. He held his cigarette in an ivory holder at a rakish angle. A superb listener, his facial expressions said, "I am the only one in the world interested in you." Encouraged, I prattled on, revealing more personal information.

"The Portland Public School system tested me ad nausium in my younger days. Because I had a spina bifida, the doctors were convinced I suffered from hydrocephalus, water on the brain. Many spina bifidas do."

"So my medical friends tell me," Professor Johnson agreed. He tapped the ashes from his pipe into a nearby basket.

"The funny part is that each time I took an intelligence test, I scored higher than the one before."

"Are you working on a degree?" he asked.

"Yes, Sir—a Masters in vocational rehabilitation," I answered. "I'm taking twelve hours this semester and nine in the spring term."

"That's quite a load for a graduate student," the professor commented.

"Oh, it's nothing. I also work nights at the UC Med Center from eleven p.m. to seven a.m. My wife is a waitress at the Koffee Kup in the financial district."

"Oh, to be young again," he mused. "Good luck." The tall, lanky professor took his leave of me. I finished lunch alone, contemplating his remarks.

A month later, early in the evening, Cassie shook me awake.

"Sean. It's five o'clock. Time for dinner, Irish stew."

I rubbed my eyes open. Her smile seduced my thoughts to visions of delights to come. Sleep drugged, I whispered, "Sounds great."

"Sean. We have to talk. You look terrible. You can't keep up this pace."

"We had a busy night. A patient died."

She continued, "You have a year and a half to go for a degree."

"I know. Let's try a little longer. I don't want to give up without a good shot."

"Yoo Hoo, Mr. Sullivan! We have Irish stew tonight. Come join us." Pauline Rose drifted by our room in a her white robe. It was badly in need of laundering.

"Okay. On my way," I barked.

I now accepted Pauline. I saw her as a unique individual rather than simply a beatnik. Although their lifestyles were alien to my value system, the Jackson Street Irregulars had become my family.

Turning to Cassie I continued, "I'm locked into a routine of work, study, try to stay awake, and damn little rest. I feel stoned half the time. Four hours of sleep out of twenty four ain't going to do the job."

"Let's go eat and we can talk more later." Cassie led the way to the community kitchen.

"Thank God for Christmas vacation next month," I muttered.

"And the end of the fall term," Cassie added.

"Hi, everybody," I called out as we entered the kitchen.

"Let's go shopping this weekend. Sears is having a sale," Cassie said.

"I don't get paid for two weeks. Sorry."

She lamented, "You're always sorry, and we never have enough money."

"Please, no arguments before din-din. It's bad for the digestion. God will provide," Pauline said. She gave her version of the Papal Blessing upon an increasingly unhappy couple.

"I wonder if God is a Republican or a Democrat?" I mused to the ceiling.

At the hospital early the next morning, my partner, Ed Novak, shook me awake. "Wake up, Sullivan. Armstrong's on her way," he whispered urgently.

I mumbled incoherently, "Blessings on him who first invented sleep. A cheap pleasure.' That's Shakespeare, you know." As a former English teacher, I misquoted "the big guys" on many occasions.

148

A small four-bed facility adjoined the admission area. It was used to observe patients on overnight status rather than admitting them to the hospital. Novak and I covered for each other when we took turns napping in the little ward on slow nights. He was a pre-med student and enjoyed a schedule as impossibly busy as my own. We snatched a moment here and there for mother academia, the unrelenting taskmaster of all dreamers.

AT APPROXIMATELY FOUR THIRTY EACH MORNING, Claire Armstrong, the night supervisor, began her nightly building inspection. She started on the top floor and worked her way down. Lookouts were posted on each floor. Phones were kept at the ready.

"Monica just called from the second floor. Hurry, she's coming," Novak urged. "She" could only be the major domo of the night shift.

"Okay, okay. It's not the second coming of Jesus Christ you know," I said.

I went into admissions, sat down and grabbed some forms to look busy. The elevator door slowly squeaked open, revealing a commanding presence framed in the doorway. A Brunhilda of a woman, whom one might expect to burst into an aria from Tannhauser at any moment, strode forth, satisfied her turf remained intact.

"Good morning Ms. Armstrong," Novak and I chorused in unison.

"Good morning, young gentlemen. And how are things this fine day.?"

I tried to stand at attention. Novak, the more assertive, stepped forward, barracks parade fashion, to make his report. He failed to stamp his feet English style.

"Everything's fine here, Ms. Armstrong, just fine. It's been a slow night." No one knew if Ms. Armstrong had ever married.

"Good." Turning to me she said, "Don't forget those ID bracelets, Mr. Sullivan."

"No, Ma'am. I sure won't." I tried not to curtsey.

"I've known Miss Huckabee a long time. We served together in the Army during the 'Big One,'" she said.

"Oh. World War Two?" I responded in all naiveté.

"No! World War One." Her bosom heaved to its full measure as each word was articulated like a cannon blast. Make that two cannons.

Novak came to my rescue. "Everything is under control, Ms. Armstrong. Not to worry."

Reduced to jelly, I gazed at her receding figure. Suddenly she wheeled, striding in step to a silent cadence of yesteryear. "Hup-two-three-four. Why not shag O'Reilly's daughter. Rub a dub dub. Balls and all," she chanted.

"Oh you dirty boys, shame!" she called out to the platoon of marching ghosts, unseen by we mortal beings. As she turned her eyes welded me to the floor. She had returned from the war.

Ms. Armstrong disappeared into the elevator with a loud "Good Night."

"Jeez, Sullivan, World War Two? She must be in her early sixties at least."

"How'd I know, Massa? I thought she was younger," I replied bowing.

"All right, Sean. I'm going to take a nap. It's your turn to watch."

"Okay. I'll let you know if anything happens," I said.

"Don't!...Oh, by the way, we're scheduled to work Thanksgiving night. Hope this doesn't ruin any plans."

"I think the gang at our house is planning a pot luck," I answered.

Novak walked away. I turned to greet Dr. Gary Roberts, the night resident. He was dressed in green, looking like the spirit of Christmas past, escorting an older gentleman into admissions.

"Mr. Sullivan, I'd like you to meet Dr. Ferguson, Chancellor of the University of California Medical Center. Mrs. Ferguson is in for an emergency gall bladder operation." Dr. Roberts paused.

"Perhaps you have some questions for Dr. Ferguson?" he prompted.

"Yes, Sir. For admissions."

I viewed Dr. Troy Ferguson as God Almighty, Ms. Armstrong as Jesus Christ, and Ms. Huckabee as something between the two. Dr. Ferguson, a portly bespectacled man in his late fifties, sat down and made himself comfortable.

"May I smoke?" he inquired politely.

"Of course," I replied.

Studying me through thick lenses, he seemed satisfied with the burn in his pipe. The chancellor could have played Dr. Defoe to the Dionne quintuplets. I squirmed under his gaze.

"I'm sorry, Sir, but we need some information regarding the care of your wife. For insurance purposes," I finally said.

"I understand. The University carries a policy for my family." Dr. Ferguson fished a card out his wallet. "Here's the number. I think this is what you want."

"Yes, thank you, Sir. It certainly is." I copied the information onto the hospital forms. We then spent a few moments in idle conversation, interrupted when Dr. Ferguson looked over to the elevator.

"I see they're taking Sharon upstairs now," he said.

"Oh, I've got to give her an ID bracelet or my boss will kill me." I started to run to the elevator.

"Don't worry. I'll take it to her." Dr. Ferguson took the bracelet and walked out.

I BECAME A ZOMBIE IN MY DAILY ROUTINE, GOING through the motions in a haze of work, school, sleep and a stab or two at the books. All I had to do was climb the rainbow and reach out for the prize. The rally cry "Go for it!" rattled unceasingly in my brain.

Cassie placed her hand on my fevered brow one Sunday morning. "Sean, You look awful! Did you get mugged or something?"

"No. I just stayed up all night admitting the dead and dying to dear old UC Med Center."

"You really should take a break. Let's have a picnic at Fort Point this afternoon, okay? We can watch the sailboats in the bay."

"That sounds great, but let me sleep for a couple of hours." I squinted at Cassie.

"Can I invite the Jackson Street Irregulars to join us?"

"Sure, why not?" I said. Magnetized by a descending Morpheus, I fell back into my much needed sleep.

"Pauline too?"

"Oh God."

Cassie hopped, skipped and jumped like a little girl into the community kitchen. She invited everyone to join us for lunch, alfresco, overlooking the bay. That afternoon, San Francisco, bejeweled and multifaceted, with a variety of tableaus, welcomed us to Fort Point.

The irregulars captured a table on a hill overlooking our own Portofino By The Sea. Cool breezes soon blew away the silver mist and ushered in a sunny afternoon. Pauline and Maggie danced hand in hand, joined by a carefree Cassie. For a brief time the real and imagined woes of our lives dissolved.

The following Friday morning the unexpected happened.

Dr. Hirth delivered the blow. "I'm sorry to tell you this, Sean, but you need to be hospitalized again. You have a bladder infection and possibly some kidney damage. I want an IVP; it's been some time since you've had this procedure."

"There goes grad school." Tears welled in my eyes. I hid my despair by changing the subject.

"What's an IVP?"

"It's a procedure where dye is injected into your vein and a series of x-rays are taken to determine if your kidneys are functioning," Dr. Hirth explained.

"Oh, yeah. I had that done a few years ago at Good Sam in Portland."

"I should ask if you're covered by medical insurance," he went on.

"Yes. The UC Medical Center carries a plan for me," I answered.

"What are you doing at the Med Center?" he asked.

"Admissions clerk. I work nights and take classes at the State College in the mornings. I'm going for an masters in vocational rehab, but I guess I'll have to give it up now."

Dr. Hirth murmured a soft, "Oh boy." He attempted to console me.

"Well, at least you won't be in the prison ward this time. Mt. Zion is the best hospital in San Francisco. You'll have a general diet with wine at each meal." He patted my shoulder.

I mustered a faint, "Sounds nice."

"You'll be on IV's day and night. Glucose."

"I understand."

"You'll be hospitalized a week at most and we should do this before Christmas vacation. Is next Monday okay? You can have the weekend."

"Thanks. Cassie's in the waiting room."

"Good, I'd like to talk to her." In reassuring terms, he explained my diagnosis and prognosis to a caring wife.

That Sunday, Cassie and I followed the Jackson Street Irregulars to the ferry building. Lloyd Aston and Carole met us there. The Irregulars decided to visit the snack bar on board.

"Saying goodbye to the ferry is like dying a little," Astin said. He leaned on the rail with me. The western sky was set ablaze by the red sunset.

"Yes it is," I mused. "Boy, I'll bet this old boat could tell some stories!"

"It sure can. Murders, babies being born, love affairs, you name it. Everything imaginable happened on the SP ferries. It's hard to believe next Wednesday will be the last ride."

"I hate to see it go. I'm glad we came today," I said. We heard footsteps approaching on the teakwood decks.

"Here come the girls," Astin turned to them.

"Lloyd was telling stories of the ferry system. Next week is the last ride." I took Cassie's hand.

"My father used to tell my brother and me bedtime stories about the old ferry systems," Carole reminisced.

"I remember one soupy night when I was a young man, I climbed to the wheel house and watched the pilot guide the PERALTA to Oakland. He stood sideways to the wheel and was almost blinded by the fog. He had to navigate using just the sound of the foghorns. What a night. And I was late for a date." Astin said.

We reverently watched the sun set over the Golden Gate Bridge. It was like meditation. The silence was broken by Cassie.

"Sean is gong to the hospital tomorrow," she announced.

"What! Again? You were just hospitalized two or three months ago," Astin said.

"Yes, well, I have another bladder infection. I may have to quit school at the end of the term."

"I'm so sorry, Sean. What will you do?" Carole asked.

"At this stage of the came, I really don't know," I answered. "But something will turn up for us. After all, God loves a sinner."

We listened to the slapping of the waves against the hull as the wind blew through the rigging.

Astin spoke up. "Hey, I have a friend who works at San Quentin. He tells me the Department of Corrections is hiring counselors. I don't know much more, except that you have to pass a written exam."

"Oh, that sounds wonderful! Don't you think, Sean?" Cassie squealed.

"Yes, it does," I agreed. He provided names and phone numbers. A loud thud caused the ferry to shiver and broke up our conversation.

"We're here." Astin raised an imaginary sword and continued, "Forward men. To the First And Last Chance Saloon where we will quaff our thirst and seduce our wenches. Har, Har. But not in that order." He grabbed Carole around the waist as Cassie as I tailgated them to our personal Camelot.

As we left the dock, Richard called out, "We'll see you guys later. We're taking the return ferry home. Stay sober!."

"We'll try!" We waved goodbye and continued on our way. A few minutes later the four of us settled into an oversize booth at the First And Last Chance Saloon. The bartender immediately began whispering double entendres over his secret speaker to the rest rooms.

"Don't forget to wash. Please flush the toilet. Thank you." We delighted in people watching. Especially ladies fleeing from the restroom. All too soon we caught the last ferry back to San Francisco.

On Monday, I found myself at Mt. Zion Hospital. I seemed to be half awake, drifting on waves of semi-transparent sleep. I became aware of muted conversations. Starched hospital whites rustled past me followed by antiseptic odors. Light filtered through my eyelids.

The first object to materialize was a metallic pole with a plastic bottle of glucose hanging from the top. Then I saw the transparent tube carrying saline solution to my right arm. Finally, I registered the catheter creeping through the sheets to a transparent bag strapped to my bed rail. Anyone could see my kidneys and bladder were functioning quite well.

A voice from afar intoned, "Sean, it's me, Cassie. Look who's here."

Pain washed over me as I tried to lift my head. Faces came into focus. "Hi Cassie. Hi Scott. Thanks for coming," I managed.

"You look terrible," Cassie said.

"Yeah, well, I had a bad night," I said.

"Sean, look, your arm."

"Its okay. The nurses had a hard time sticking the IV needles in me. Elephant skin you know. Hypodermic needles are less painful." I offered my left hand to Scott.

"This is the second time in six months I've been hospitalized. It's disgusting," I groaned.

"I know what you mean," Scott agreed "It reminds me of Korea. When I got wounded they dragged me to a field unit, then jeeped all us injured to a MASH outfit."

"What happened?" Cassie asked.

"I was hit by mortar fragments. We were ambushed near the Choson Reservoir in North Korea. It was the winter of 1952."

Cassie pressed for more information. "That must have been terrible."

"Cassie." I attempted to change the subject in case Scott was getting uncomfortable.

He continued, "In the dead of night two-hundred thousand Chinese troops chased us out of our encampment. Bugles blared. Bayonets gleamed cold blue steel in the moonlight. I woke up in a Tokyo hospital flat on my back."

"It must be difficult for you to come here," I sympathized. "I appreciate it."

"Yes." His eyes drifted to the ceiling painted hospital green. "I wanted to die but they gave me medals instead. The general called it heroism in the face of barbarism." Six years later the word 'Vietnam' crept into the vernacular of the day.

A few days later Cassie sat cross-legged on our bed leafing through a worn out Sears Roebuck catalog. "I don't know what to get my brother and sister for Christmas," she said. "There isn't much time left."

"We don't have any money," I pointed out, bracing myself for an argument.

"We never do!" Cassie exclaimed. She threw the big book across the room.

I tried to mollify her. "Tomorrow I'm going downtown to sign up for the prison counselor exam. I'm sure I qualify." I said.

"I hope so. We can't go on like this. But I am sorry you have to leave grad school," she said.

"Well, why don't we go over to Sears this afternoon and window shop?" I suggested.

"Okay. I'll get dressed."

"You look good in jeans," I prompted with a grin.

"It's Sunday. I want to look nice."

We arrived at Sears an hour later. As we strolled by the lingerie counter, Cassie picked out a pair of nylons and held them up to the light. She fondled them. "Oh, Sean, look! And they're on sale. I really need them," she pleaded.

"Go ahead, buy them."

"No, we can't afford it now," she said with a sigh, pulling me away from the counter.

"Are you sure?"

"Yes."

Moving on to the glassware section, we saw sunbeams dancing through vases of green and blue. Delicate figurines of leaded crystal surrounded by transparent cloisonné transported us in our imagination to ancient Cathay. This special corner presented the aura of celestial lighthouses transmitting a rainbow of hues. Ghosts disappeared at the wave of a hand.

We lingered to enjoy a few minutes of silent browsing. My eye fixed on the vases. I held up a large V-shaped green vase.

"Hey, Cassie. This would make a great mantle piece. If we ever get a mantle."

"Oh, that's a great idea. Let's get it." She smiled at me.

"Are you sure? It is on sale."

"Oh, yes, I'm sure."

That night, I presented our buy of the day to the Jackson Street Irregulars. The gang had gathered over coffee and doughnuts in the community kitchen.

"It looks like a phallic symbol to me," Richard snorted as his iron cross danced with each movement of his head.

"I kinda like it," Scott commented.

"It does say something, but I'm not sure what," Maggie frowned.

"What's a phallic symbol?" Marge asked.

"Sex," Richard replied.

"I might have guessed," she retorted.

"Hey, it'll make a great paper weight," Mickey offered. "Just kidding, Sean."

Cassie brooded. This was out of character with her usual bubbly personality. Maggie and Marge both tried to engage her in conversation.

Finally she turned to me, teeth clenched in rage, and stammered, "Why didn't you buy me the stockings? You knew I wanted them." Everyone focused on my wife of two years.

"Because you said not to buy them."

"We can buy this thing but not my stockings? You know I need them for work." Cassie made a lunge for the vase.

Maintaining a death grip on our purchase, I said, "I'm sorry, Cassie. Come on, let's go to our room."

Embarrassed, the Irregulars engaged in trivial conversation in an attempt to ignore us. We argued, Cassie jumping on the bed as I stood looking out the window. Our loud voices pierced the partition for the next forty minutes. Bits and pieces of garbled phrases passed through the wall to the kitchen.

In frustration I thundered, "I'm going to the state office tomorrow to find out about correctional counseling. The fall term ends after

Christmas so I can work full time then." Cassie was drowning in a sea of unfulfilled promises and I had thrown her a life preserver.

I continued. "And maybe we should move. Living in one room is too confining. Community facilities are okay for awhile, but I need my privacy. I want my own bathroom for a change."

"So do I," she agreed. "Richard mentioned a small apartment down on Steiner Street. We should look into it."

"Okay, fine with me," I said wearily. I climbed into bed.

"Don't you dare go to sleep on me," she threatened.

"I'm tired," I said, and was then surprised to hear my voice murmur, "Maybe we should separate for the time being." She ignored my suggestion.

"How much does it pay?"

"What?!"

"The prison job."

"Oh, $400.00 a month."

Exhausted, Cassie finally joined me in bed and we embraced in a tangle of arms and legs. Later, when we had just begun to fall into a dreamless sleep, Cassie jerked upright. "Sean, you really don't want to separate do you?"

"I think we need a break," I replied. I slipped out of bed a few hours later without awakening her, dressed and left for work.

At four-thirty the next morning, an apparition manifested itself in Admissions, proclaiming, "My wife is going to have a baby!" An anemic young man, cheeks pinched with hunger, his appearance betrayed his status in life. I assured him that he had come to the right place.

"Don't worry. I know exactly what I'm doing," I assured the teenage mother-to-be. My duties as admission clerk included taking women in labor to the eleventh floor delivery room.

"Why the eleventh floor?" I had asked Huckabee one morning.

"Because some man, who has never been with child, put it there," Nurse Huckabee barked. End of conversation.

The nervous young husband and I managed to get his wife into a wheelchair.

"Oh my God! Oh my God!" stuttered the father-to-be. We got into the elevator. Stabbing button number ten, I took note of the elevator slowly creaking upward.

"Why are we going so slow?" The husband wheezed in competition with his wife's gasps for breath.

"Because I forgot to use the express key," I muttered.

"Oh my God!"

The elevator came to a standstill and the doors slowly squealed open. We raced down the green halls of the tenth floor. I maintained a death grip on both handles of the wheelchair.

People yelled, "You're on the wrong floor!"

Another series of "Oh my God! Oh my God!" erupted from the husband, along with hysterical hiccups.

I made a hasty U-turn, causing the wheelchair to teeter on one wheel. The patient spilled onto the floor in a heap of outstretched hands and tangled feet. The wailing and weeping seemed unending. Soothing voices took over finally, guiding parents-to-be and their frantic admissions clerk to the eleventh floor OB-GYN. On my return to admissions Ed Novak greeted me.

"Hey, Sean. What happened?" I relayed the story of chaos and confusion. Novak broke away.

"Tell me about it later. I'm going on break. They want you in exam room three."

I met the house doctor on his way to E3. "Mr. Sullivan, I understand you are to remove ID bracelets from patients who have expired," he said. A young man dressed in green, he stood motionless, studying a chart. His face looked like it was carved in marble. He gave no sign of recognition.

"Yes," I answered.

"Mr. Gianinni has left this world."

I opened the door to the examination room, took one look and stifled a scream. "He's dead," I cried to no one but the corpse. Cautiously, I entered the room and approached the body.

Swallowing dry mucous, I gaped at a hole where a stomach should have been but wasn't. I stared at the bandaged face, mouth agape, frozen it seemed in mid-conversation. Orbs of opal glared at me asking, "Why?" The hollow cadaver tried to tell me something. I stumbled towards the door.

The doctor walked into the room with the nurse. "Oh, sorry. I forgot to drape him. First gut wound this month," he said.

The resident glanced up at the ceiling. In short bursts he continued, "The son-in-law shot the old man. Used a twenty-gauge shotgun. Probably a family argument." In a voice that grew older each night, he turned to the nurse on duty.

"Mary, please cover the patient in number three."

Not wanting to wake the deceased, I whispered, "He looks so small. So naked."

"Death disrobes us all." The old young man in green shuffled out of the emergency room.

13

"SAND CASTLES"

A neurotic builds sand castles
A psychotic lives in them
The psychiatrist collects the rent

CHRISTMAS HAD COME AND GONE. I TOOK THE test for correctional counselor, scoring eighty-six. On Monday, December 29, 1958, I reported for duty at the California Medical Facility in Vacaville. I handed a letter confirming my employment to the Correctional Officer (CO). A trustee escorted me to the supervisor's office.

We took a long walk down "main street," through the heart of the prison, past electronic gates, security cameras mounted on the wall, and glassed-in stations. We arrived at a gate which opened to a world I had never seen or imagined.

I had the obligatory chit-chat with Wendell Carruthers, my new supervisor. He introduced me to some fellow counselors before my grand tour.

"Hi there. My name is Sean," I said to everyone.

"I'm a little busy. Felix here will take you on a short tour of the facility. We can talk when you return. This will be your introduction to CMF." Carruthers shook my hand in dismissal.

A small slender patient materialized before us. Inmates at CMF were called patients, or sometimes patient/inmates.

"I'm Felix," my escort grunted. We shook hands. When he looked the other way, I wiped a sweaty palm on my pant leg. Our first stop was the reception center.

We entered a large room lined with benches and showers at one end. A Department of Corrections bus, painted green with barred windows, had backed into the huge enclosure. Cantilevered doors of aluminum rolled up noisily behind the bus, announcing the end of life and liberty as the occupants had known.

Inmates with leg irons handcuffed to each other clanked into the holding area leading to the main reception center. Showers, a medical examination, and psychological testing awaited the new fish that had been caught. Interviews with the counselors would follow in a few days.

"Shorts off, Hadley!" Correctional Officer Gonzales yelled. His moustache twitched. Eyes darted from Patient No. 93401 to prison clerks scribbling on notebooks. Patient No. 93401 hesitated. I saw a tear trickling down his cheek.

"It ain't that bad, Hadley," a patient clerk shouted. Giggles and nervous laughter ricocheted throughout the reception center. Clerk No. 1 inspected the new man. Tiring of his present amorata, he desired something different. Hadley could be sold for a few cartons of cigarettes or a favor if he proved unsatisfactory.

Hadley, James, San Francisco, California, age thirty-one, married, two children, embezzlement, no previous record, indeterminate sentence of ten to twelve years, broke down and cried. Trying to cover his nakedness, he staggered to the other end of the center, turned his back to the audience, and attempted to cleanse away the sins of yesterday.

In the free world, Hadley had reeked of success. An outwardly adoring wife and a four bedroom home in the Forrest Hills district of San Francisco, overlooking the foggy Pacific Ocean, completed a picture of success. The mini-mansion came equipped with an elevator. The social lion of Herb Caen's "Baghdad By The Bay" had earned a Masters of Business Administration from Stanford University, passing the CPA exam at the tender age of twenty-six. A "workaholic" approach to his job at the bank had kept him in favor.

After several satisfying sessions of bedroom gymnastics, his demanding mistress, a bottle-blonde who didn't really care, encouraged him to dip into the till.

The next patient walked to the center of the room. Leg irons and handcuffs were removed. He took a turn at the shower.

My euphoria at landing the job as a correctional counselor began to rapidly dissipate. Having viewed the lowest level of the moral hierarchy, I now reflected upon my place in the sun. The dehumanizing of patients shattered my sensibilities. My thirty-three years of following the rules of society seemed a complete waste of time. Generations of Presbyterian virtues disappeared one layer at a time.

My thoughts turned to Cassie as I watched the receiving process. Our marriage was foundering on the shoals of frustration. We had agreed to a trial separation.

I found a trailer home near the prison in Vacaville and, on a stormy Saturday afternoon, helped Cassie move into an apartment on Steiner Street in San Francisco. It had been recommended by one of the Jackson Street Irregulars.

Irregular itself, the apartment had once been a small family theater owned by a Basque family. As you entered, a ramp lead down to the living room which boasted a small stage with curtains. In the rear was a dining area and bathroom, leading to a flowered courtyard and lawn. It had since been converted to a first floor flat.

"Why a family theater?" Cassie asked.

"They were quite popular in the old days—a sure sign of status. Many Italian and Basque families put on plays and musicals in their homes," I explained.

We walked down a ramp to the living area. What had been the stage was now walled off, separating the family room from the kitchen, bedroom, and bathroom. The back yard was festooned with hanging plants and flower beds, creating an illusion of tranquility. Shielded from street noise, it became my personal Shangri-La when we reconciled.

"I scored well on the exam for prison counselor," I offered.

"Good for you," Cassie said. She patted the settee, inviting me to join her.

"How far is Vacaville from San Francisco?" she asked.

"About thirty-five to forty miles. A long commute," I answered. "Maybe I can carpool with Jack Barr, the assistant counseling supervisor. He lives in the Marina."

I sensed a reconciliation. Three weeks had passed since the spilt.

"Why don't you stay the night?" She planted a kiss on my lips. I accepted her offer with glee.

"Oh, by the way, I bought a new car." I thought the news would make her happy.

Suddenly she stood up, pointing an accusing finger at me. "How did you finance a new car? You haven't been paid yet, have you?"

"The State employee's credit union loaned me the money after verifying my employment at the joint. They were quite nice. Nothing down, but the payments are a little high."

"How high?"

"$265.00 a month, including insurance due on the first of each month. We get paid on the fifth."

I pulled her down on the day couch. A short embrace preceded a much needed night of love making. The next morning I slipped out of the apartment without waking her.

I drove over the Golden Gate bridge to Vallejo then on to Vacaville and the California Medical Facility. In my office, I picked up a two-inch binder entitled, "Rules and Regulations, State of California, Department of Corrections, Sacramento, California." Gold on blue. Engrossed in a never ending compendium of "Thou Shalt Nots," when I finally glanced at the wall clock it read eleven-fifteen.

The Prisoner's Dictionary contained definitions, abbreviations, and musings on language used in state correctional institutions. Language is ever-changing. This is particularly true in prisons, where there is the motion of people coming and going, a culture based on a unique set of circumstances, and the need to speak in words that often carry varying depths of meaning. There are some expressions that can never be fully understood by the outside world. This list will never be complete, nor is it intended to be exhaustive. I read.

The prisoner grievance or administrative appeal process (CDC Form 602). This process provides three formal levels of review, beginning with institutional levels and progressing to the Director's review in Sacramento. Although the appeals process provides a means for prisoners to express complaints, there are many problems with the system and appeals are frequently at the informal levels of review.

AB: Aryan Brotherhood, a white right-wing prison gang. This abbreviation can also refer to the Department's administrative bulletins.

AC: Adjustment Center, a segregated control unit. In theory, the unit was to provide an intensive rehabilitation program. In practice, such units remained the hole. A landmark case challenging conditions in San Quentin's Adjustment Center was filed in 1973. The challenges were upheld and the case continues to be enforced as a permanent injunction.

Ad Seg: Administrative Segregation. Placement in a controlled unit for the safety and security of the institution, for situations such as allegations of gang affiliation, investigation of a disciplinary offense, or repeated misconduct.

Beef: A disciplinary charge, as to "catch a beef."

BGF: The Black Guerrilla Family, an African-American prison gang that originally started as a left-wing organization influenced by George Jackson.

Broadway: The first floor of some tiers. A wide area where patients come and go. Occasionally inmates are housed here if the prison is particularly crowded.

Camp: CDC minimum security facilities for fire fighting and conservation work. In the juvenile system, a camp is a long term (under one year) detention facility operated by the county probation officer. Sometimes called "the Ranch."

Cat-J: A prisoner who needs mental health treatment.

C-file: The central file. The critical information maintained on each prisoner. Sometimes called the "yellow jacket."

Chrono: Informational notes by prison officials documenting classification decisions, minor disciplinary offenses, medical orders, and just about everything else that might be recorded on a prisoner.

Click up: To join a gang.

Convict: A prisoner with traditional values. One who has pride and respect, who maintains integrity. A convict differs from an inmate.

Date: A prisoner's release date.

Debrief: A procedure by which prisoners who wish to establish that they are no longer associated with a prison gang must provide information regarding gang activities and pass a polygraph examination. The prisoner must give names and identify criminal activity. This is the only means available to prisoners to establish that they have left a prison gang and should be released from segregation. Having become an informant, the prisoner must then rely on the Department of Corrections for protection. It is an extremely dangerous pact. Prisoners who are wrongfully identified as gang associates may have nothing to offer in the debriefing process.

EME: The Mexican Mafia, a southern Hispanic prison gang.

E.P.R.D.: Earliest Possible Release Date. A prisoner's release date if he or she earns credits and stays out of trouble. Computing this date can be difficult since it is based on a complex formula. The prison's computation can be reviewed through the Legal Status Summary Sheet.

Fence Parole: Escape.

Fish: A new inmate.

Fish Line: A line used to pull items from one cell to another.

Hack: A prison guard.

Hall: The hall, Juvenile Hall. A short term detention facility operated by the probation department housing minors who face pending adjudication as well as minors found unfit for juvenile court who are under 18 and have been ordered by the court to be housed there.

Home boy: Another prisoner from one's hometown or neighborhood. Seth Morgan's book by the same title remains a classic piece of writing about prisoners and prison culture.

House: Cell.

Inside: Behind the walls.

Jacket: Central File.

Jody: The anonymous lover taken by a wife or girl friend.

Kite: Notes or letters.

Lifer: A prisoner serving a life sentence.

Lock down: The policy of confining a group of prisoners or an entire prison to cells. This is generally done in response to unrest or emergency—although some lock downs are instituted for extended periods of time.

L.W.O.P.: Life Without Possibility of Parole.

Mainline: The general population.

Missive: I am not sure why this term became popular, but an amazing number of prisoners refer to correspondence as missives.

Nester: A member of Nuestra Familia.

NF: Nuestra Familia, a northern Hispanic prison gang.

PC: Protective custody. Prisoners may be placed in protective custody for many reasons—they snitched on a gang; their offense was one looked down on by the prison population (child molestation, for example) and became known, or they display some weakness that would make them a victim.

Pile Weights: Weight lifting, as in the iron pile. A favorite pastime.

Pruno: Homemade alcohol, fermented juice, the classic prison drink.

R-Suffix: A designation for sexual offenders that limits placement decisions. For obvious reasons, this suffix is to remain confidential.

Shakedown: A search of a cell or work area. The most common complaint by prisoners is that property is lost, destroyed, or left scattered after a search.

Shank: Handmade prison weapon, generally a stabbing instrument. Also called a shiv or a piece.

SHU: Segregated Housing Unit. The Hole. Prisoners may be placed in the SHU for limited disciplinary terms or on an indeterminate basis for posing a general threat to prison security (such as alleged gang affiliation). The most notorious SHU unit in California is at the "super-maximum" Pelican Bay, and is characterized by isolation, sensory deprivation, limited access to programs, and the use of force.

Slam down: To place in segregation or to lock up an institution or unit.

Snitch: An informant. Rat. One who has given up names or activities. In theory, the use of confidential information against a prisoner has certain procedural safeguards. In practice, prison officials rely upon shadowy information in a context prone to manipulative deception.

Ticket: A transfer order.

Turnkey: A guard who is there just to open doors, who cares about nothing other than doing his or her shift.

Walk alone: A prisoner who cannot exercise on a yard with other prisoners not so designated. San Quentin's death row has a yard for "walk alones" to exercise together.

Warehouse: An institution with overcrowded conditions and little or no rehab program. Housing may be in a dormitory or a gymnasium converted to living space.

Yard: The exercise area. In segregation, the yard may be nothing more than a concrete "dog run" with no equipment. Other units may have a basketball court, weight lifting equipment, or grassy areas.

Now I can communicate in the local jargon.

My thoughts were interrupted by, "Good morning, Sean." Mr. Carruthers strode into my office with a rolling gait suggesting years of sea duty. "Have you been reading the regs?"

"Yes, Sir. But I haven't finished all of them yet."

"That's not so important. Just so you get the idea."

"Yes, Sir."

"Your orientation continues today. First lunch with the prisoners, then a visit to maximum security. Next week you and Josh Elliot will take a field trip to Folsom."

My colleague, Folsom, was a young man with a Masters' degree in Social Work. He had reported for work the same day I did.

"I think I already got the grand tour," I said.

"Not yet, but you will," my supervisor said. Carruthers, a big man, had survived World War II as the captain of a cargo ship. Prone to story telling, he launched into another anecdote.

166

"Reminds me of the time I reported aboard the JONATHAN O'BRIEN as the new skipper. I rounded up the crew and gave them one of my little talks." His "little talk" lasted into the noon hour.

Warden Carruthers neglected to explain, nor did I ask, how he had progressed from a sea faring man of adventure to the confines of a state penal institution. The keeper of the gaol, a lonely man, he possessed an ego that hindered close friendships. His braggadocio blocked intimacy with friends and co workers. I viewed him as a someone who liked to "talk story."

"Come to my office. It's more comfortable there." I tried to keep pace with Carruther's long strides. We arrived at a large well furnished room appropriate to his rank and nautical in flavor.

"Sit down, Sullivan. Make yourself at home."

He pointed to several balsa wood models of sailing ships. "I made those in my spare time." Next he turned to a mahogany framed picture of a cargo ship behind his desk. "That's the JONATHAN O'BRIEN, a World War Two Liberty Ship from one of Kaiser's killer yards, near your home town of Portland," he said.

Carruther's had studied my personal file.

Turning to his desk, Carruthers picked up a gold encased compass and fondled it for a moment before returning it gently to its place. "My crew gave this to me when I left the Merchant Marine Service," he explained.

A large ship's bell cast in iron and gold plated, mounted on a stand made of oak, completed the sea going flavor of his office. "That's the original bell from the O'BRIEN," he explained.

"Interesting," I said.

"Now for business. Let me give you a thumbnail sketch of this institution."

"Yes, Sir." I sat at attention.

"The medical facility was opened in 1955, three years ago, at a cost of twenty million dollars. It currently houses fourteen hundred inmate-patients, all male. Three-hundred are classified as psychotics, one-hundred seventy-five as homosexuals, three-hundred as various other sexual deviants, and three-hundred as pyromaniacs, alcoholics, psychopaths and anything else you can name in the family of mental illness. The rest are just miscellaneous."

"I'm impressed."

"You should be. To continue—we also have fifty tuberculosis patients in the medical wings."

"I worked as a counselor at the Eastern Oregon Tuberculosis Hospital in The Dalles, Oregon for several years," I chimed in.

He changed subjects for a moment. "Group therapy is a technique of modern psychiatry in which emotionally disturbed people meet in a semi-circle of seven to nine individuals and talk out the experiences that led them to their confused state in life.

"There are another six-hundred men in the reception center committed from the forty-seven counties of Northern California. They are given both mental and physical exams, tested for intelligence, education and aptitudes, and then sent on their way to the various institutions of the State prison system."

"Until recently, I wasn't even aware that this place existed," I commented in admiration.

Suddenly Carruthers jumped to his full six-feet two-inches, reached over and grabbed a small braided rope, and rang the ship's bell twelve times. "1200 hours. Come on, Sean. I'll take you to the dining hall."

"Yes, Sir." We began to walk the four hundred and seventy yards down the corridor called "Main Street."

Carruthers picked up his monologue. "We get the cream of California's criminal crop here. The roughest, toughest prisoners in the State. We also get those who are obviously mentally ill—the psychotics, compulsive neurotics, and psychopaths."

After passing through the usual gates, slamming open and then shut behind us, we arrived at the mess hall. Seating capacity 600. "The patient population has doubled in size since the facility opened in 1955. Now each meal requires two shifts," Mr. Carruthers explained.

Ten or twelve patient cooks and servers mingled near the front entrance. Dressed in white, with colored bandannas around their necks and food stains on their serving aprons, they waited for the lunch hour. An oversized patient called out from the kitchen, "Sit anywhere, Mr. Sullivan. We'll bring you a tray." His right ear ring, glittering in the fluorescent lighting, caught my eye.

"Thank you. How did you know my name?" I hollered back at the big guy. More grins by the kitchen crew followed by complete silence answered my question. It was my first experience with the prison grapevine.

"It's the prison telegraph, Sean. They know all about you five minutes after you enter the joint. You'll get used to it," my supervisor explained.

Every security station, guard post, office and gate had at least one "gofer"—"go for this" and "go for that," hence the world's greatest telegraph system. Little could be accomplished with secrecy. Wherever there was a CO there would also be a clerk dressed in the standard uniform of denim blues or gray.

"What are those?" I pointed to security stations built into each of the four corners of the dining hall.

"Observation and control. That's two inch bullet proof glass. The portholes are used to dispense gas during a riot."

I pondered this information. "This is certainly a whole new world to me. I think there's an element of danger to this job."

"Oh, not really," Warden Carruthers replied. His soothing tones did not dispel my apprehension.

Suddenly a six-foot-four patient loomed over me, flexing a musculature envied by his colleagues and grinning a toothy welcome. Both his sleeves had been cut off, revealing an American flag tattooed in red, white and blue on the right shoulder. His black arms stood in stark contrast to the white uniform.

"My name is Fred. Some call me Fearless Freddy," the behemoth announced. More giggles and one or two "ha-ha's" echoed from the kitchen. A small jeweled cross hung his left earlobe, swinging back and forth with each movement of his head and mesmerizing me. He held out a huge paw. I turned away, seeking the protection of my mentor.

"Where is Mr. Carruthers?" I pleaded.

"He left," the patient responded.

"Oh God!" I whispered.

I tentatively reached out for his outstretched hand. I expected a bone crusher of a handshake, but was surprised by his delicate grip. "Hi. I'm Sean Sullivan, the new counselor," I said.

"Yeah, I know." He scrutinized my face for clues to my personality. Satisfied with his analysis, the sovereign of the dinning hall retreated to his domain just as the doors to the dining room opened. The great hall became the Tower of Babel.

"Here's your lunch, Mr. Sullivan." A young man of slender stature appeared, placing a tin tray, a tin cup and a large metal pot of coffee before me. Divided into three parts, one large and two small, the receptacle resembled the TV dinners of the near future. Spaghetti, peaches and white bread were the afternoon fare. The patient/server continued to hover above my table.

"Is everything okay, Mr. Sullivan?"

"Fine, fine. Any sugar or cream?" I asked.

"Coming right up, Mr. Sullivan." He ran at a half trot to a nearby counter, returning in record time. "You didn't say which one so I brought both."

"Thanks." I looked upon felons as untouchables, heathens in their blindness to the realities of life. Suddenly I became aware of the rattling of metal cups and trays. The overwhelming din of voices soon faded into sounds of slurping, swallowing, and little civility. Five patients of diverse hues and cultures joined me at my round table.

I greeted them. "Hi, fellas."

I was greeted in return with grunts, groans and one "Howdy." A silent lunch followed. Thirty minutes later, I waited until everyone had left before I walked down the long corridor, through the series of gates clanging open and shut.

"Mr. Gonzales, what are you doing in the counseling center? I saw you this morning at reception," I said. Gonzales stood up, coffee cup in hand.

"They transferred me. Now I'm nothing but a clerk." He groaned. One could see the bile rising up in his throat.

I offered my condolences, "Sorry."

"And after three years, I really knew how to run that reception center," he continued.

"Yes, I could see that."

Rule No. 1: Familiarity breeds collusion. Department of Corrections policy stated that all personnel should be rotated between a variety of duties on a frequent basis. Too many opportunities for wrong doing otherwise. A fact of life I would learn to my everlasting regret.

"Let me explain a few things to you," Gonzales offered.

"Okay."

"Your job is to interview, diagnose, classify and assign patients to the appropriate facility."

"Yes. I know."

"You will see patients according to their crime. On Mondays, armed robbery, assault and battery with a weapon or any felony committed while possessing a deadly weapon. On Tuesdays, attempted rape, rape or kidnapping. On Wednesday, murder, attempted murder or bodily harm. On Thursdays, arson or breaking and entering. On Friday, sex beefs. It's a great way to end your week. You'll feel like you are climbing out of a sewer on Fridays."

"Sounds interesting."

"One more thing. If you need help, knock the phone off the desk and we'll be down here ASAP. Understand?"

"Yes. But I hope that won't be necessary."

"You never know…Now, let me call someone to escort you to max. It's part of your orientation."

"Max?" I repeated.

"Maximum security."

"Oh."

"It's located on the other side of the reception center." My escort, a slender young man with a slight involuntary eye twitch, arrived in a few minutes. A black patch over his left eye announced, "prison fight." We walked the main line to max. He slowed so I could keep pace.

"Can I ask you a personal question?" he said. His right eye squinted at me until he focused a questioning glance at my feet.

"Sure." Here it comes, I thought.

"What happened to your legs?" he asked.

"Spina Bifida. A birth defect in the lower spine," I answered simply.

"You're getting your exercise today."

"That's for sure," I agreed.

Another electronic gate banged opened. We entered maximum security. I saw a row of cells on the right, with security stations at each end of a long corridor. Gas ports were located in the center of each station.

The CO walked over and extended his hand. "Welcome to Max, Mr. Sullivan."

"Thank you."

Large barred windows on the left allowed the sun to create as slight illusion of cheeriness not shared by the patients. Few areas in the joint were open to daylight. I tried not to stare at the patients. I saw freedom on the left with caged animals on the right.

"To your right are twenty-five six by eight single cells containing the bad boys of the joint. They are here for any number of reasons." He droned on for several minutes explaining the do's and don't's of the California Medical Facility and maximum security in particular. The pride in his voice almost disguised his contempt for felons. To quote Mr. Carruthers, he ran a tight ship.

Suddenly the CO yelled, "Watch out!"

A hairy arm shot out of a nearby cell, thankfully grasping only air.

"He almost got you. Stand clear of the cells," the CO advised.

"Sorry." A challenge was one thing; physical danger was another. The patient and I exchanged questioning glances as he slowly drew his paw back through the bars.

"They can grab you faster than a cobra in mating season. The bad guys are always looking for a hostage. I'm sure you don't want be held prisoner by a prisoner," my guide said.

"No, not really," I sighed.

The CO banged on the cell bars with a night stick. "George, you know I have to put you on report now," he said. The patient flipped the finger in the officer's direction. My inspection of maximum security ended a few minutes later.

"That concludes our tour of Max. How about a cup of coffee, Mr. Sullivan?" The CO smiled, twirling his baton like a high school cheer leader.

"Oh, no thanks. I should get back to my office and finish reading the regs."

"Ah, yes, the regulations. What would we do without them? Well, some other time then. And good luck—you'll need it in this joint."

"Yes."

"You can find your way back? Just turn left and go straight down Main Street until you come to the counseling center on the right. You can't miss it."

Officer Gonzales greeted me at the gate. "Well, what do you think of the joint so far, Mr. Sullivan?" he asked.

"Words fail me. I've never seen anything like this place."

He opened gate number nine leading to my office. For the next twelve months and five days I would live in fear of being sandwiched between gates. My thoughts were interrupted.

"Mr. Elliot is waiting for you," the officer said.

"Thanks." I walked a few steps to the small room on the right—my new office. It was a windowless room containing a steel gray desk complimented by two straight back chairs not designed for comfort or counseling. Fluorescent lighting overhead gave the impression of an operating room in a small hospital. A poor rendition of Vonnoh's "In

Flanders Field Where Soldiers Sleep and Poppies Grow, 1892" had fallen to the floor.

"Hello, Mr. Elliot. I'm Sean Sullivan." We shook hands.

"Call me Josh," he said. A red-haired six footer, with gold rimmed aviator-style tinted glasses, he assumed the grim-faced pose of Hoover's finest.

"Have you ever worked for the FBI?" I inquired.

"Why do you ask?"

"Oh, never mind."

Ignoring my question, we exchanged perceptions of our first day on the job. Jack Barr soon joined us. He was an experienced correctional counselor with dark curly hair and deeply tanned skin. His green eyes looked at me curiously.

"You must be Sean Sullivan. Mr. Carruthers told me about you," he said.

"Nothing bad, I hope," I joked.

"Oh, no. I think he likes you. Either one of you gentlemen live in San Francisco?"

"No. Well, my wife, or maybe I should say my bride, found a three-bedroom double constructed home over in Dixon for $19,500," Elliot answered.

"I'm living in a trailer house on the edge of town but I may move back to the Big City," I said. I did not discuss my marital problems with strangers, although I could have used some advice.

"Well, just let me know if you want to car pool. I live in The Marina. It's a long commute." Barr shook his head. "Trailer houses are uncomfortable."

"Yeah, I know. It's a long walk to the bathroom and showers."

"Don't forget, you guys—field trip to Folsom on Monday. We can take my car." Barr left the room.

At five o'clock I began the long drive to San Francisco. Car pooling with Barr appealed to me.

On the way to San Francisco one weekend, I contemplated several ways to negotiate a peace treaty with Cassie. I vowed to myself there would be no more fights. Two hours later we ate a make-do supper of Spam sandwiches and soup made of leftovers.

"Good soup," I said, presenting my best face.

"Thank you. But if you had called, I could have gone shopping and made something better," she said.

"Oh, this is fine. I could eat a bear," I commented truthfully.

"How's the new job?" she asked.

"I think it's going to be okay. Quite a change from taking ID bracelets off dead patients."

"Do you like living in a trailer house?"

"No, I don't. Is that a new blouse?"

"Yes. It was on sale at the Emporium."

"It's very pretty, very feminine. You look good." Cassie's eyes narrowed with suspicion.

"Thank you."

"Here, let me help you with the dishes." I said. An expression of "you don't really expect me to believe this" flashed across her face.

"That's okay, Sean. I can manage."

We returned to the theater living room. I invited her to join me on the day bed.

"Cassie, I'm sorry about the arguments. It seems like something has died in each of us. I think it's hope."

My awkward apology was met with silence. Hot tempers, angry words, and accusations could not easily be forgotten. She put a restraining hand on me.

"I can't stand the fighting. No more, Sean." Her body stiffened.

My heart cried out, "My dream, my dream." There was a fire in my belly.

"Sean, I know you worked hard at the Med Center and grad school. A masters would have been wonderful, but we need things. I need things. Tips have been down at the Koffee Break. I'm thinking of quitting and looking for something else."

Jolted into silence by Cassie's remarks, I sat down on the sofa. My moral compass wobbled all over the spectrum.

"Come on, Sean. Things aren't all that bad." She put her arm around me.

"I have a good job. I'm working full time and making over four hundred dollars a month. That's good money for these times," I said.

"That's fine. Good for you."

The phoenix in me attempted to rise from the ashes. "I'll make it up to you, Cassie." I begged, "What can I do for penitence?"

A lascivious smile passed over her face. "Don't tempt me. I forgive you." We shared a caring embrace.

A small voice in me bravely ventured forth. "Can I come home Cassie?"

"Yes."

I exploded with joy. "A celebration is in order! Let's go to the Hungry I tonight. Ada Moore is featured."

"Sure, Sean."

On a more practical note, I added, "We're going on a field trip to Folsom Prison on Monday. I can pick up my things after work."

An hour later we walked down the stairs to our favorite bistro. We ordered drinks as the chanteuse began the last number in the first gig of the evening, "Won't you Come Home Bill Bailey." Cassie and I babbled the whole evening through. The word love never entered our conversation.

A week later Jack Barr, Josh Elliot and I were seated in a semicircle in front of Carruthers' desk at the California Medical Facility. Mr. Carruthers made a steeple of his fingers and assumed a judicial expression before beginning his little talk.

"Gentlemen, you will find Folsom a most interesting place. Warden Heitman is a remarkable man. Governor Warren appointed him Warden of Folsom in 1944. He has somewhat of an ego but is in complete command of the facility." The supervisor talked for some time. A timepiece in the center of a fully rigged model sailing ship chimed twelve.

"Well, enough for now. I am sure Warden Heitman will fill you in on the history of Folsom." Carruthers stood up, thus concluding the conference. We excused ourselves.

Elliot took his own car since he lived in Sacramento. Barr and I went together in his car and pulled up an hour later in front of a walled stronghold made of rock. Elliot was waiting for us in his car. We surveyed the scene before us with sinking hearts.

"My God, it looks like a fortress." Elliot's eyes widened in wonderment.

"The rocks are from a nearby quarry. They used prison labor." Barr responded.

"You mean the inmates built their own joint?" I asked, wondering at the irony. Stunned, Elliot and I gaped in silence.

"Yep," Barr confirmed. Gawking in disbelief, we slowly approached the rock-walled prison.

"You'd think just seeing this place would keep a person on the straight and narrow," I said.

"Let's go." Barr hustled us into the receiving area. He warned us, "Be prepared; Heitman is quite a character." He did not elaborate.

Our ID's were checked as Barr explained the purpose of our visit to the CO on duty. He studied his clipboard for a few moments before the first gate slammed open. A trustee escorted us to the Warden's office.

A few minutes later, Robert Heitman entered the room like a pirate taking over a Spanish Galleon. "Good morning, gentlemen. Welcome to Folsom State Prison." He waved us to straight back chairs. He had discovered that visitors tended to shorten their stay when the furniture was plain and uncomfortable.

He stood before Elliot and I, a rotund man whose labored breathing and beer belly betrayed a man older than his fifty one years. His small brown eyes squinted in a pale and drawn face that was carved in lines of brutality. Heitman looked more the ancient mariner with a story to tell than the keeper of the jail. Clothed in a black suit, a costume compatible with execution day in the old West, Heitman appeared an echo of an 1850's Hangtown Sheriff.

"So, you're the new counselors at Vacaville?" he commented.

We made no response to his rhetorical question.

"I never had much formal education myself. I made it up the last few years with experience in this joint," he beamed.

Jack Barr ventured, "Experience is a great teacher."

"Sure is," Heitman boomed. "I started driving the Superintendent of Corrections when I was seventeen and in 1944 I took over here when Mr. McGee became Director of Corrections."

"I met him. He was on the orals board when I interviewed for the counseling job at Vacaville. I had just received my Masters in Social Work. Nice man." Elliot offered.

Barr shot Elliot a glance. He had spoken out of turn. Heitman had little tolerance for people with degrees; he referred to them sarcastically as "college boys." His education had taken place at the university of the five senses.

"Well, now, time for a little history to make your day complete," Heitman said. He lit the stub of his cigar for the third time.

"But first let me show you this." Flashing a grin, Heitman slowly and theatrically opened one of his long desk drawers. Standing to one side he announced, "Confiscated contraband, Gentlemen. A real no-no in this place or any joint." I threw Elliot a startled look as his blue eyes registered dismay.

"And this represents collections for just the last two weeks," the warden said almost proudly. He invited us to look in the drawer. It contained shivs fashioned from an assortment of picks, screwdrivers, grappling hooks, and tools stolen from the prison shops. Heitman studied our facial expressions.

Slamming the drawer shut, Warden Heitman next launched into a soliloquy that took us well past the lunch hour. Barr looked bored. Elliot and I teetered on the edge of our seats trying to look interested.

"Three hundred acres of land on the banks of the American River were purchased from the Natoma Water Company in 1868. It took twelve years to build the prison. On July 15, 1880, Thomas Pockman was appointed warden. Folsom opened on October 17, 1878 when two-hundred prisoners were transferred from San Quentin to Folsom. There have been over six hundred deaths here since 1918 of all causes, including executions. California is the most dangerous state in the union." Apparent asthma caused him to gasp for air.

"In the early days a gang of convicts built a stone structure to be commissioned as Folsom State Hospital. It was known as "the bug house" until 1942 when another generation of convicts tore down the partially finished stone walls." He paused. "Mr. Barr, I know you've heard this story. It is important."

Heitman wheezed, shifting his weight. Barr straightened up in his chair. Heitman went on.

"I question the abilities of my predecessors. A 1944 investigation revealed that the chief inmate nurse carried a key to the drug closet. It turned out he was a narcotics addict. This unhappy event occurred several months before I took over. Nothing of the sort has happened since I became warden." A knock on the office door gave us a reprieve.

An office clerk announced, "Warden, Roscoe is waiting."

In an aside to Elliot and me, Warden Heitman whispered, "Let me tell you something about Roscoe. In his confession he said, 'Then I would undress them completely. Nothing gives a man such a feeling of Almightiness as viewing the naked body of a women he has just strangled'." Heitman paused for theatrical effect.

"His confession concluded, 'I loved wiping up the blood after the murders. It made me feel as though I were drinking it in, as though I were assimilating the person and thereby gaining new strength. I think there is something to vampire stories'."

Heitman slumped into his chair. "I've talked too much, as usual."

A thin man, eyebrows twitching, slithered into the office. "This is Roscoe. He'll be your guide," Heitman said. Roscoe was a short, stooped wisp of a man, fifty-ish, with the eyes of a sick mongoose. He certainly didn't look the part of an evil doer. The scrawny inmate greeted the "college boys," shaking hands with each of us.

Nothing stirs the inner recesses of a convict's heart like meeting someone new. Be it inmate or free personnel. The opportunities boggle the mind.

Barr pulled back his hand, murmuring, "Hi, Roscoe."

"Oh, that's right. You two already know each other. Roscoe's my favorite tour guide. You're a good guy, right Roscoe?" Heitman asked, highlighting his question with a fraternal slap on the prisoner's back.

"Yes, Sir, Warden Heitman. Thank you, Sir."

Barr stood up to leave. "I've taken this tour several times. I'll just wait for you two in the snack bar."

Warden Heitman escorted us to the outer office. Roscoe led the way from there through the usual locked gates. He was instantly recognized as we were granted "open sesame" to the maximum security cell block near the dreaded back alley of old days.

The trustee explained, "This is Siberia, max." We nodded our heads.

"About the same as Vacaville," I offered.

"Yes," responded Elliot.

"What is that thing?" I pointed to an overhead block and tackle hanging from a large hook at the end of the corridor.

"That's the derrick." Roscoe's lips curled in disgust. We stared saucer-eyed at the contraption, unbelieving what we thought we were seeing. Roscoe confirmed our fears.

He whispered, "An inmate was first handcuffed. A rope was then passed underneath his arms, and he was pulled off the floor feet first. The inmate would be stretched two hours in the morning and two hours in the afternoon, followed by confinement to his cell for several days to contemplate the error of his ways."

"My God!" Elliot let out in a strangled cry.

"The State stopped corporeal punishment when Mr. McGee took over the Department of Corrections," Roscoe continued. "But they keep that here as a reminder of the good old days."

Our tour continued past shops, laundries and the mess hall. We entered a large area containing rock hewn cells. "This is the original cell block," Roscoe explained. He peeked through the bars of a nearby cell.

"Hi, Jimmy. How're you doing?" Roscoe asked. A youngish blonde man put down a balsa wood model of an eighteenth century sailing ship.

"Just finished shaping the hull." He waved a razor blade in our direction.

"See yah," Roscoe said. We walked on for a few minutes.

"Look, an empty cell. I didn't think we would see one. This place is crowded," I said. We peeked in between the bars. The cell floor, painted a putrid green, seem to be in a state of disrepair.

"This cell is empty because it's not usable. Years ago the floor was covered with chloride of lime which becomes an acid. The bad boys were thrown in for two or three days at a time," Roscoe explained.

"Jesus! Why?" Elliot pleaded.

"For punishment! The fumes would suffocate the guy and burn raw the inside mucous membranes of his nose, mouth, and throat," Roscoe whispered.

Our tour ended in solemnity despite Roscoe's attempts to brighten up the conversation. Cautious handshakes were exchanged between free personnel and felon. Heitman signaled Elliot and me into his office. Barr joined us.

"Well, how do you like Folsom?" The warden grinned. "I suppose Roscoe took you by the derrick and the lime cell."

"Yes, Sir," Elliot said. "Interesting."

I swallowed a lump in my throat. "I can't believe what I've seen."

Heitman flashed a superior grin. "To misquote the bible, Son: 'The judgments of the Lord are true and righteous'." He stood up to bid us goodbye. "Don't believe everything you see or hear. Mr. McGee, the director, abolished corporal punishment in 1944."

"Yeah, we heard," Elliot said.

"Sorry folks, you're too late for lunch. You're welcome to stay for dinner, though. Here's today's menu." The Warden handed us a sheet of paper.

Dinner - Monday January 12, 1959: combination salad with Thousand Island dressing, beef stew with fresh vegetables, buttered noodles, beans, corn, bread, fruit turnover, hot tea.

Barr replied, "No thanks, Warden. We have to check in at Vacaville before five o'clock."

That evening I finished off a large plate of fried jumbo shrimp over a bed of steamed rice. Sweet and sour sauce enhanced the fruit from the sea. A shimmering glass of Chablis completed the meal. Cassie watched in delight as I ate the last bite followed by our dessert wine of choice.

"What a great dinner, Cassie! What's on TV?" I motioned her to join me on the day bed.

"Lockup' is on Channel Four," she answered.

"I think I've had enough prison for one day," I sighed. I lit my corn cob pipe as a finale to a perfect meal. I studied the TV Guide. "How about 'You Asked For It' on Channel Two? It's a fun program."

"Okay...Sounds like you had an interesting day at the joint." Cassie had acquired the habit of using prison slang. She blushed, "Now you've got me saying it."

"What?"

"The joint. What happened today?"

"You wouldn't believe our tour of Folsom. I never knew such things existed."

I turned to Channel Two. Cassie's macabre curiosity, however, begged to be satisfied. At her urging, I related the day's experience in detail. In due time she changed the subject.

"How about an evening at Easy Street?" she finally suggested.

"Not tonight. I work tomorrow. Remember?"

"Sorry. I thought it would cheer you up."

"How about Friday night? Okay?"

TGIF finally arrived. We proceeded to Turk Murphy's club on Powell near Bay early in the evening. "Memphis Street Blues" split the night air as the San Francisco jazz band began their first gig. Seated at a front table, I ordered a scotch and soda, Cassie a white wine.

Turk Murphy took up his trombone to begin the first set. He growled a fierce but subdued "Tiger Rag." Cassie swayed back and forth to the beat of the music. I jumped up at the start of "Just a Closer Walk With Thee," a slow piece.

"Let's dance." I grabbed her hand.

"Sure."

After a few moments it became apparent that I couldn't maintain my balance. "Sorry, Cassie." I resigned myself to the realities of life once again.

"It's alright, Sean," she said soothingly. We strolled hand in hand to our table. The band finished in the style of the legendary Lu Watters Yerba Buena Jazz band of 1940's fame.

"Lloyd Astin and Carole spoke with reverence of Hambone Kelly's Bistro in El Cerrito, across the bay, where Watters, Bob Scobey and Turk Murphy indoctrinated a generation of fans to his style of traditional jazz," I mused.

"What happened to Lu Watters?" Cassie asked.

"I read in the Sunday paper that he retreated to Stinson Beach. He refuses to take part in any musical activity so Murphy has carried on the tradition."

The band took another break. Turk Murphy sauntered over to our table. "Having a good time folks?" he asked.

"We sure are," I replied enthusiastically. "This is my wife, Cassie,. and I'm Sean Sullivan."

He shook our hands. "Turk. Call me Turk. Everybody does, but don't ask me how I got the moniker."

"We sure enjoy your music." More profound words failed me.

"Any requests?"

Cassie's joy turned to ecstasy. "Oh! Will you please do 'Silver Dollar'?" She beamed.

"You got it," Murphy said.

Turning to Cassie, I commented, "Mad Mary in Eureka sang that every time she got drunk."

"Hey, I've been there a couple of times. The Redwoods are beautiful," Murphy said. "Well, back to work. Not that it is." He kissed Cassie's hand and ambled back to the bandstand. Her unsinkable spirit sparkled happiness.

Thad Vandan, the current tub thumper, came down front to sing while Murphy took over on the drums. We enjoyed another superb evening at Easy Street.

"It's getting late, Sean," Cassie finally said.

"Yeah, but tomorrow's Saturday—no work. Let's stay for one more set and then we'll go," I replied.

The room soon rocked with "St. Louis Woman With All Her Diamond Rings," followed by "Shake It And Break It." The evening closed with "When The Saints Come Marching In." The musicians circled the room, leading all the jazz aficionados in a conga line. The thundering climax of "Oh When the Saints" ended a perfect night.

I put my arm around Cassie as we walked to our car. She drew me closer. We stopped and kissed and she gave herself up to the sensation. I knew that when Cassie kissed a man, it was usually part of a transaction for her—something she gave in return for whatever she needed from him. Tonight it was different. She wanted to kiss me for me.

"I really enjoyed myself tonight," I exclaimed. "No derricks, no lime cells, no banging of gates. Nothing but sweet Dixieland jazz San Francisco style, and the company of my lovely wife."

"I had a wonderful time, too," Cassie bubbled.

The following Monday, Barr and I continued our daily commute between San Francisco and Vacaville. Over time we became friends. We eventually exchanged personal thoughts and ideologies.

"What do you think of having a black man for a supervisor?" Barr blurted out during one morning commute.

"Well, Ted Jefferson seems like a nice guy," I replied. "I've always felt a kinship between the physically handicapped and the minorities. Especially the blacks," I said.

"The Department appears to be changing it's hiring policies," Barr said. His screwed up face betrayed the turmoil of his inner thoughts. Silence prevailed until we pulled up at the gate.

I wanted to pursue the conversation but I sensed Barr might be a racist. I had been raised in the 1920's, with a Mississippi-born father. I had ambivalent feelings concerning the "coloreds," as Daddy had called Afro-Americans.

The next morning was full with back-to-back interviews. I read yellow jackets, listen to the stories, and suggested either minimum, medium or maximum security, subject to review.

I had taped the Vonnoh painting opposite a water color of a garish circus poster depicting elephants in single file grasping each other's tail. After three months of contemplation, I had yet to understand it's meaning. My meditations on the elephants were broken by Officer Gonzalez.

"Mr. Sullivan, this is L.C. Harrington."

The patient seated himself before me. He had the face of a biblical prophet with dark eyes staring our from under a creased brow. Bushy eyebrows and a prominent nose with flaring nostrils, all topped by thinning red hair made for a somewhat familiar face. He was a lookalike for Red Buttons of "Sayonara" fame.

Harrington began an immediate litany of woe. "I don't know why I'm in this joint. I did a little gambling." When I opened his file, he said, "You won't find the truth in there."

His facial muscles twitched causing an excessive eye blink. The patient hunched his shoulders and studied the elephants on the poster. Maybe he would figure them out.

I read aloud from Harrington's file. To the client this action seemed an implied threat.

"This is the fifth time you've been sentenced for illegal gambling, book making, running numbers and other offenses too numerous to mention. Indeterminate sentence of one to five years." I declared.

"So I took a few bets. Everybody does," he complained.

"You have been convicted five times for the same offense. The judge thought it serious. He gave you one to five." Oops. I had used one of the "Thou Shalt Not's"—never discuss the nature and length of a patient's sentence.

"I wanted to ask you a favor," Harrington said. He pulled his chair closer to me.

The word "favor" should have rung bells, blown whistles, set off rockets. It didn't. "Sure. What can I do for you?" I replied politely.

"Today is Monday. My wife is going into surgery at the University of California Medical Center Wednesday morning for a heart operation. I'd really like to be able to talk to her on the phone." His time-furrowed face squinted at me.

"Well, I'll ask Mr. Carruthers about it. But no promises," I said.

Patient Harrington shook my hand with vigor. Smiling, he left the office. At lunch I relayed the morning activities to my supervisor, Theodore Jefferson.

A former San Francisco Forty-Niner linebacker, Jefferson stood six feet two with broad shoulders. Long limbed and rangy, his face featured high cheekbones, an aquiline nose and dark eyebrows. He could not quite be described as handsome. An accent, articulate and melodious, with the softness of the South, was in contrast to his awesome physical presence. I thought he was a little over thirty.

"Call me Ted," he insisted. "And how was your morning Mr. Sullivan?"

"Call me Sean," I replied before describing my interview with Harrington. I was happy to have an audience.

"Rule No. 1—never express an opinion of a patient's sense of morality," he cautioned. "Never read from a yellow jacket to a patient. Everyone has a different value system. We are not here to judge."

"Yes, I understand. I'll be more careful in the future."

"Another thing. When you hear the phrase "do me a favor," watch out. You know the rules. You'll get the hang of it…pardon the pun."

"Mr. Carruthers suggested I take some Sociology courses," I offered.

"That sounds like a good idea."

I didn't mention my experience with Janet Pensky in Eureka. Or quitting graduate school. Prison counseling was my new start in life.

"Penology can be an interesting vocation," Jefferson commented.

We shook hands as I stood up to leave. "Excuse me, I have some paper work to do. I'll talk to Mr. Carruthers regarding Harrington. See you later," I said.

The days and weeks followed in fairly routine succession. The long commute between the apartment in San Francisco and Vacaville eventually proved costly and tiresome. I began to lobby for a transfer to San Quentin.

"Sean, do you think you have a chance for San Quentin?" Cassie asked one evening. She had became mellow in our relationship. The marriage remained intact throughout the spring and summer of 1959, with an occasional outburst when one of us perceived a threat.

"I've only been at Vacaville two months but the commuting is really getting to me. Not to mention it's expensive—thirty, forty dollars a month in gas alone. And it's hard on the car," I said after a particularly long day at the joint.

"I want to stay in San Francisco," Cassie frowned. "There's lots to do and my friends are here."

"Don't worry. I'm not going to force you to move to Vacaville," I said. I was curious as to who her friends might be.

She continued, "And the night life in this town is fantastic. The Hungry I, Enricos, Bocce Ball and the Purple Onion."

Cassie walked to the kitchen. "Carole called this afternoon. She and Lloyd invited us to join them next Saturday night at the Hungry I. The Gateway Singers and Professor Corry are on the bill," she called out. Cassie no longer viewed Carole as a predator. They became fast friends and would share a similar fate in the near future.

"Fine. Call Carole and tell her we'd be glad to join them for the evening. Sounds great. I get paid Friday." I said.

The phone rang. "Hi, Jack. What's new?." I said. I listened to his brief message. "Oh, sorry to hear that. Hope you feel better. See you next week, same time same place. My turn to drive."

"Barr's sick. I have to drive alone tomorrow," I announced.

"See what you can do about a transfer," Cassie said.

I felt her arms slip around me. She reached for the light switch. Her lips were upon me. Another carpet of dreams took off for paradise.

AFTER LUNCH THE FOLLOWING WEDNESDAY, FRED Janus announced to the small group gathered in the CMF lunchroom, "Today's Wednesday, hump day in this joint. Mid-week. We're half way home."

I saw an aging counselor in his late forties. His face spoke of his years of experience. His ears had been strained by the now silent volumes of stories he had heard. In a place like this there is always lost hope, degradation, and a slow descent into the inferno.

He had a pleasantly deep voice with an accent hard to identify— perhaps New Zealand. He had heavy eyebrows and steel blue eyes laced with crows' feet. Those eyes were haunted by some inner anxiety.

"Yeah," I responded. "I'm sure looking forward to Saturday night! The Gateway Singers are playing at the Hungry I with Ada Moore."

"We're fixing up a nursery this weekend," Elliot grinned.

"You're expecting? I mean your wife?" Janus flushed.

"Yep, next September."

"Congratulations!"

"A son is a man's immortality," Elliot proclaimed. "Or so the philosophers say."

"How about you, Sullivan?" he asked. "You and I are about the same age."

"Well, it just hasn't happened yet." It was my usual evasive answer to an often-asked question.

"Hmmm." Janus managed to inject a wealth of compassion and understanding into such a simple sound.

"Well, folks, I should get back to the salt mine. Harrington is coming to see me," I said.

"That old gambler," Janus laughed. "They finally got him. He is the most notorious bookie in the valley."

"Yeah. The judge socked it to him this time—one to five," I said.

"Watch out. He is a con's con. He'll have you believing there is cheese on the moon." Janus laughed as he picked his way around the lunch table.

"You mean there isn't any cheese on the moon?" Elliot chuckled.

I left the lunchroom and navigated down the street back to my office. Traveling between the ever present gates. Bang bang, slam slam.

"Harrington is waiting for you, Mr. Sullivan." Gonzales stood as I entered the counseling center. I took this as a sign of respect or courtesy. Real or feigned, I appreciated the gesture.

"Good afternoon, Mr. Sullivan. How are you this fine day?" Harrington's voice had an Irish lilt to it.

"Good news, Harrington. You can make your phone call to the hospital. Your wife isn't going into surgery until two o'clock this afternoon," I said.

"Thank you so much. I've been going crazy all morning not knowing." Harrington actually hugged me. "You don't know what this means to me."

"See Officer Gonzalez for your pass," I said.

"May the Good Lord smile upon you Mr. Sullivan, and your lovely family," he intoned graciously.

CO Gonzales appeared. "What's with him?" he asked. A twitching moustache gave way his curiosity.

"Mr. Carruthers approved a phone call to his wife. She's going into surgery this afternoon," I explained.

"What's her problem?"

"Heart."

Rule No. 3—never discuss an inmate/patient's confidential affairs with another individual unless it's your supervisor.

I interviewed several patients, finished the paper work, then took a coffee break. Walking down Main Street, I encountered Harrington on his way back from Mr. Carruther's office. He was all smiles. Pointing to me between gates he said loud and clear, "Talked to the wife. She's going to be okay. Thanks again, Mr. Sullivan."

Heads turned. Crimson faced, I replied, "You should thank Mr. Carruthers." Patient and free man continued in opposite directions.

As I walked back to my office, the CO thrust a phone in my face. "For you, Mr. Sullivan. It's Father Dubocek."

I put one hand on the desk to steady myself. "Yes?"

A European accent slowly articulated, "Mr. Sullivan, we haven't had the opportunity to meet but my name is Dimitri Dubocek. I am the Catholic Chaplain."

"Yes, Sir," I answered. The educational priests at the University of Portland flashed before me one by one.

Attempts at the University to provide me with a humanistic education with overtones of the Renaissance had proved somewhat successful. My undergraduate days could be characterized as an unholy Bacchanal consisting of one part womanizing and two parts Chivas Regal. Or was it the other way?

Father Dubocek continued. "Sorry to bother you but John Dortice, the Protestant Chaplain, and I are late for an interfaith conference in San Francisco. Cardinal Mahoney is speaking."

His voice, sadden by years of ministry in a prison where screams ricochet from the bowels of the institution in the middle of the night, murmured in ghost-like tones. "Would you be kind enough to inform Jimmy Harrington his wife passed away? I believe in surgery." He concluded with a whispered, "Peace be with you."

"Yes, I will," I assured him.

"I'm sorry to be asking you to do this, but you were listed as his counselor."

"It's okay, Father. I'll call him in right now."

"We thank you so much. God bless you. And please tell Mr. Harrington I shall pray for his wife's soul."

"Yes, Father." God didn't visit the joint often, I thought.

Turning to Gonzales I said, "That was Father Dubocek. Harrington's wife passed away. Both chaplains are unavailable."

"Ah, yes. The God Squad. You can always depend upon them." The rancor in his remark caused me to flinch. The CO sent a gofer to fetch Harrington.

"What's up, Mr. Sullivan?" Harrington seemed to sniff the air, sensing bad news. He sat on the edge of a chair, primed to explode.

"I don't know how to put this but Father Dubocek just informed me that your wife passed away in surgery a few minutes ago. I'm truly sorry." I stood up. I thought a hug might be in order.

"No, no!" Harrington screeched, pushing me away. Apoplectic with rage, he went berserk. He howled like the hounds of Hell. The fabric of his life was splitting before me one thread at a time. Faster and faster.

He screamed, "Why? Why?" Reduced to jelly in the face of such emotion, I retreated to the other side of the room. He pounded the walls with his fists and his head until blood ran slowly down the wall. The red on gray created a Salvador Dali hallucination.

Rule No. 4—knock the phone to the floor. An officer will respond.

Harrington fell to the floor crouched in the fetal position. His wail of pain reverberated throughout the center and down the hallway. He swiped at his face and hair with his bloody hands until he looked like a gargoyle out of Hell. Grotesque in form, pathetic in perception.

Officer Gonzales charged into my office, slamming Harrington against the blood-stained wall, then handcuffing him. He started to drag the hysterical patient out by the wrists. "I'll take care of this. Stand aside," the CO ordered.

"No, you don't understand. His wife just died," I explained. Appalled at the ferocity of events, I pleaded for compassion.

"Don't you worry, Mr. Sullivan. We know what to do."

The CO retreated to Main Street, dragging patient Harrington off to Siberia. Harrington's moans and groans faded away as the sound of gates opening and closing echoed up and down the street. His voice, shrill with horror, continues to penetrate my dreams in the wee hours of the morning.

Three hours later I was home picking at a pot roast. To me the dinner were the remains of the day.

"Sean? You look unhappy," Cassie said. "What's wrong?"

"Man's inhumanity to man," I answered. I started to relate in detail the Harrington episode.

"But first, I need another drink."

"You had two before dinner," she reminded me.

"You're counting?" Cassie knew well not to argue over my drinking.

"Sorry," I said. She blinked surprise.

I went to the kitchen and filled a glass with ice as I poured a double Chivas Regal. Returning to the front room I turned on the phonograph, seeking solace in classical music. A scratchy version of Beethoven's Fifth Symphony squealed a prelude of rumbling drums. Clutching my glass, I looked at my fingers turning white. A mask of fury hid my loss of innocence in a world which should not exist.

"I guess experience provides many lessons in life, not all of them positive," I philosophized.

"It does," Cassie agreed. "Sean, you always think people are better than they are. You have to develop a tough hide in your job if you're going to survive."

"You're probably right. I wish I could."

"To you life is classical music, jazz, opera, art and nice people."

"I can't change."

"Then you're in the wrong profession." Cassie had peeked into the future.

My head jerked. "Enough of this. The Gateway Singers are featured at the Hungry I with Professor Corey, the world's greatest authority. What do you say, Pal?"

14

"HEAR NO EVIL"

HEAR NO EVIL,
SEE NO EVIL,
SPEAK NO EVIL.*

(*Legend relating to the "Three Wise Monkeys" carved over the door of Sacred Stable, Nikko Japan, 17th Century.)

A ROUSING RENDITION OF "DON'T BURY ME IN my Overalls" filled the night air as we walked down the stairs to Banducci's basement bistro. The Hungry I, on a misty Saturday night, became our Mecca for G.B. Shaw's "Brandy of the dammed." A balm to salve the wounds of the week.

Lloyd and Carole joined us for another San Francisco evening at the Jackson street club. Folk songs, ballads and spirituals for the beatniks rang throughout the room. The Gateway Singers were accompanied by a distinguished group of jazz men. Now enshrined in a mythical San Francisco Pantheon of jazz music are such luminaries as Lu Watters, Turk Murphy, Kid Ory, Red Calendar and Thad Vandan, to name a few.

The ensemble had just finished their second set with "Sally Don't You Grieve," when Professor Irwin Corey, the world's greatest authority appeared. True to form, Corey supplied laughs aplenty. He had a unique brand of humor and was blessed with perfect timing. Nothing was sacred to him. He took on the Babbits and the Elmer Gantrys of the 1950's.

Hair dripping over his forehead, torn baggy pants and a yellow print tie, flopping back and forth, punctuated his irreverent satire and quick wit. Cassie tried to suppress fits of giggling. The wee hours of the morning were wrapped up with a rowdy rendition of "The Rock Island Line."

"Let's have a nightcap at Pierre's," Astin suggested. He stubbed out a cigarette. We walked the three blocks, arm in arm, to Banducci's newest creation on Broadway.

AS THE DAYS PASSED, THE SHIP OF OUR MARRIED LIFE stabilized on calm seas. Cassie became the anecdote to the poisons of prison work. The feeling of being protected and cherished gave me warmth. The occasional frustrations of counseling caused silent dinners followed by Cassie asking, "What's wrong, Sean?"

"Oh nothing, Cassie."

"Well, something's bothering you."

I mouthed the familiar, "I don't want to dump on you, but." Every tale condemned a value system to the garbage can of immorality. My reflections of the day ended with, "I will never understand why people behave the way they do. The things they do to each other are unbelievable."

"That's just the way the world is, Sean," Cassie advised.

The next morning, I bellowed to Officer Gonzales, "Who's first?"

"Jeff Conklin, involuntary manslaughter. On his way."

"Okay." I drummed my fingers on the desk while staring at the elephants in the circus poster picture. I read the yellow jacket.

Jeff Conklin, Salinas, California, involuntary manslaughter, indeterminate sentence of ten to twelve years, married, age thirty five, two step-children, truck driver, tenth grade education, no hobbies.

"Have a seat, Conklin," I ordered.

He stood in the doorway, a tall man, over six feet, in prison blues. His head was held down in obeisance; his hands hung at his sides. Hairy arms were connected by excess knobs of bone. Flecks of silver glittered at his temples.

"Yes, Sir." His soft voice bespoke a self-effacing personality quite in contrast to his rugged features. Frequent coughing and throat clearing betrayed a man trying to control himself. You could see he had gone to pieces, or maybe he'd always been in pieces.

I shuffled papers, using the bureaucratic approach to the interview. Or did I simply want to impress myself?

"You have been committed to the California Correctional system for an indeterminate sentence of ten to fifteen years."

Conklin was well aware of his sentence. "What about..." He was going to say "parole" when I interrupted.

"The purpose of this interview is to review your test scores, look at your adjustment to incarceration, and determine minimum, medium, or maximum security." I droned on for several minutes, finding the technique of a bureaucrat uncomfortable.

191

"I didn't mean to do it," he said.

"What?"

"Hurt the boy." I recognized a desire to articulate. Conklin found an audience in me.

"I dropped out of school in the tenth grade when my girl friend got pregnant. We married and had a boy, Jeff Junior. I found a job that paid pretty good, driving trucks long distance. For a time we were happy. To make the big money I took on long hauls. The money is good as an independent trucker, if you can stay awake. Soon, we bought a new house on the outskirts of Salinas. I also made payments on my rig. It was all silver and shiny." Conklin paused.

"At first Heather didn't seem to mind my long absences. She seemed to be a good mother." I pushed an ashtray toward Conklin as he lit a cigarette. Smoke rings drifted to the ceiling. My eyes focused on his ill-fitting dentures stained yellow with nicotine.

"I came home late one night and Heather wasn't there. The babysitter said she was at the local bar. I ran over to the Roundup and caught her dancing with a stranger. I yelled at her, 'What are you doing here?' The guy she was dancing with was a weasely little man with a scraggly beard and 'Mother' tattooed in red and blue on his right arm."

Conklin paused to stare at the circus picture poster. Most patient/inmates identified with elephants holding each other's tales and walking in a straight line. He picked up his story.

"Everyone had stopped dancing and formed a circle around us. Heather looked at me and hollered, 'No, Jeff, don't!' She made a futile attempt to keep me away. I put the guy in the hospital and the next day my wife moved out. I got custody of our boy but she had visiting rights. I don't know why the judge gave her the right to see my boy. She missed a few weekends."

Conklin continued his monologue. "I continued making long hauls across the country. I took Jeff Junior to New York one summer. Finally I met Sharon. She had two kids by a previous marriage and they seemed to get along fine with my boy."

Conklin chained smoked another cigarette. "Every time I came home Sharon complained about his behavior. Her kids could do no wrong, though." he said. I drained the last of my coffee.

"Then one evening I got home early. I was dog tired, hoping for a little TLC. Sharon met me at the door and announced, 'You've got to do something with Junior. The school counselor called. He wants us to come in tomorrow.' I asked her what had happened and she just said how he was always getting into trouble at school and at home. She said I had to do something about it.

"Then the door banged open and Jeff Junior walked in. He said 'Hi, Dad. When did you get home?' He ran over to me and jumped on my lap. He was a towhead, all arms and legs still. He'd just turned twelve. Anyway, Sharon snarled something about him always being late for dinner and how she ought to just not feed him to teach him a lesson." Conklin slowly caressed the large buckle on his belt, lost in his memories.

"Then I proceeded to throttle the boy into the next world. Sharon's children ran screaming out of the room. She stayed, though, and a little smirk crossed her face. I kicked and lashed the boy in a frenzy of rage. My frustration increased as I hit him in the ribs and pounded his head with my belt buckle.

"He managed to cry out, 'No, Daddy, no!' He tried to get out of my grip. Finally Sharon yelled 'That's enough!' She seemed kind of dazed, standing there like she'd been shot or something." Conklin took a long draw on his cigarette before continuing his story.

"Finally I threw the belt on the floor and sat down. 'My God! What have I done?' I said" His eyes took on a wounded look. "Then Sharon said 'I'm calling the police,' and ran to the phone."

Conklin said, "He was a nice boy. We had such good times together. I guess we won't go fishing anymore."

My client stood up to leave. I saw tears cascading down cheeks of red. "I murdered my own boy," he stammered as he walked out of my office.

I contemplated the vagaries of human behavior for a few minutes then walked the "Street" to the lunch room. Fred Janus was there sipping a cup of coffee. Sunlight beamed shadows through the bars, tending to silhouette a cell from inside the prison. Was God trying to tell me something?

"You wouldn't believe the session I just had with a truck driver." I retold Conklin's story, adding layers of emotion with my theatrics.

"Don't worry. You'll get the hang of it." Janus walked out.

That afternoon I interviewed a drug dealer. I was falling behind schedule so I wanted to hurry this session. After I read the yellow jacket, I launched into my philosophy of the drug scene with Harry "The Horse" Zenter.

"The thought that drugs can be beneficial is a dangerous one," I began. "Society objects. The waste of human resources is phenomenal. Look for the answers within yourself not dope."

Rule No. 5—never philosophize or debate with a patient concerning his crime.

Harold Zenter, also known as "Harry the Horse," was aware of his second-to-none intellectual acumen and as he pondered my words, made himself comfortable in an uncomfortable chair. I anticipated a thought provoking discussion. After all, the yellow jacket included two counts of possession of heroin, one count of possession of marijuana exceeding six ounces, three counts of distribution in or near a public school, and one count possession of an unregistered firearm.

He had received an indeterminate sentence of three to five years. Age twenty nine, single, two years graduate work in Sociology at the University of California, Berkeley, his hobbies included classical music and anthropology. He had scored in the ninety percentile on the MMPI (Minnesota Multiphasic Personality Inventory), and eighty five percentile on the SVIB (Strong Vocational Interest Battery.)

"Ordinarily they don't give the MMPI or SVIB to newly committed patients. Just the Wide Range Achievement Test and/or the Kuder Preference Test," I said.

"Yes, I know. The Kuder is designed for people with less than a college education," he responded.

"What's a guy like you doing in a place like this?" I asked. Fascinated by the young man, I enjoyed a conversation worthy of a college bull session in the student coffee shop. The patient possessed a personality Dale Carnegie, of "How to Win Friends and Influence People" fame, would have been proud.

"You appear to be conversant with tests and inventories," I went on. Impressed with Zenter's credentials, I expressed my curiosity with a little sermon. "You're an intelligent young man. You know drugs are illegal, as well as harmful to your health and well being. Why spend your life in this or any other joint? You'll only come to no good if you continue this lifestyle. You will experience the depths of degradation." I steepled my hands together in a reverent pose.

He took a deep breath, morphing into a teacher explaining the facts of life to a schoolboy. "Your dogma is inconsistent with the cynicism you express," he said.

"What cynicism?" I asked. Ignoring my question, Zenter continued.

"Doing drugs on a casual basis is not seeking a cure to anything; it's just like playing softball on a Saturday afternoon. I don't smoke marijuana very often anymore. It doesn't make you stupid, unless you spend all day every day stoned out of your mind."

"But you deal to school kids," I pointed out.

"Business is business. If I didn't, someone else would."

"You might be eligible for Federal and state financed training and/or education programs. The state and the Feds offer all kinds of programs."

"Why should I go on welfare for three hundred dollars a month when I can make five hundred a day pushing dope?"

"You got me there," I said.

"Clearly you have never done any hallucinogens. In my humble opinion, the experience is important to every thinking person's education. It opens you to a broader consciousness, expands your insights. Read Huxley, read any of the Fabulists of the last thirty years. Even the post-Freudian psychoanalytic philosophers will give you a perception of the possible," he said.

"You know, the skeptic in me wonders if you're a true zealot for your cause, or if it's just the money talking," I responded.

"Money talks, of course," he admitted. "But you're not ranting against drug use so much as serious addiction and morality in particular. Using marijuana does not rob you of consciousness, does not distract your attention, or do any of the other hogwash things you mention. It's just fun and it sets you to looking at the world in a slightly eccentric way."

I retorted, "To me, life is a blast without drugs. Sure there are good days and bad days. But I believe doing drugs to be among the most dangerous fads in vogue. The American character, as portrayed in the history of the West, is fast disappearing. Is this hyperbole?" I wanted to rest my case but the patient continued the debate.

"Surely the Krushchevs, the Batistas and the Hitler imitators of the world are of more concern than the so-called drug problem. Intolerant Fundamentalism and the Civil War, which we are still fighting in this country between blacks and whites, between the rich and the poor, and our futile attempts to be the policeman of the world, should be of greater concern." Harry "The Horse" Zenter smiled at having scored more points.

195

"But people are unwilling to take responsibility for their actions. This is an essential element in the makeup of the American character," I replied.

"Casual drugs are just that. If people kill themselves over them, don't blame the individual consumer. There are plenty of people out there who smoke marijuana, shoot heroin, smoke opium, heat up coke, drink moderately, and do hallucinogenics. But they don't threaten the fabric of our society as much as fundamentalist Christians or Jews or Muslims."

"I still say the idea that drugs can be beneficial is dangerous. We're always looking for cures. With drugs, the problem is a spiritual one, whether it be boredom or grief or physical pain. I had six surgeries on my back and legs before I was fifteen. I never took a pain killer. It symbolized defeat to me," I said. I shifted my weight to ease the pain in my legs.

"Smoking marijuana, having a scotch and soda, or having sex are in no way escapes for personal responsibility. And don't tell me that legalizing drugs would take the profits out of peddling and reduce crime."

"I won't, but it would. Strange as it may seem, coming from me, the only argument in favor of continuing this costly and bloody drug war may be more people would use drugs if they were decriminalized. Otherwise, the pleading for legalization must be simple and to the point," he said with conviction.

"Ten years of teaching, guidance and counseling has left me empty. For every mile I walk, I lose two in the quick sand of illiteracy, illogic and ill-gotten gains. Drugs make people dumber, unable to learn. They encourage apathy and irresponsibility." I wanted to end the interview.

"What about the Civil War going on today?" Zenter persisted.

"Well, I think it's a plot to kill the blacks by flooding their neighborhoods with all kinds of drugs. Drugs rob the user of a little bit of consciousness with every use," I answered.

"Repressive sentences will never stop crime," Zenter noted.

"Drugs can be found people's bones twenty years after their last use. Drugs drain our resources, distract our attention. Drugs reduce society's ability to handle the big problems."

"And what are the big problems?" Harry asked.

I didn't answer for a moment. "If your house is burning down and you're so stoned you don't even notice the flames, don't you wonder about the use of drugs?"

Zenter peered down his nose at me. "Using drugs doesn't mean getting so smashed you don't notice the fire. I think the only people you've ever seen using drugs must be totally whacked out. Would you ban alcohol like those Prohibition fools in the 1920's to prevent the abuses of the addictive class?" He started to leave the office.

"I feel like a voice in the wilderness," I said.

"Well, unfortunately, you're not. You're in the majority. Probably the reason you feel all alone out there is that you're screaming so loud you can't hear all of your brothers screaming just as loudly."

Trying to staying in control, I proclaimed, "I enjoy a good bottle of wine or a glass of Chevas Regal now and then, but I don't get so sloshed I loll in the gutter, pissing in my pants like some beatnik wino!" As an afterthought, I added, "I will always be for education over legislation."

Beelzebub made an appearance in the form of Harry "The Horse" Zenter. "There is too much Puritanism going on in our society for anyone's good," he proclaimed.

He gave me a sidelong glance as he walked out of my office. The gladiators of good and evil retreated to their respective lifestyles, each feeling content that he had won the battle.

I took a copy of the <u>San Francisco Chronicle</u> out of my desk drawer. Turning to page two I read, "Drug Legalization Movement Makes Gains. The drug legalization movement has been making significant gains in the last several months in spite of electoral losses and allies in the Eisenhower administration."

I put the paper down and picked up Zenter's file. A piece of paper fell to the floor. Bits and pieces of something were always falling out of yellow jackets. I read,

<u>*Urine Nation*</u>
Urine, Urine Nation.
We have become a Urine Nation.
Drug tests on parole, drug tests on the job.
All this has encouraged me to become a drunken slob.
I cannot eat a poppy bagel, or take a puff of pot.
So I drink my Jack Daniels straight,
My brain and liver's shot."
By Nkrumah Fubar
(Parolee in New York City)
Copyright <u>Prison Life</u> magazine, 1995.

Gonzales interrupted my meditations. "Mr. Sullivan, they want you in the art room. It's at the other end of the joint. Go to the street, turn right, then walk about three blocks. It's a long way."

"That's okay by me. I'm getting claustrophobia in here—no windows. I feel like an assistant coach of something. They never have windows." I walked to the art room deep in the prison. Several "Hi, how are you's?" greeted me along the way.

I speculated on the pros and cons of a career in penology. Despite Zenter's elocution of the drug scene, I felt good. He hadn't penetrated my moral armor.

"Good afternoon, everybody," I called out as I entered the room. My forced cheerfulness failed to elicit a response. Six patients mentally diagnosed the "new guy." Their instant analyses was confirmed and conclusions drawn.

CO Henderson and his minions passed by me in single file, each offering a vigorous handshakes. "We've been expecting you, Mr. Sullivan," he said. Henderson seemed like a man to whom I could bond.

A patient pushed his face into mine. "Would you like some coffee and cookies, Mr. Sullivan? Or would you prefer tea?" he asked. One look at his toothless grin caused me to slide over to Mr. Henderson for protection. The patient scurried over to a large coffee urn, filling a mug labeled "Property of California Medical Facility" in gold flecked gothic script. A good example of California's efforts to rehabilitate the dammed.

I balanced myself against a desk while holding a cup of coffee and a small plate of brownies. We all engaged in a few minutes of trivial chit chat. My eyes scanned the art room. It's overall décor seemed like a huge fading portrait in silhouette outlining the good guys gone bad. Cassie's art commentaries had given me a slight knowledge of Shakespeare's "A Pretty Mocking of Life." I often referred to her fellow artists as the "artsy fartsy gang."

Officer Henderson, a small man, pale and wrinkled in the twilight of his years, looked the fatherly type who enjoyed his work. A mother hen by nature, the CO reveled in his student's victories at the annual art show. It was opened to the public once a year, from twelve noon to four p.m., Saturday and Sunday. No strollers or children under the age of sixteen. please.

"All right, boys," Henderson began. "I have only four spatulas. One is missing. You know it's closing time."

He turned to me. "They get a little playful now and then," he laughed. "Spatulas make an excellent shiv as you can see."

A search for the missing weapon began. I surveyed the patients. I saw sheepish grins and giggles all around the room.

"Nobody leaves until we find the spatula," Officer Henderson boomed.

"Mr. Sullivan, we would like you to award first, second and third place," he announced. "Here, place these ribbons above the paintings you favor." He added, "Go ahead. Just take your time."

A patient approached me sporting the usual tattoo, earring and broken nose. Yard fight no doubt. Through his drooping mustache a voice blared, "I am me. I am unique." I thought it was an attempt to escape his world and join mine. A few days later he was forced to shave the soup strainer. Prison rules.

"Would you like me to show you our little studio?" he asked.

"Sure," I replied calmly. My brief experience as a correctional counselor had taught me to expect the unexpected. The patient led me on a personalized tour through a maze of art paraphernalia and people. Students holding easels, paint boxes on the floor, an assortment of tubes scattered here and there, sketchbooks, oil paintings, charcoal drawings, water colors on the stands and on the walls, and a collection of various scraps all made up the clutter one would expect in an art studio.

There were seascapes, landscapes, cloud scapes, river scapes, exterior and interior. All kinds of escapes. My eye caught a large oil in a burnished sheen of sepia and brownish yellow.

"This is my dream," my guide said. He picked up a painting and held it aloft as in victory.

"Beautiful, wonderful," I said. At a loss for words, I continued my examination.

"It is a triumph of light emulating the luminous magic of Rembrandt," my guide explained. "And I say this in all modesty." The canvas was a self-portrait depicting the patient as a bodily spirit floating past correctional officers through a gate on his way to heaven. A chained inmate nearby applauded the escape.

Officer Henderson joined us in viewing the painting. "To me it shows the horror of prison as expressed by the young patient bound in chains between two CO's," I said.

A second patient elbowed his way to my side. "The shining splendor of the angel in the dark shadows of the night brings out the details. When you look at the picture, it lights up your face," he said.

"The prisoner looks like you," I said to my guide.

"It is. I come out of prison accompanied by an angel as if this were all a dream rather than reality."

"You'll notice the CO with a flashlight waking the other patients," Officer Henderson pointed out.

"What the flashlight does not touch, the light of the moon does," murmured the second patient.

"I tried to paint different night effects competing with the living light. I wanted to show the vapors of the flashlight, the splendor of the angel, and the dark shadow of the night." My guide critiqued his own work.

"It's all so real and natural. It doesn't seem like a painting in the usual sense of the definition," I opined.

"Definitely first place," patient number three chimed in.

To the everlasting joy of the patient artist, I pinned the blue ribbon to the top of the picture frame. My action was met with a flickering of applause. I continued my stroll around the room, tailgated by the student artists.

A patient held another painting in my face. "This represents Art Nouveau or new art. Notice the riot of disjointed colors in the water color splashing before us."

"Picasso hallucinating," I branded the offering.

"How about this one?" Officer Henderson pointed to a framed charcoal.

"It looks like the ash can movement to me," patient number three sneered.

Patient number one held up an oil. "What we have here is what is known in the art world as a classical abstraction. Notice the balance of colors," he pointed out.

"Personally, I think it's early Salvador Dali," patient number three suggested.

"Well, I think it's 'between a thought and a thing,' as Coleridge might say," I commented. I delighted in misquotes.

"What have we here? I haven't seen this painting before." Officer Henderson picked up a framed oil from the floor.

"I just finished it this morning, Mr. Henderson," explained patient number three.

"Must be psychedelic," I suggested. "I detect the fine hand of a beatnik."

"Well, it is mind expanding." Number three added, "Just like mace or a hot pot of inhalers."

I failed to appreciate his remark. I finished my rounds and pinned a red ribbon on an oil for second place. A white ribbon placed over a pencil drawing indicated my choice for third place. My duty done, I started back to the office.

"Good news, Mr. Sullivan. We found the missing spatula," the CO said. Officer Henderson waved the instrument high for all to see. Looking straight at one patient, the gray haired den mother taunted his charge. "Naughty, naughty Jose. I don't want to have to put you on report."

In the summer of 1964, I would have the opportunity to visit the Vatican in Rome, Italy. After an exhausting walk through a maze of museums, alcoves and libraries, my eye caught a Raphael. Labeled "The Deliverance of St. Peter," it looked strangely familiar.

On my return to the counseling center, I encountered security people scurrying towards me on the "street." I stopped the Lieutenant of the watch.

"What's going on here?" I asked.

Lieutenant Joe Santee, Jr. yelled, "Murder! Talk to you later." He ran in the opposite direction towards the art room. By the time I reached my office a buzz of conversation could be heard up and down the street.

"What happened?" Elliot asked.

"Who did it?" Officer Gonzales pushed into our circle.

"Why?" I asked.

"Oh, don't be naïve, Sean. Although oral sex is perfectly acceptable between consenting partners, it's a no-no in the joint," Fred Janus explained.

The prison telegraph enjoyed it's finest hour. The details of the deed were known by all by the time I arrived at the counseling center.

"One patient tied up another patient. With a shiv in hand, he proceeded to perform surgery without benefit of anesthesia. Throat to pubic hair," Jack Barr explained.

"I've never heard of such a thing," I said.

"Didn't you just come from the art room?" Barr asked.

"Yes, why?"

"Well, the murder took place next door in a supply closet," Janus answered. I held back vomit.

"So that's what happened to the missing spatula. Someone used it while I was judging the contest and returned it before I left the room."

When I recounted the day's activities to Cassie after supper that evening, she said, "I'm glad you waited to tell that story until dinner was over." And then, "I think the prison is getting to you, Sean."

"You have to admit it's an interesting way to make a living. Tomorrow I'm going to ask for a transfer to San Quentin. At least it's closer to home."

"That sounds good to me," she said. "What do you think your chances are?"

"I don't' know, but it doesn't cost anything to ask." I answered. "So, what's new?"

"Well, the gang is going to join us Saturday night at Easy Street."

"What gang?"

"The Jackson Street Irregulars, as you call them. Maggie, Marge, Richard and Scott. Turk Murphy is on vacation but Kid Ory and his Creole Jazz band are taking over for two weeks."

That Saturday night we joined our friends at a large table facing the band. The godfather of Creole Jazz, Kid Ory, shuffled his seventy-one year old skinny frame onto the stage. The combo included Thomas Jefferson on trumpet, Gene Cedric on piano, Bobby Oldban on drums, and Bill Shay on clarinet. Charlie Odim, the bass man, strolled to the bandstand behind the Kid.

The group opened with "Yamma Yamma Man," a bluesy number much appreciated by the generous audience. Rousing renditions of "Basin Street Blues" and "Memphis Blues" followed. The set ended with a moving "Gettysburg March."

To no one in particular, I mused, "My father would have enjoyed the last selection. He could, after a libation or two, dance a Southern shuffle second to none. The old man departed this veil of tears in 1971, loyal to a Confederacy which no longer existed."

The night closed with a magnificently moving performance of "Just A Closer Walk With Thee," Joe Watkins on lead vocals.

My love of Jazz would be revived in the summer of 1986 when the Preservation Jazz Hall Band toured Honolulu, Hawaii. Sitting in the front row, a burned-out teacher, I would experience bittersweet memories of Cassie as the band began "Just A Closer Walk With Thee."

My thoughts were broken by Cassie squeezing my shoulder. "Sean, I'd like you to meet Peggy Tolkin. You remember, she owns that club, the Tin Angel, on the Embarcadero."

"Sure, I remember. My pleasure, Ma'am" I shook hands with the short blondish lady of thirty-something standing before me. Our fragile friendship was cemented. We parted after a few minutes of trivial chit chat.

"Give us a call. We're in the phone book." Cassie said.

"Drop by the club anytime," Tolkin countered. Then she leaned over and whispered, "Confidentially folks, I think Kid Ory may buy the Angel." Index finger over her lips signaled a secret. She disappeared into the vapors of the night.

"We should have offered her a ride home," I said belatedly.

"Oh, no. She can take care of herself. Peggy also acts as bouncer at the club. She's a tough lady."

"There's something about her," I mused.

"Peggy has been trying to sell the Tin Angel. She had a deal but the buyer reneged. It was in the Chron last week."

"Where did you meet her?"

"At the Koffee Kup. We also had a chat in the ladies' room just now."

"That's nice. Lets go home."

Cassie and Peggy Token would be roommates at the Napa State Hospital several years later, along with Carole.

Four days later Ted Jefferson, my supervisor at CMF, invited Cassie and I to dinner. "Bring the missus," he said.

"I don't know what she has planned for Saturday night, if anything," I said.

That evening I discussed the invitation with Cassie. "He's black, you know," I pointed out.

"So what, Sean? This is 1959 not 1859. I thought our little stay at Jackson Street had opened your eyes."

"Well, I was kinda getting the hang of the beat generation. But it's hard to adjust to different cultures."

"Just tell him we will be happy to accept his kind invitation," she said.

That Saturday evening we parked in a section of Vallejo labeled ghetto by those who lived elsewhere. Welcomed by my supervisor, we were introduced to his wife and children. His kids soon disappeared. I had been afraid of a resurrection of "Uncle Sean."

My inhibitions disappeared as Cassie joined Althea Jefferson in the kitchen. The women interrupted our analysis of the football season by placing plates of barbecued chicken, beans cooked in molasses, corn bread and mashed potatoes before us. On the way home I declared the evening a success.

"Yes, they're nice people," Cassie agreed. "It was fun." She mouthed, "I told you so."

The following Monday morning, Jefferson walked back to my office with me after the staff meeting. "Have you ever observed a group therapy session?" he asked.

"No, I haven't," I admitted. "It's something I should do soon since Mr. Carruthers and Dr. Kloss are both big on group therapy."

"Dr. Kloss, the superintendent, put great effort into promoted the funding for this institution. He's considered a pioneer in modern penology. And Dr. Kloss views law breakers as sick people and treats them accordingly. That's why we refer to them as patients not inmates," Jefferson explained.

"He may have a point," I said. I tried to keep up with Jefferson.

"Do you have anyone scheduled this morning," he asked.

"No, not yet."

"There's a therapy session set for ten thirty. Officer Gonzales will give you an escort." We parted.

By the time I arrived at the conference room, institution personnel were clustered in little groups according to rank, engaged in a buzz of chatter. I entered the large theater-style room which easily seated seventy-five to a hundred people. Austrian style curtains concealing the stage reminded me of the Paramount theater in Portland.

I had no idea what to expect as I found an empty seat in the back of the room. Blending in with the decor gave me a sense of security. The house lights dimmed as the curtains slowly raised. I expected a silver screen to descend at any moment followed by a popular "Looney Tunes" of the day.

A well-lit stage showcased eight patients seated in a semi circle. They sat on straight back chairs with the leader in the center. To my surprise, Jack Barr officiated as the moderator. It was his job to guide rather than direct; to stimulate and prod.

At first, I thought it would be like any other bull session except that the patients came to understand their purpose. They did not waste time on idle conversation. One man, doing time for assault with a deadly weapon, was anxious to get talking before the group was even seated.

"Should I take what people say to me seriously?" he asked.

Tony, a twenty seven year old murderer, laughed. "Just don't take anybody seriously," he said. "When a guy says something you don't like, just figure he doesn't mean it. Or maybe he doesn't mean it in the way it sounds to you." He concluded, "I used to get tied up in the belly, but now I just figure it's only words."

James, the man who asked the question, wasn't satisfied. The group followed the conversation with interest, all except the dark haired man who sat to one side. A sex offender. He stared at the floor.

"I don't really mean what I said," James pleaded. "Everything is okay, then you see the guy on the main line. You get a the knot in the stomach.

A husky young fellow who looked like a lifeguard on the beach interrupted. "You've been going out of your way to get sore at people ever since you've been here, James."

A long silence followed, broken by Jack Barr. "How about it, James?"

"Maybe so," James answered. "When I came here I hated everybody."

"That's a lot of hate, James," Barr said.

"Yeah," the man replied. "I even hated you, Mr. Barr." He looked for peer approval from his fellow patients. "Imagine hating a guy like Mr. Barr here."

"Well, we're all human. Maybe you thought you had a reason for hating me," Barr commented evenly.

"Yeah, I guess I did," said James. "But now I don't hate so many people.

Barr turned to the sex offender, "How do you feel today?"

"All right," said Eugene. It was the first time he had said anything in the month he had been attending the group sessions. "What I want to know is, why we don't have groups of all one kind, like one group of all sex offenders?" he asked.

"I'll tell you why," said the lifeguard. "Because it's better to have all different kinds of men in a group. It helps to show that all people are alike." He paused. "Take me. I'm a child molester, but I find many of the guys think I would do anything."

"You got it made in this joint," said Bill. He was doing twenty-five to life.

"I got it made, do I? I don't get pains in the belly at everyone." The lifeguard's voice rose sharply. "I'll tell the truth to anyone who asks me right. And if a man can't understand, I just won't waste time talking to him. That's all. Nobody's going to push me."

"What do you think, Pete?" Barr asked the elder statesman of the group.

"I think we should form a group made up of intelligent men so you can learn something of yourself. In the process you can change and improve. Most men doing time want to change. They just don't know how to make the change," he said. I labeled Pete as going along with the program.

The session continued to probe for answers to human understanding and conduct. Tony spoke eloquently of young black men having no sense of direction. "Black people oughta accept responsibility for their actions. Let's be honest. It's on us to change. It's not the government's responsibility."

Wilbert, who has already done eighteen years of his twenty to life said, "Black people can get on the radio and use the words 'nigger' and 'bitch.' To me it's serious. If you think white people are going to stop calling us 'niggers' and 'bitches,' you're crazy. We have to stop degrading ourselves."

Pete, the elder statesman, joined the conversation. "We created the problems. It's up to us to stop this."

Eugene added, "The world only stops for courageous people. These are the people who deserve our respect."

I observed occasional asperity, some laughter, and much bantering, with surprisingly little profanity. All of the group smoked cigarettes except Barr and the narcotics user. In time, the curtains lowered and the audience dispersed. I waited for Barr on the main line.

"Hello, Sean." Mr. Carruthers startled me by appearing out of nowhere. "Well, what do you think of group therapy? Think you could handle a session?" he asked.

Evading his question I said, "I can't make up my mind if it's Freud's 'talk therapy' or something new."

"A rose by any other name." My supervisor took note of my failure to answer his second question.

"Hi, everybody." Jack Barr was smiling when he joined us. The three of us headed back to the counseling center.

"Mr. Sullivan and I we were discussing the value of group sessions," Carruthers explained.

"Let's stop for coffee," Barr suggested. He added, "Mr. Sullivan is contemplating taking a group session."

"I stood in front of a classroom for a year so I guess I can handle a small session," I said.

"Therapy groups are a step toward change. I think we've found a way to break the cycle of violence." Barr leaned back in his chair.

Mr. Carruthers relit his pipe. "If the public could observe our program they would see it's a positive way to diminish the punitive attitudes perpetuating violence," he said. "Prison doesn't have to be just a warehouse where bodies are stowed. It can be a place for rehabilitation, a place where men can transform themselves so they can return to the community. They're ought to be a program like this in every prison."

"I agree," Barr said. "The present system is going nowhere. I'm not saying men shouldn't be incarcerated and punished for their crimes, but they shouldn't just be discarded and forgotten."

Carruthers finished his coffee. "I've witnessed some heart rendering transformations over the last few years. Men on whom society has given up are achieving insight, proving anyone can change in the right setting."

I ventured in. "Group therapy is a beacon of light, but we have to remember the quality of our character is more in what we do than what we say."

Carruthers turned to Barr. "Good news, Jack. You've been promoted to assistant supervisor at the counseling center in San Quentin. They want to talk to you Wednesday morning. Take Sean with you. Consider it a field trip for the day."

"Congratulations, Jack!" Turning to Carruthers, I added, "And thank you. I would like to see the joint."

"Sullivan, you might make a good penologist some day, if you're headed in that direction." Carruthers walked away.

"Sean, I'll meet you outside the main gate of San Quentin at nine Wednesday morning. There's no need to come here first," Barr suggested.

"Okay. You know, I left my request for transfer on Mr. Carruther's just desk this morning while he was out," I said. "No guts. Couldn't face him."

"He may not take kindly to the idea. I think he likes you." Barr replied.

"The eighty mile commute is getting to me. Besides it's expensive. And Cassie won't move to Vacaville," I complained.

"I know what you mean. See you Wednesday morning."

When supper was over that evening, I went into some detail explaining group therapy. Cassie's attention wandered. "Sean. I'm tired. I think I'll go to bed early," she said.

"Okay. I am going to watch a little TV." I flipped the knob to Channel Five. On the black and white screen slowly rolled the words, "Zane Grey Theater, presented by General Electric. Tonight's feature, 'The Ghost,' starring Mel Ferrer. Your host, Ronald Reagen."

"Tell you what, Cassie. How about dinner tomorrow night at the Chinese restaurant on Grant? You know, where they have clay pot porridge."

"Okay, I'll meet you there at six.."

I kissed her, briefly at first and then, when she made no attempt to draw away, more persistently. My desires became urgent and demanding. We let the past drift away like the sands of time.

"Let's go to bed," I whispered. That night we had old memories but young hopes.

After work the next day, I enjoyed the pleasure of Cassie's company at the Bow How Grant Street restaurant. We ordered steaming bowls of porridge accompanied by Chinese doughnuts. Clay pot cooking, usually found in Southeastern China, was a specialty of the house. It was easily digested.

"How was your day?" Cassie smiled.

In between gulps I answered, "Great. Jack Barr and I are going to meet at San Quentin tomorrow morning. He's been promoted to assistant counseling supervisor there."

"There goes your car pool."

"Maybe not," I said.

"Sean, you know I'm not moving to Vacaville. I love San Francisco. All my friends are here." She gazed into her chicken porridge seeking solace from the restraints of life.

"Okay, okay. I think my chances are good for a transfer. Mr. Carruthers isn't too happy with the idea, but I like the Bay Area," I said reassuringly.

After dinner we walked to upper Broadway, stopping in front of "The House That Jack Built." The garish exterior in greens, red and brown put me off but we ventured into a den of adventure. The small audience was made up of couples and singles scattered throughout the room. A waiter appeared from out of nowhere once we were seated. Cassie ordered the usual white wine and I had a scotch and soda.

"Do you like opera?" our waiter asked.

"He does," Cassie said, pointing at me.

"I love it," I seconded the thought.

"My name is Guiseppi—Joe to you. And this is my wife, Giovanna." He waved a dark-haired young woman over to our table. Joe disappeared for a few minutes while we visited with Giovanna.

I recapped the day's activities. "I think my chances of getting transferred to San Quentin are good. I'm going to meet Barr there tomorrow morning."

"Who would want to work in a prison?" Giovanna commented. She huffed her way back to the kitchen.

"Oh, Sean, I sure hope they'll accept you." Cassie uttered a girlish chuckle.

Joe reappeared with a guitar. Joined by Giovanna, they serenaded us with well known operatic arias. Their voices blended in some lovely duets. His bell-like tenor rejoiced in perfect pitch to "O Solo Mio" and

Puccini's "Turnadot." Next Joe sang the clown song from "Vesti la Giubba." It was the perfect finale to an evening I would remember into the sunset of my life.

"It's getting late, Sean," Cassie finally prompted. We walked out on to Broadway into the night air and headed back to the parking lot. On the way, we stopped in front of "The Visuvio." It was an odd looking building. A large yellow sign on top of the building proclaimed in brown letters, "I wish I were in Portland, Oregon."

Peeking in the window I declared, "Weird. It looks like a beat hangout to me." I started to walk away. Cassie kept looking.

"Look at the hanging baskets. You can sit in them! And the walls are covered with psychedelic paintings and poetry," Cassie squealed. "Oh, let's have a nightcap," she pleaded.

"You've had enough to drink," I admonished.

Cassie dragged me into the Vesuvio. She was immediately taken with a large rattan basket. I sulked in a small booth.

"Evening, folks. What will it be?" A tall slender man in his late twenties, stood over Cassie. We ordered the usual.

"My name is Bruce," the bartender offered. We introduced ourselves. Cassie wandered through the room eyeballing each painting. Bruce engaged her in idle chit chat as she passed by him, oblivious to my stink-eye stares.

Returning to the table she announced, "I can't make any sense out of some of them."

"Who can?" I said. "Come on, let's go," I demanded.

Cassie responded, sulkily. "Okay, if we have to." We drove home in complete silence.

"I'm tired. I'm going to bed," she announced as soon as we got home.

I picked up that morning's <u>Chronicle</u> and turned to Herb Caen. I failed to notice Cassie sitting in the dark end of the room. I heard an almost imperceptible groan followed by soft weeping. Her hand brushed away a tear or two.

"I'm sorry," she said.

"I thought you had gone to bed."

Her sobs shook her shoulders. I sat beside her, my arm around her waist. "What's wrong?" I asked.

The flood gates opened. She blubbered, "I lost my job today."

15

"STAND ASIDE. DEAD MAN COMING"

"I rob the rich to pay the poor,
Which hardly is a sin.
A widow ne'er knocked at my door,
But what I let her in.
So don't blame me for what I done,
I don't deserve your curses,
And if for any cause I'm hung,
Let it be for my verses."*

(*Black Bart, a/k/a C.E. Bolton
Inmate #11046, San Quentin
November 1883-January 1888.)

A SADNESS, THAT HAD BEEN HIDDEN ALL DAY, came bursting to the surface. "Why?" I asked.

"I spilled hot coffee on Jake."

"Jake? Jake who?"

"You know, Jake The Rake."

"Oh God!"

"What's wrong?"

"He's the best known attorney in San Francisco." I proceeded to give Cassie a thumbnail biography.

"He said I ruined his new suit," Cassie moaned.

"Don't worry. We're in pretty good shape money-wise." I kissed her damp cheeks.

We walked the few steps to the day bed in the living room near the stage. Cassie averted her eyes while I undressed and climbed in beside her. When I was done, I turned over and went to sleep. She awoke early the next morning feeling more refreshed than she had been for a long time.

I met Jack Barr in the parking lot at San Quentin promptly at nine. Our ID's were checked. We were escorted through a series of gates leading to a conference room.

Warren Mallachey, newly appointed supervisor of the counseling center, met us at the door. Standing behind him was the prison psychiatrist, David G. Schlicter, M.D. After a cup of coffee, the meeting turned to business.

"Come with me, Jack. I want to explain your new job. Oh, and I think Dr. Schlicter wants to talk with Mr. Sullivan." Mr. Mallachey led Barr out of the room.

Before me sat a square-jawed man in his early fifties with a receding hairline and a pince-nez balanced on the bridge of his nose. Schlicter had Teutonic features, which in no way matched his current hobby, restringing a pawn shop banjo. Many of the free people at Q engaged in hobbies that were in contrast to their prison duties. Anything to take your mind away from the joint.

Schlicter's facial expression shifted from open to uncomfortable to assertive. Too many years probing the mindless depths of the purveyors of atrocities had taken their toll.

"Well, Sullivan," the doctor said, "I understand you want a transfer to this joint." He took off his glasses. Reptilian orbs, cold and dangerous, locked me into a trance I could not break.

This man was my "Open Sesame" to a career at San Quentin and ever lasting happiness with Cassie. His influence was pervasive through out the Department of Corrections. I began to feel ill at ease in his presence.

"Yes, Sir. My wife and I live near the Marina in San Francisco. The eighty-mile commute to Vacaville is getting to me."

"Move to Vacaville," he barked.

Beads of sweat began to form on my forehead. "That would be a good solution, except that Cassie likes San Francisco. And so do I."

"Well, that's your choice. This joint is much different from Vacaville."

"I understand."

My anxieties were increased when the doctor only murmured, "Hmmm." He managed to inject a wealth of doubt into a simple sound. He finally broke the silence with, "I don't think you'd be happy here...Well, I have to go back to work." Then he walked out, tossing a "Nice to meet you" back at me over his shoulder.

Later that evening Cassie listened as I embellished my encounter with Dr. Schlicter. A sense of compassion caused her to "weep with him who weeps."

"What will we do now, Sean? I'm not moving to Vacaville."

"Well, I won't quit my job. I'll just keep on with the commute and hope the car holds together," I said.

"I'm going to look for another job. Maybe it will help." With that, Cassie became her cheerful self again.

"What can you do besides wait tables or serve drinks in a bar? You don't have any job skills." I said.

She glared at me, then turned and made a show of stomping to the kitchen. The clatter of banging pots and pans answered my question. A sleepless night left me short tempered the next day.

"Top of the mornin' to you, Sean Sullivan. And how goes the battle this bright and sunny day?" Jack Barr said.

"Oh, okay, I guess. Another day, another dollar." It was the best I could mutter.

"Uh, oh. The good doctor Schlicter must have given you a bad time. Don't take him seriously. He's been at San Quentin since 1932."

"He must have political influence or knows where the bones are buried," I said.

"Now, now. Mustn't talk that way. Good news; we're here. Our home away from home," he said.

We walked down the Main Street of CMF, encountering Mr. Carruthers "tween gates." "Sorry about Dr. Schlicter, Sean," he said sympathetically. "He's a powerhouse. Just remember, 'The enemy of my enemy is your friend'." I mulled over the proverb for a minute.

"I haven't given up on a transfer," I said.

"Why not take my suggestion and finish a masters in Sociology at Sac State. It may take some time, but it'll be worth the effort. I'm sorry I can't offer you a scholarship or a loan, but I do see a future for you in Penology," he said.

"Thanks, Mr. Carruthers. I appreciate your kind thoughts." I left my supervisor shaking his head.

The buzz of conversation at lunch time centered on congratulations to Barr and condolences to me. Everyone was familiar with Dr. Schlicter's modus operandi.

"Don't give up, Sullivan. Schlicter isn't the last word," Fred Janus offered.

"I'm not."

MY TRANSFER PAPERS ARRIVED EARLY IN APRIL OF 1959.

"They called me with the news a week or so ago. I was going to tell you then, but I wanted to wait for the paperwork." Mr. Carruthers towered over me on a foggy Wednesday afternoon.

"Thank you so much," I said sincerely. "This will make things so much easier."

"Well, I hope it's what you really want, Sean. Sure you won't change your mind and stay here?"

"Yes, it is, and yes, I am. I'll do my best, Sir." We stood up and shook hands. Mr. Carruthers saluted me as I walked out.

Promptly at six o'clock, I walked into our little theater apartment on Steiner Street brimming with the good news. Cassie rubbed the sleep out of her eyes as she awakened from a drowsy half dream.

"Taking afternoon naps now, are we?" I chided.

"I looked for work this morning. I have to transfer twice to get downtown, you know."

She had gotten up and was now standing, hands on hips, prepared to square off in another row. Cassie and I had been sniping at each other for days on end. The frustrations of her job hunting were rendering the seams of our marriage.

"I got my transfer to San Quentin." She rushed into my arms, her eyes now gleaming with joy.

"Now we can settle down to a normal life with a future!" she exclaimed.

"I sure hope so. I start to work Monday."

I reported for duty at San Quentin on April 13, 1959. My ID and car were checked. The hub caps were removed and inspected for contraband.

Prison architecture dating back to the gold rush days, greeted me as I walked toward the gates. Round stone towers with conical roofs and narrow windows, suitable for archers, commanded my attention. My building had a turret at each end with silly crenellations on top dating it pre-Renaissance. A good sixty five feet high, it looked out of place in the potpourri of architecture. The moat was missing. I expected knights of old to appear at the ramparts shouting, "Stand and deliver!"

The pleasant marine vistas of San Pablo Bay facing San Quentin were in contrast to the sweltering stone barrens of Folsom and the heat of Vacaville. The flesh pots of San Francisco and Cassie were now only twenty miles distant. The employee housing in the upper reaches of San Quentin Village gave the place a Southern California resort appearance, much like any suburban neighborhood in America. It is a place of beautiful tree-lined streets with modest homes. The sounds of children can be heard on hot summer days.

The first gate clanked open. "Turn to the right, go to the next station, then take the stairs on the right. Second floor. Mr. Mallachey is expecting you." The turnkey stared at me in curiosity, muttering as I walked by, "This joint is no place for a cripple."

I entered a world of concrete walls and chain-link fences laced with razor wire. I heard loud bells and voices over the PA. A gun tower silhouetted against a blue sky dominated the skyline. A solitary inmate swept the long walk way to the next gate. I climbed the stairs to the counseling center.

"Good morning, Mr. Sullivan. Welcome to San Quentin." Warren Mallachey extended his hand.

"Gentlemen, this is our new counselor Sean Sullivan. Sean, shake hands with Phil Kinser, Chuck Fleming, Mike Weaver and, of course, you already know Jack Barr." I resented being told to shake hands.

We stood in a semi-circle. The mandatory inanities followed. "You married? Where do you live?" And always the zinger, "Any children?" Followed by, "Do you think you'll like San Quentin?"

"I don't know. It looks interesting," I answered.

"Harley Teets said 'San Quentin is a blindfolded elephant lumbering along the edge of a precipice'," Mallachey quoted.

"Who's Harley Teets?" I inquired.

"The former Warden. He died on the job two years ago. Heart attack."

I did an eyeball analysis of my colleagues.

Kinser, tall and slim, with aquiline features, got his way by smiling. Deeply attached to the refinements of San Francisco, he fancied stylish clothes and his stunning wife. He exhibited polite manners and was rumored to be a party-goer of major stature. Kinser had pitched baseball in a triple A league for several years until his rubber arm gave out and he remarried. The Kinsers do not have children.

Chuck Fleming, the senior counselor, was older, shorter and plumper than the others. He sported a mane of white hair over sad blue eyes. Reading glasses gave him the mystique of an academic. An unpretentious demeanor, coupled with a pleasant personality, made him an agreeable co worker. He was a quiet man whose facial expressions revealed the stress and strain of years in prison counseling. On the minus side, Fleming had the personality of a turtle. His character was not unlike mine. Slow but sure.

A former football player for the Los Angeles Rams, "Iron Mike" Weaver proved difficult to engage in conversation. Always on the defensive, he anticipated questions concerning his ex wife. "As you know, my divorce from Kathleen was not amicable. The novels took precedence over her wifely duties," he would recite on occasion. Otherwise, Weaver seldom discussed his ex-wife. She was a celebrity in the manner of Grace Metolius whose "Valley of the Dolls" had bought her fame.

Kathleen Weaver had written the best seller, "Forever Faithful." The movie version had played sixteen weeks at the Mason Street Theater in downtown San Francisco. The book and the film were considered adult, somewhat risqué for the times. Today it would be labeled "Miss Goody Two Shoes."

The counselors drifted back to work. Mallachey walked me to his office. The San Quentin Counseling Center was located on the second floor of the main building above the visiting room. My office, at the end of a long hallway, had an outstanding view of San Pablo Bay. A small desk, two chairs and an old Underwood Royal on a nearby table, gave the room an appearance of austerity.

Mallachey had recently been appointed supervisor of the counseling office. Unsure of himself in his newly acquired status, he soon learned rank has it's privileges. Fifteen years of loyalty to the system were rewarded by promotion. He waved me to a chair.

A balding man in his forties, he could be anyone's kindly Uncle Herman, offering advice only when asked. A man of the old school, he always wore a three piece suit, favoring dark brown. He swiveled in his chair and pointed out the window. "That's the yard. Stay out of there if you can."

I saw a huge open area surrounded by cement walls reaching heights of one hundred and twenty feet. Thirty or forty picnic tables for the card players and escape plotters were partially sheltered by a v-shaped roof. Six or seven hundred inmates could be found in the yard on any given day, rain or shine.

Mallachey pulled out a three by five card from his vest as he tapped ashes from his Missouri Meerschaum. Relighting, he took slow draws as he contemplated a painting on the wall. An oil of a 1938 supercharged Cord convertible hung in a place of honor. The fragrance of sweet Virginia mixed with a Turkish aromatic tobacco filled the room.

"I am required by the rules to read you this statement," Mallachey announced, and proceeded to do so. "I must inform you that should you become a hostage, the State of California and the authorities at San Quentin will not negotiate for your freedom. We will do everything possible to secure your safe release, however, neither you nor your family or heirs or assigns will be allowed to take legal action against the State of California, officials of San Quentin Prison or any law officer."

I contemplated my future.

"In other words, Sean, if they grab you—tough luck."

"Yes, Sir."

"Good. Now we can proceed. Coffee?" Mallachey reached behind his chair for a thermos.

"No, thank you. I am kinda coffee'd out," I responded.

"San Quentin is one-hundred and seven years old. Capacity is five thousand and we are always full. We have a staff of approximately fourteen-hundred. Fifty-five percent of the personnel are correctional officers."

After a sip of coffee and a pull on his pipe, Mallachey continued, "We have funding for four correctional counselors, including you, an assistant supervisor, myself and three inmate clerks. The counselors interview and prepare progress reports on the rehabilitation of inmates up for parole. We cannot recommend parole. A thorough knowledge of the English language can result in a slanted report." He winked.

My supervisor labored on for a few minutes with statistics. Bored, I maintained a fixed smile on my face. Finally he finished.

"That's enough of the regs. We have a temporary office for you to use during your first week of orientation."

"The first week? I anticipated a short period of indoctrination due to my experience at the California Medical Facility."

"Well, every joint's different. It'll take a week or so here. There's lots to do and see."

Mallachey handed me a two inch binder of state regulations. "This will keep you busy. There are many unwritten rules but the most important one is survival." He lit his pipe again and added thoughtfully, "For us as well as them."

My temporary office faced the yard but I couldn't see it through my window. Rolls of barbed wire, circling the top of every building in sight, blocked my view. I could stare at a sea of piano wire, razor wire, barbed wire, and gun towers. Or I could study the regs.

Within the fortress San Quentin, I developed a sense of futility. Uniformity, uniforms and regulations by the book erased any identity. By the numbers. No names please. I fantasized about the possibility of escape—not only for myself, but for my fellow human beings.

I tried to concentrate on the regulations. Mallachey might ask questions. I began to read, skipping whole sentences or paragraphs.

"On July 7, 1852, twenty acres of land were purchased for $10,000 at Point Quentin. It was named after an Indian warrior. On July 14, 1852, the Bark Waben, the stern of an old sailing ship, or 'wabau' as some historians have it, was towed to Point Quentin and converted to a prison. Four hundred and nine people have been executed at San Quentin to date, including four women since 1852. Executions are usually held on Fridays at 10 a.m. Thus, execution days are called 'Black Friday' by the inmates.

"In March of 1938 the gas chamber was built at a cost of $5,000. Also in 1938, Robert Wells helped build the gas chamber in which he himself was executed in 1942. The last group of women prisoners left San Quentin in the fall of 1933. A new cotton mill opened on the facility in 1955. Skills learned in the mill are useless as there are few cotton mills in California." I kept on reading.

"How about a break, Sean? We're going across the street for coffee." Mr. Mallachey and Mike Weaver stood in the doorway.

"That sounds great to me. Between looking at barbed wire and studying the regs, I think I'm going blind."

"Take your time. No need to hurry." An engaging Mallachey exuded charm. "There's a snack bar outside the gates. We go there for morning and afternoon breaks. It has a beautiful view of the bay."

"Calms the nerves," Mike Weaver added.

"I could use some tranquility. I feel like I'm living in the dark ages," I commented.

Mallachey led the way through the gates to the outside. Stepping through the last barrier, I inhaled deeply. "Ah. Pure air." A half hour later we returned to the office. Refreshed, I resumed my study of the regs.

"Upon arrival at San Quentin, an inmate is stripped of all clothes and possessions. After a shower he is given an orange jumpsuit and his legal paperwork. He is known as the 'new fish' because he has just been caught. The inmate is assigned a cell and given state-issued toilet paper, comb, linens, towel, soap, toothbrush and blanket. Later he is led under escort to the West Block where he is maintained under strict security. For the next two weeks the new fish undergoes medical and physical examinations, as well as educational testing and staff evaluation. Then he is dressed in prison blues. San Quentin offers educational classes in everything from the GED (General Educational Development) to medical science."

I caught myself dozing off from time to time and had to slap my face to stay awake. Frequent trips to the rest room carried me though the day. At five p.m. I got up to leave.

Mallachey appeared in my doorway. "Sorry, Sullivan, you can't leave just yet. The count is short one inmate. Some idiot is probably hiding."

"Can I phone Cassie? She's probably waiting dinner for me."

"Sure. Use my phone." A few minutes later we got the all clear. The daily count did not always agree with the roster.

Cassie sat entranced that evening as I treated her to the delights of my day. I don't think she ever fathomed the true meaning of my job.

Barr popped into my office on Friday. "Good news, Sullivan. Your permanent office will be ready Monday." He sat down and started to say something.

I interrupted. "Good. I think I've figured a way to get over barbed wire and out to the free world."

Barr sneered at my little joke. "Bad news. They want you to walk the walls as part of your orientation."

It's always "they." "You're kidding," I said. "I'll fall off and bust my ass. No balance, you know."

"I'm sorry, that's what they said. When you get back I'll introduce you to your gofer. He's in for life. No parole."

"That's nice."

Barr then explained how to get on the wall. On my way to the door leading to the first gun tower, I speculated on who "They" might be. David G. Schlicter, M.D., prison psychiatrist, loomed large on my list of suspects.

I didn't ask to be excused from walking the walls. I accepted the challenge, hoping to be considered "one of the boys." Grasping the handrails on either side, I started for the first gun tower. The walk way was two feet wide. Thank God I had something to hold on to. The walls soared to over a hundred feet above the ground in some places. I told myself not to look down. I looked down anyway.

The yard teemed with inmates planning an escape. I saw an anthill of felons relegated to the garbage dump of society. At the first tower, the CO, with his right foot on the rail, made 180-degree sweeps of the yard with his weapon.

Hearing my asthmatic wheeze, the officer wheeled. "What the hell are you doing here?" he demanded. I starred into the barrel of a 30.06 canon. Risking life and limb, I let go of the rails. Before he could get off a shot, I raised both hands.

"Don't shoot!" I yelled. He laughed, pointing his gun back out at the yard. "My name is Sean Sullivan," I continued. "I'm the new counselor. They told me to walk the walls."

"Come into my office," he said. "Have a cup of coffee. Take a seat." The CO poured coffee into a tin cup. The metallic taste lingered in my mouth the rest of the day.

"Who told you to walk the walls?"

"My boss." I neglected to mention his name since I considered Mr. Mallachey to be a good guy.

The CO studied the yard for a few minutes, "Uh-oh." He blew a whistle that had been dangling from his neck. We looked down at a scuffle between two inmates that was turning into a full scale altercation. Thirty or forty prisoners quickly surrounded the combatants, shouting encouragement.

"Kick him in the balls!" The smaller of the two men was clearly losing the battle.

Drawing a bead on the melee, the CO shouted, "Stand off or I'll shoot." Five seconds later a loud bang whistled past my ear. Seven hundred felons froze in their tracks. A tableau of the misbegotten stared at the source of the blast in stunned silence. Four or five officers hurried to the scene and quickly dispersed the onlookers.

"I think the bullet ricocheted," the marksman said.

I suppressed a, "Good shot, old boy!"

Across the yard, I saw an inmate fall to the ground, his body locked into the fetal position. He waved an obscene gesture in our direction.

Blood oozed from his right leg. The inmate sued the State of California for hazardous living conditions. He lost.

"Well, I guess I'd better finish my walk," I said.

The CO said, "You don't have to do this. Go on back."

"Okay, I did my duty." I quick-stepped back to my office.

"Oh, there you are," Barr said. Beside him stood the Svengali who, in the next few months, would lead me to my final seduction.

"This is Manuel Ramirez. He'll be your gofer."

"Pleased to meet you, Mr. Sullivan," the man said with a smile. Gold filled cavities sparkled in my eyes. Could I have foreseen the future, I would have turned right then and ran out of the building, through the main gate, back to Eureka, California.

"Hi," I responded. "Well, back to the regs. I'll be glad when this is over," I said.

"Cheer up, Sullivan. Your new office overlooks San Pablo Bay. It has the best view in the joint. I'll see you later." Barr headed out the door.

Ramirez asked me, "Did ya hear about the fight in the yard?" Any kind of action to him was like an orgy in a whore house.

"Yes, I was up in the gun tower," I answered.

"The gun tower? What were you doing there?" he asked.

"They told me to walk the walls. Part of my orientation."

"Somebody's just pulling your leg."

"That's what the CO said," I agreed.

Later, as my marriage entered a sea of troubles, Ramirez played me like a harp, knowing exactly which string to pluck. He was a con's con.

"It doesn't matter. I'm anxious to finish this week and I'm looking forward to moving into my new office. This barbed wire is getting to me."

Ramirez smiled. "Let's take a look."

I turned the handle. "It's locked. I don't have a key."

Ramirez smiled again, and slid an ID card in the crack of the door. He jiggled the door handle a bit and popped it open.

"I'll be right back." He returned with a cup of coffee. Sugar, no cream. After a few minutes of conversational probing by my gofer, under the guise of establishing a new friendship, we left the room.

TUESDAY, APRIL 21, 1959, WAS THE DAY OF THE hostage taking. I had been working at San Quentin a week. I prepared to interview my first inmate. We auditioned our clientele by crime category.

Mondays: breaking and entering, armed robbery, any crime involving a weapon. Tuesdays: arson, extortion, illegal gambling, usury (Mafia-type crimes). Wednesdays: kidnapping, rape, assault and battery, manslaughter, murder. Thursdays: fraud, embezzlement, white collar crimes. Fridays: sex crimes, incest, child molestation. I crawled out of a sewer every Friday afternoon promptly at five, assuming the count was correct.

Ramirez fetched the first inmate of the day, an arsonist. Twenty minutes into the session, the man leaned over my desk to share his innermost secrets. He looked to the ceiling. No cameras. I would soon know the whereabouts of Blackbeard's treasure.

"Every time I torch a place I ejaculate," he confessed.

"What does lighting fires have to do with a sexual experience?" I blurted out in amazement. "I've never heard of such a thing."

"I dunno. It just happens. Sometimes I think I do it more for the sensation than the money. I'm a pro you know." He smiled. Here was a man who took pride in his work.

Kinzer stuck his head in the door. "Come on, Sullivan. You should see this." He pointed to the opposite end of the hallway. I dashed out, completely forgetting my inmate interview. My client joined the gofers at the reception desk.

I looked out the north window to see a bevy of prison CO's, the California Highway Patrol, Marin County Deputies, and an assortment of civilians running out the main gate. Police helicopters whirling overhead were joined by two United States Coast Guard patrol boats on San Pablo Bay.

Mr. Mallachey ambled by our group. "I just got a call. Two inmates are holding an elderly couple hostage at the end of the Marin Rod and Gun Pier. They've threatened to slit the hostages' throats." The counseling staff, trailed by the office gofers, gathered at the big window. We could not see the pier, but the activity resembled a bee hive.

"What happened?" I asked.

"Probably an escape," Weaver replied.

"Look. Here comes another helicopter," Kinzer said. Someone produced binoculars.

"I think the CHP has stopped traffic on the Richmond-San Rafael bridge," Ballachey said. Twenty minutes later the banter between the onlookers slowly diminished.

"I guess we'll find out the details on the news and in the papers," Carr concluded.

I finally remembered the patient I'd left back in my office. "I have to finish an interview," I said. "Where did he go? I'm not through with him yet."

Ramirez popped into my face. "He went back to work on his mural, Mr. Sullivan. He is an artist you know. Want me to go get him?" His condescending ways made me uncomfortable. He knew which button to push.

"No, that's okay," I barked. "I can write a report based on what I have."

I returned to my office and left the door open. As I completed the paper work a spirited dialogue between the office gofers caught my ear. The clerks had gathered at the receptionist desk nearby.

Inmate/clerks Chapin and Frantz were new to the job. Ramirez had been the chief clerk for the last six months. Clarence Chapin's desk was located at the top of the stairs facing Warren Mallachey's office. Clerking in the counseling office was a duty envied and sought after by the other five thousand inmates.

An Afro-American, with the physique of a football player, Chapin didn't have much going for him in the personality department. His round face and questioning eyes constantly begged understanding. Short, but broad shouldered, he took every opportunity to press weights in the recreation yard.

The counseling office had been his domain until November 18, 1959, when Ramirez challenged him for territorial rights by provoking an altercation. Despite his slender stature, Ramirez had continued flailing at the larger man with his fists until two CO's appeared. Chapin was sent to the hospital; Ramirez was confined to Siberia—maximum security.

I overheard, "Hey, Chapin, what's your beef?" It was an unwritten rule of the prison to never ask another inmate why he was in the joint.

"Arson, and you know it," Chapin answered.

Ramirez was all powerful in Q. Feared by the lessor beings of the San Quentin society, he held the title of Chairman and CEO of the Hispanic gang. The knife was their weapon of choice.

"I hear the cops found you in the closet of your apartment with fifty pairs of ladies shoes," Ramirez taunted his co-worker in his bully manner. Chapin's fetish was well known. I could never understand the relationship between women's shoes and arson.

Years of self-induced suffering were written on his face. Chapin broke the silence. "Get off my back, Ramirez," he pleaded.

"Come on, Manuel. Have a heart," Frantz said.

A tall cadaverous man with a constant involuntary twitch in his right eye that caused his eyebrows to jump up and down, Frantz actually possessed quite a gentle nature, especially for an inmate. A suspected informer, he was shunned by many of the inmates. Strange things happened to snitches in the middle of the night. Rumor had it that Frantz enjoyed a monthly pittance from the local police department, which enabled him to pay for a bodyguard.

"At least I'm not a snitch," Ramirez retorted, turning to Frantz and giving him the San Quentin stink eye. The only thing lower than Frantz, a snitch, in the prison hierarchy was a child molester.

Frantz had had been the enforcer for a local loan company. He often stuttered his favorite jingle, "You late one time—broken arm. You late two time—broken arm and leg. Next time you see me, you won't see me. Goodbye." His whiney voice branded him a loser in the truest sense of the word.

Ignoring Frantz, Ramirez turned to Chapin and laughed. "And you got stuck in the air vent when you tried to torch Sears."

Unsuccessful in his efforts to burn down the building, Chapin had slithered out of the vent, bypassed the office safe, and ran the few blocks to his apartment.

I had made the mistake of reading Manuel Ramirez' yellow jacket. Ramirez was in for life without parole for multiple crimes including, rape, kidnapping, and armed robbery. Muscular and compact as a pit bull, he enjoyed intimidating people.

I finished the day and went home. Cassie met me at the door. "Jonathan Winters is coming to the Hungry I. Can we go?" she asked.

"Sure. I got paid a few days ago."

We took in Mr. Winters' performance the following Saturday night. A genius at improvisation, he showcased his talents to a full house. The basement bistro rocked with laughter. After the last show, we left the Hungry I and walked to Pierre's Sidewalk Café on Broadway.

Opened in October of 1958 by Enrico Banducci, Pierre's Café is a world class coffee house. A first for San Francisco. A real Parisian cafe.

It was a great place to sit at sidewalk tables and peruse the local newspapers, play chess, or just watch the world go past.

Pierre's boasted a handsome interior with Grecian columns and marble tables for those who were not the outdoors type. Light meals were served in the continental tradition. Home baked French and Italian pastries were featured with a choice of coffees. A well stocked bar completed the ambience.

A few minutes later, we finished our drinks and were just started for home when we heard scuffling and shouts of, "Get him! Get him!" On top of nearby marble tables stood Jonathan Winters and his adversary, Paddy O'Sullivan, engaged in an imaginary duel to the death. Winters threw his tie to an appreciative fan, opened his shirt, and prepared to do battle. Paddy O'Sullivan, dressed in his usual black cape, plumed hat, ruffled shirt and velvet pants, threw down his glove, thus accepting Winter's challenge.

Cassie and I sat at the bar hypnotized by the action. The commotion carried through the room. A crowd formed a circle around the combatants; tables and chairs were pushed aside. Late night onlookers cheered and chanted. Make believe swords flashed in the air.

An occasional "Touché!." followed by an improvised repartee accompanied the gymnastics. Winters threw his phantom blade to the ground in victory. He raised both hands in triumph. The blond lady sitting next to us asked, "Would you like to meet him?"

"That would be great," I replied.

Winters broke off the engagement and strode toward the bar.

The lady spoke up. "I should warn you, though. He's in a bad mood. He got into a hassle at the club last night. It was in the newspapers."

"That's okay. We'd really like to meet him," I repeated. She nodded and led us over to the bar.

"Johnny, meet Sean and Cassie Sullivan."

We were greeted with firm handshakes and, "Hi, how are you?" Perspiration bathed his forehead. Cassie and I attempted casual conversation.

Winters rolled his eyes at his companion. "Come on, baby. Let's go back to the hotel." We had met our first celebrity. Next year, Charles DeGulle.

Wednesday, May 13, 1959, the headlines of the <u>San Francisco Chronicle</u> read, "Police Take Top Comic To Hospital." A companion article announced, "Girlfriend Attempts to Rescue Boyfriend. Shirley O'Neil, a pretty teenager, attempted to rescue Albert Kogler from a great white shark at Baker's Bay yesterday."

Two weeks later Cassie and I enjoyed a Sunday picnic at Baker's beach. We visited the Jackson Street Irregulars on weekends, with occasional forays to the Buena Vista Cafe to sip Irish Coffee with Lloyd and Carole.

On Monday mornings I steeled myself for the daily plunge into the pit. With conscious effort on my part, San Quentin slowly became bearable. As I walked into my office that Thursday morning, Ramirez brought in coffee and the newspaper. Leafing through the first section, my eye stopped at page four. "Killer Of Two Dies Today."

My next client, a young man in his late twenties, stood politely at attention.

"Have a seat," I offered. "How are you?" We began.

I had just completed the interview with the bank embezzler when Mr. Mallachey stepped into my office. "I don't know why, but they want you in the visiting room now," he said.

"Okay, I'm on my way."

He muttered, "I've never had a request like this."

The CO in the visiting room introduced me to a Mrs. Bledsoe. Her son, James Bledsoe, whom I had just interviewed, had briefly enjoyed a $500,000 windfall. A creative bookkeeper, his reward was a five to ten year indeterminate sentence plus reimbursement to the Bank of America and the court.

The officer said, "I understand you talked to Mrs. Bledsoe's son James this morning."

"Yes. How did you know so soon?" I asked.

"The wireless." I think the grapevine at Q is faster than Vacaville.

A woman in her fifties in print dress, Mrs. Bledsoe held out her hand. We sat down in a quite corner. She pulled her glasses down from the top of her head and put them on, searching my face for something, I don't know what.

"Jimmy shouldn't be in this place. It was all a misunderstanding. Can't you do anything?" she pleaded.

"No, I'm sorry, I can't. I'm just a counselor. You should talk to your lawyer," I suggested.

"That son of a bitch. He's the reason my Jimmy is here in the first place." Spittle began to form on her lips. Her red face exploded, "He didn't defend Jimmy. He just sat through the whole trial looking at the floor. Please, please…can't you do something? James is a good boy." Panic stricken, she gasped for breath.

"Mrs. Bledsoe, I am only a correctional counselor. The trial is over. The only people who can help you are a good lawyer and maybe a political connection," I said.

"Have you read his file?" she demanded.

I made the fatal mistake of answering, "Yes." Complicating the situation, I added, "I wonder why they sent a first time white collar offender to a max joint."

"There. There, you see? He doesn't belong in this horrible place. You just said so."

"Well, I don't see many bank embezzlers," I admitted. "Newly committed white collar felons are usually sent to a minimum or maybe a medium security institution."

Mrs. Bledsoe, refueled by my latest verbal faux paux, went ballistic. She jumped up, waving her arms.

"Hallelujah! I knew it. I just knew it. I'm going to tell my Congressman what you said. Oh, this is wonderful! I know we can get him a new trial." She became dizzy with glee.

"Mrs. Bledsoe. Mrs. Bledsoe, please…" I pleaded.

"Oh, thank you so much!. I feel so much better." She grabbed me by the shoulders and smashed me into her ample bosom. The crushing bear hug left me breathless. I unlocked myself from her grip and gave up on further dialogue. She raced out of the room in a flurry of "Thank you's."

After Mrs. Bledsoe flew through the gates, I scanned the visiting room. Whispering voices were planing the future, "When I get out." A father, choking back tears, apologized to his son for past misdeeds, "I'm sorry, son. So sorry." Whines in high pitched tones protested, "I didn't do what they said. They got the wrong guy." And one inmate said to his wife, or lover, "How's the cat? Have you been feeding her." I liked that man. He knows what's important, I thought.

As I walked through the second gate leading to the counseling center, a voice behind me boomed, "Stand aside—dead man coming." I flattened myself against the wall. Two muscle-bound, six-foot-plus CO's, half guided, half carried a slender five-foot four inmate to a private visitor room.

I related the experience to Barr. "They were probably taking him to the lawyer's room. He's scheduled to be executed tomorrow morning and his lawyer is one of his last outside visitors allowed, except family and the chaplain," he explained.

"What's 'Stand aside - dead man walking' mean? I don't understand," I said.

"Tradition. The CO's on death row always holler, 'Dead Man Walking' when they open a cell, as if the inmate didn't know his status in this life," he answered. "Well, I've got some paperwork to do." Barr left.

Friday morning Barr reappeared in my office door. "If I were you I'd find a place to hide," he advised. "They're looking for witnesses."

"For what?" I asked.

"The State of California requires twelve witnesses for an execution. Riser goes this morning and so far they only have nine witnesses."

"Well, I guess I'll head over to the snack bar for a coke then."

"Good idea."

As I entered the snack bar, I bellied up to the counter and ordered a coke. Three inmate clerks immediately turned their backs and froze in a time warp. Five thousand or more felons in fortress San Quentin stood motionless in a huge tableau. One of their brethren is leaving this world.

I looked at my watch. Three minutes after ten a.m. The pellets are dropping now. The brotherhood continued their mute observance of the unseen punishment. I could hear Father Dingberg intone, "For I am the resurrection..."

One witness fainted at the rail surrounding the Green Apple Room. Two deaths this week. One by gas, the other by a hungry shark. I went back to my office and joined my co-workers at the South window overlooking the entrance to the execution chamber.

"Here they come," Fleming announced.

Twelve tried and true witnesses staggered out of the chamber into the light of day. Some gasped for air. Several threw up on the ground. Two hugged each other for solace. The other counselors returned to work while I lingered at the window.

The Warden walked out alone, stretching his arms as if petitioning to the Gods for forgiveness for his part in the death of a fellow human being. The law requires that he officiate at each execution. Clinton Branigan, his predecessor, had presided over ninety such "going away parties." He had claimed that "nary an innocent man was sent to his just reward."

A few days later I found a note clipped to a file on my desk. "Sean, please interview this inmate. He is up for parole next week. Thanks, Warren Mallachey."

"Good morning, Mr. Sullivan. Coffee, one cream, two sugars. And the <u>Chron</u>." Why did I always fixate on Ramirez' gold fillings? They glittered in the sun, that's why.

"Thanks, Manuel," I said. He stood behind me at the window. Gazing out at the bay was his daily morning ritual. Maybe he saw it as his reward for bringing the coffee and newspaper.

Ramirez spotted the file on my desk marked LPFN. The name of the inmate was printed in bold letters, red on yellow. I asked, "What's LPFN?"

"Lost privileges until further notice," he barked. "I know the guy. He's in the hospital. Somebody stuck a shiv in his back. He's in a wheelchair for life."

"I have to interview him. How do I get to the hospital?"

"Go down to the front gate. The turnkey will point you in the right direction. See ya." Ramirez left for the day.

A few minutes later the CO at the bottom of the stairs gave me directions to the prison hospital. I had to walk the yard. There are many yards at San Quentin, some big, some small.

The recreation yard is where track and field events as well as softball games are held. Then there's an exercise yard for weight lifters. The main yard is a huge open air area with forty or fifty picnic tables. Usually there are five hundred to a thousand men milling about in the main yard, nothing but time on their hands.

"Good luck," the CO opened the gate.

I spotted the hospital at least three city blocks in the distance. Remembering Confucius, I took the first step of a journey of a thousand miles. I became a knight of old walking the gauntlet. Perspiration dripped down my forehead as I scanned the yard from right to left, anticipating an attack from any quarter. I now understood the meaning of fear.

"Hi, Mr. Sullivan. What are you doing out here?"

I did a three-sixty, seeking the source of the sound. Panic washed over me. I thought a spider was crawling up my back. Regaining my balance I identified the felon smiling at me from a picnic table. I had interviewed him last Wednesday. Voluntary manslaughter one. Ten to fifteen.

He appeared to be holding an object behind his back. He started towards me in a leisurely fashion. I picked up my pace, hurrying in the direction of the hospital. Spurts of adrenaline shot through my veins.

"I'm going to the hospital to interview a patient," I called back in his direction.

He stopped walking. "Just wanted to shake hands," he said. The windmills of my mind slowed as I walked through the hospital door. The staff provided me with an empty office.

A gofer wheeled in a pasty-faced young man who hadn't seen the light of day for some time. I saw shadows filtering through the bars onto the ceiling. The pattern reminded me of Rorschach ink blots.

"What significance does this have for you?" the doctor had asked me.

"I dunno. It looks like an inkblot to me." My answer years before, during one of the many "I wonder if he's hydrocephalic" examinations I had endured at the Shriner's Hospital.

The inmate, desperate for companionship, was a talker. Captured by my curiosity, I listen to his story. A first timer, he had been caught with a gang of teenagers holding up a mom and pop grocery store. Mom was shot. She died. He denied being the shooter. "And then the gun went off."

Every murderer I ever interviewed at San Quentin always finished their story with something like, "And then the gun went off," or, "When I woke up I had a knife in my hand." The one I liked best was, "When I came to, I saw poison on the table." Cons could not bring themselves to articulate, "I did it."

I never heard, "I pulled the trigger," "I chopped her up with an ax," or "I poisoned him." It was always, "I woke up with the ax in my hand," or "the bottle of poison spilled on the floor next to me." One client had even said, "I saw the cat sniffing the rat poison on the table." Murderers were the most fascinating of story tellers.

I tried to motivate people to take responsibility for their actions. The psychology books stated that if one verbalized a desired behavior, behavior modification would eventually take place. It was possible to return to one's rightful place in a forgiving society.

As I started to leave the hospital a white coat blocked my way. "Well, Mr. Sullivan. What are you doing here?" A sardonic grin, worthy of Bela Lagosi, greeted me.

Feeling victorious, I said to Dr. Schlicter, "I got my transfer to San Quentin." I turned to leave.

"Don't go. Let's have some coffee." He affected a smile. I weathered fifteen minutes of idle conversation carefully calculated to probe my psyche.

"Well, I've got to get back to work. Please excuse me." I started for the yard.

"No, use the outer exit. Circle the joint to the left," Dr. Slichter suggested.

"I was told to come this way," I said.

"Somebody is putting you on." This was becoming a familiar phrase by now.

"Thank you," I said.

I arrived back at my office in time to go to lunch with my co-workers. The employee dining room was near the entrance to the execution chamber. An uneasy feeling came over me every time I sat down to lunch. The inmate waiters were courteous and well managed, but of a dubious background, of course. My parents had always told me that con artists, murderers and the like were people to avoid at all costs.

Adding to my apprehension, my fellow counselors jokingly identified the inmate waiters according to crime category. "See the man bringing your soup?" Fleming murmured. "He's in for murder. Poisoned his girl friend." Giggles and smiles would follow.

"Maybe this isn't such a good job after all," I said.

Weaver was just sitting down when Warren Mallachey approached our table. "May I join you?" he asked. "Please do," Weaver replied. Mallachey eased his Lincolnesque frame into a chair.

After a leisurely lunch we went back to work. As usual I was the last to climb the stairs. I glanced towards Mr. Mallachey's office. The gofers seemed agitated.

As I passed by his office and glanced in, I saw Mr. O'Conner, Captain of the Guard, along with Jack Barr, the assistant supervisor, and Mallachey. Seated before them was an inmate waving a book of prison regulations. The office clerks were noticeably titillated. I saw smiles, and heard soft laughter along with the question, "What's he trying to prove?"

Apparently a first-ever event in the history of San Quentin had taken place that May of 1959. "Did you see him? Did you see him?" Ramirez asked me when I reached my office. An excited Givens and Frantz joined us.

"Yes, I did. He was completely naked. I wasn't thrilled; voyeurism is not my cup of tea."

16

"HAVE YOU FOUND GOD?"

I RELUCTANTLY RETURNED TO WORK. I STARED at a stack of yellow jackets on my desk. Since it was a Friday, I turned off my value system and waded through interviews with pedophiles, child molesters and "Uncle Harrys."

Ramirez floated into my office a few minutes before quitting time. "Did you hear? The guy in Mr. Mallachey's office has been studying the regs. He couldn't fine any rule against going naked."

"Creativity and initiative at it's best," I commented dryly.

"I guess they'll have to change the rules now." His sad face twisted in anguish.

"What's so great about taking off your clothes?" A wounded look answered my question.

Ramirez gazed out the window. Sail boats drifted on the water with puffy white clouds floating overhead. He saw through his mental looking glass a tantalizing picture of freedom. Like the touch of a woman in his dreams, forever out of reach. The frustration of incarceration did not equal the punishment of the nearness of all he now valued.

Out loud Ramirez directed a haunting soliloquy to the cool sea breezes of San Pablo Bay. "Prison is an attempt to get into our brains. It's a crazy mixture of boredom and terror. Boredom, because nothing happens. Fear, because anything could happen. Any time." I didn't respond.

"They don't just strip you. They go deeper. They take what little dignity you have. They make you live, eat, sleep and even shit next to other men. You can't wear anything that says 'This is me. I'm separate from the others'."

"They" were always the unseen enemy.

I began to bond with Ramirez that summer of 1959, completely unaware that he was leading me down the path to self-destruction. "Remember all my brothers and sisters who rot in these steel tombs," he said. His eyes held me hostage. "Think of us as you cross the Golden Gate Bridge tonight on your way home to Cassie's arms."

I had never mentioned Cassie by name, always referring to her as "my wife" or "the wife." His eyes narrowed in disdain. "When will you become a mistake like me?" he asked. Ramirez knew the answer as he walked out of my office.

I picked up his yellow jacket. LWOP was stamped in bold red. Life without parole. At the bottom in gothic print, red on yellow, "Manuel Phillipe Ramirez."

Later I had my first glimpse of the newspaper. "Duncan dies for two rapes, murders." That evening Cassie asked, "What's new at work, Sean?"

"Another day, another dollar, another execution," I replied. The last of May soon became the middle of June 1959.

"I CAN'T FIND A JOB. WHAT AM I GOING TO DO?" Cassie lamented one foggy Sunday afternoon. She sounded depressed so I turned down the TV. Half time analysis bored me anyway. The Forty-Niners were losing.

"Just keep looking. You find something," I responded.

"I think I've been blacklisted or something," she complained. The look on her face tugged at my heart.

"I doubt that. It's a big town. How about school?. Maybe you can complete the requirements for a degree."

"No." She didn't elaborate nor did I pursue the subject.

"Phyllis Diller is at the Purple Onion this weekend," I offered as a diversion.

"Oh, that sounds like fun! She'll cheer me up."

The following Saturday night, we parked the car on Broadway and walked over to the Purple Onion. At the three-way intersection of Columbus, Montgomery, and Broadway are two of the more interesting institutions in San Francisco—the Vesuvio and City Lights Bookstore.

Guiding Cassie away from the Vesuvio and Bruce the bartender I suggested, "Lets check out City Lights."

"Okay," she agreed.

We were greeted by a bearded beatnik type. "Can I help you folks?"

"No thanks," I said. "We're just browsing."

Cassie pointed to a staircase. "What's in the basement?"

"More paperbacks. Let me show you." Our guide took us on the grand tour. Cassie warmed quickly to strangers. I usually maintained a "wait and see" attitude.

"My name is Freddy Fischette," our friendly tour guide said. A warm handshake cemented the new relationship.

"Hi. I'm Cassie and this is Sean," she responded.

The basement resembled a catacomb, complete with monastic brick arches decorated with religious phrases in gothic letters. We encountered the first one—"If ye believe not that I am he, ye shall die in sin."

"I've got to put that on my desk. Maybe I can save a few people," I said in jest.

Not understanding my attempt at humor, Fischette asked, "What kind of work do you do?"

"I'm a correctional counselor at San Quentin," I replied.

He chose to change the subject. "Before World War One this was a Holy Roller Meeting Place," he said.

I spotted another inscription over an archway—"Remember Lot's Wife." I blurted out, "Who's Lot?". My heathen background was revealed to all. Beady eyed glances shot my way.

On a door leading to the next alcove was the statement of the century—"I am the door." Redundancy at it's finest, I thought.

"When we opened the store in 1953 we found cases of Chinese back scratchers. Here, take one, or two if you want," Fischette said. He reached into a nearby box and pulled out a handful of bamboo back scratchers painted red.

"Thank you," I muttered. I was beginning to like the poet Fischette.

"I'll bet this place has quite a history," Cassie commented. She poked at a small ceremonial dragon sitting in the corner.

"It sure does. The previous owner was a Chinese electrician," Fischette began. We went back upstairs as our host continued his story. "As I said, my partner and I opened this place in 1953. I bought him out last year and he left for the East Coast. We trade in nothing but paperbacks and we've just begun publishing our own titles."

"I notice you have some foreign language books," Cassie said. She picked up a paperback in French.

"Yes. We just started stocking French and German entries. They're doing quite well," he said with just a hint of pride.

"Do you have Ginsberg's Howl?" she asked.

"Yes. The San Francisco Police labeled it as obscene last year. They arrested me but I beat the rap. We sold thirty thousand copies.

I picked up a paperback. "My God, you have <u>Beat Zen</u>. Alan Watts, the guru for Zen Buddhist philosophy, wrote this one. Do you have any Kerouac?" I asked.

"Yes. Jack stops by now and then." Fischette smiled. Cassie and I were impressed.

"It's getting late. Phyllis Diller, remember?" I guided Cassie out of the book store. "Thanks for the tour," I called back to Fischette.

Cassie eyed the Vesuvio bar but the Purple Onion was in the other direction. We hurried to our director chairs to enjoy another evening with Phyllis Diller. Green hair and all.

A WEEK LATER JACK BARR GREETED ME AS I REPORTED for work. "Sullivan," he said, "It's time for you to start leading a group therapy session. We've selected six inmates for you. Be at the conference room at one o'clock this afternoon."

"Okay," I replied. I wasn't too happy about group counseling but I figured the experience would be worth the effort.

"Now keep in mind, this isn't the family counseling they've been talking about it the papers. This is similar to the sessions at Vacaville," Barr explained.

"As you know, I sat in on some of those dialogues. I think I've got the idea," I replied.

"Good. Come into my office afterwards and we'll critique the session."

"I'll be there."

After lunch I made my way back through the gates and up the stairs towards my office. As I opened the door to the conference room, I faced a collection of inmates of varying shapes, sizes and colors. Their arms were adorned with the usual tattoos. Earrings and nose clips on the younger men silently challenged, "I dare you to help me. I'm a bad dude."

I glanced at my list of inmates. Inmate No. 1: Albert, age twenty-seven, murder, twenty-five to life. Inmate No. 2: Tony, age twenty-seven, second-degree murder, twenty to life. Inmate No. 3: George, age thirty-five, narcotics - third offense, seventeen to life. Inmate No. 4: Allee, age forty, armed robbery, rape, twenty to life. Inmate No. 5: Willy, age forty-four, manslaughter, armed robbery, has completed seventeen years of a twenty to life sentence. Inmate No. 6: Robert, age fifty- four, assault with a deadly weapon, attempted murder, ten to fifteen.

"Good morning gentlemen," I squeaked. A sudden shot of anxiety ricocheted through my stomach. I made a great business of searching for my pen.

I intoned, "Gentlemen, we are gathered here today to realize the value of conversation, verbal interaction. Anything you say will be kept in complete confidence. Perhaps we can resolve some problems." I was attempting to perform a marriage between the unwashed and a society that had cast them out. A few quiet snickers, burps, belches and mutterings of "Oh God" followed my opening statement.

The big guy with the nose clip stood up. "Mr. Sullivan, I don't quite understand. What we are supposed to do here? Maybe you can explain it."

I wish I could, I said to myself. To the group I said, "Certainly. It's talk therapy. You talk out your problems—what happened, why you're here, whatever. Maybe we can come to some conclusions. If you'll pardon my vulgarity, a vocal bowel movement."

A skinny inmate flashed a corn kernel grin. "Yeah, sure."

"Well, who would like to begin?" I said. I expected a buzz of scintillating conversation exorcising the demons from the minds and bodies of my clientele. My boys would go forth into the world never to sin again.

Silence. I tried to draw them out. "Remember, this is just between us. Not a word goes out of this room," I offered in confidential tones.

The longest fifty-minute hour of my life crawled by one excruciating minute at a time. Twice the skinny guy began his story. Twice he was stared down by the "bosses."

I threw in an occasional "I'm here to help you," without success. The more I babbled, the less they talked. My years of study in counseling and guidance failed me. To my great relief the big guy finally said, "It's two thirty. How long do we have to stay here?"

"You don't; our time is up. Hopefully we'll have better luck next week. Same time, same place." The big guy led the parade out of the room. I walked to Barr's office in disgrace.

"Well, Sean, how'd it go?" he asked.

"It was a complete failure. Freud is turning over in his grave," I said chagrined.

"He can't be; his body was cremated."

"That helps."

San Quentin's oldest inmate walked into the office. "Hi, Tony,." Barr jumped to shake his hand. Before us stood a man with a straight back and the dignity of his eighty-two years. I stood in deference to his age.

"Take a seat, Tony," Barr offered.

The old man sat down and slowly removed the cellophane from the biggest black Italian cigar I've ever seen. Barr and I simultaneously offered him a light. "I thought you were a pipe smoker, Tony," Barr commented.

"I am, but the Warden gave these to me at the parole hearing yesterday," Tony answered.

"You're getting out this time?" Barr inquired.

"Nope. I'm an old man. Too old to start life again on the outside."

"Why stay in this place?"

Irritated, he fired back. "I don't want to leave. I got nobody outside. I want to just sit here in my rocking chair, smoke my pipe, and listen to music until the big boss calls me."

"Well, what can we do for you?" Barr asked.

"I can't find Mr. Mallachey. He said he would loan me some old Enrico Caruso records."

"He's at a conference but he should be back later today. I'll tell him you were here," Barr said.

"Thank you. I'll come back later." He stood up to leave. The wrinkles in his face deepened and twisted. I finally realized he was smiling. Old Tony shuffled past the inmate clerks standing at the reception desk in a silent salute. Ramirez engaged him in a few minutes of respectful conversation.

Barr gave me some history on the old man. "He's been in this joint since 1919. He murdered his wife. I think he found her in bed with a neighbor."

"The Italians take marriage vows very seriously," I offered.

The following Saturday I picked up the morning <u>Chronicle</u>. Buried on page four, the word "execution" nevertheless caught my eye. "Killer of Two Goes Calmly To Execution." I thought the headlines on page one should shout, "They did it again!" I was developing an anti death penalty attitude.

Another news item grabbed my attention. "Red Cross Gives Highest Award To Shirley O'Neill." The contrast between legalized murder and a nineteen-year old heroine facing the jaws of a Great White Shark remains in my mind to this day.

Several Tuesdays later, the State Parole Board met at San Quentin. They rotated meeting sites between the various correctional facilities throughout the state. An inmate could be set free on a Tuesday or executed on a Friday.

Mr. Mallachey briefed me on the procedure for Parole Board Hearings. "Sit in the back row, don't take notes, and smile."

"Yes sir." I said.

"Have fun. Mike Weaver is going to join you," he added.

A few minutes later 'Iron Mike' appeared at my office door. "Hi, Sean. Ready for the big event?" he asked. A taciturn man of few words, his expressionless face usually remained as passive as an ice sculpture.

As we entered the front office of the administration building, three inmates sat on a wooden bench chaperoned by two CO's. One of the felons studied the ceiling at great length. Another examined invisible mutations on the floor. The third thumbed his pocket bible with a nervousness approaching palsy.

The Parole Board consisted of three members: an educator, a minister, and former Warden Clinton Branigan. Mr. Branigan had been appointed to the Adult Authority of the Parole Board in 1951. Born in the San Quentin hospital where his father worked as a guard, Branigan had served as warden from 1940-1951.

An office secretary and Chaplain Koberg sat with the parole board. Sitting to one side was the current warden, Fred Dickey. Warden Dickey, a large beefy man, had been appointed in 1957 following the unexpected death of Warden Harley Teets.

The morning session began promptly at nine. Chaplain Koberg intoned the prayer for the day, thanking God and the State of California for the opportunity to consider the plights of those wrongdoers who had strayed off the beaten path.

"Let's have the first man," Mr. Branigan ordered.

The bible carrying inmate was escorted into the room and seated on a chair facing his inquisitors. Unseen, he put the good book on his lap. He couldn't control the muscle spasms in his legs. The questioning began, with each member taking his or her turn based on seniority.

The lady educator asked, "How much education have you had? Do you have a job skill? Are you married? Do you have a hobby?" The inmate answered the volley of questions in an evasive manner. Plainly uncomfortable, he mumbled.

Weaver leaned over and whispered, "He's losing ground. He won't make parole."

"Doesn't look like it," I murmured.

The minister from the Fundamentalist church began his questions with a sonic boom, "Son, have you found God?"

The inmate whipped out his Bible and jumped up, slamming the book onto the table as he announced to one and all, "Yes, Sir, I have. Hallelujah Brothers and Sister!" He danced his way back to the chair. Having found the Supreme Being within the last five minutes, he sat down grinning.

The lady educator and Mr. Branigan spotted a spider on the wall weaving a web for its latest victim. The minister made Klaxon-like noises straight out of the silent service. He sounded like a submarine surfacing.

Weaver whispered, "Maybe we should look for God."

"I'm with you." We both struggled to keep a straight face.

Mr. Branigan regained control of the meeting. "Perhaps we should adjourn at this point," he suggested.

"But I haven't completed my examination of this good Christian." The minister stood up and grabbed the pocket Bible, waiving it for all to see.

"Proceed." A weary Branigan sat back down in his chair.

We were treated to a twenty minute tale of how the inmate had saved himself from the evils of the world, all thanks to the latest King James version of the Good Book. The meeting ended with a pyrotechnical speech summing up the inmate's personalized philosophy. Weaver and I headed for the snack bar. A few minutes of quiet serenity, meditating on the San Pablo Bay, and we returned to our respective duties.

The first client of the day had asked for this counseling session—an unusual request since the inmates typically didn't trust the free personnel. His yellow jacket indicated a crime of usury. He and his brother had run a bail bond business with loan sharking as a sideline. Two to five.

Ramirez escorted a pale young man into my office. He was clean shaven with white blonde hair. He studied me with hooded eyes that darted back and forth.

"Maybe I shouldn't be here," he muttered. Shrugging, throwing caution to the winds, he began his story. "I'm going to be paroled in ten days to two weeks."

"That's good. Bet you're looking forward to the day," I said.

"I am. But I got a problem."

"Yes," I prompted.

The inmate looked sick. The words came out slowly and haltingly. "My family has paid for a bodyguard the last two years." I knew better than to ask why.

"The money ran out."

"I wish this guy would get to the point," I said to myself.

"They're after me," he said, finally getting to the meat of his problem.

"Who's after you?" I asked.

"You know I can't give you names."

"Then how can I help you?"

"You can have me put in the isolation cell. I'm trying to save my life."

I jerked forward. He now had my complete attention. I began to notice his effeminate mannerisms—the wrist motions, searching eyes, and lilting quality to his voice. To me, in my prejudice, these were stereotyped affectations of "l'amour bleu" or those who engage in a love which dare not speak its name. Homosexuality.

"I'll talk to the duty officer. No promises," I said.

"Oh, thank you so much," he said. "I'll never forget this." He continued to shake my hand. I broke loose and walked down to the main office. Lt. Zweig listened to my story.

"Considering the circumstances, could he be placed in isolation?" I asked.

Oliver Zweig, who stood six-feet four and weighed in at two-hundred and fifty pounds, exploded in my face. "Are you crazy or something?" he yelled. "He probably owes cigarette money. You've been here long enough to know what goes on in this joint."

Correctional officers, particularly lieutenants and captains, are a special breed. Part Lone Ranger, part school yard bully. Their eyes constantly search for trouble before it happens. They have institutional stares which can penetrate walls of cement and people. I backed away from the lieutenant.

"Sorry. I was just trying to help the guy."

241

"He conned you." Lieutenant Zweig slammed a file on his desk, indicating the interview was terminated. Embarrassed, I shuffled back to my office reflecting on the many events that had occurred at San Quentin since my arrival.

Ramirez appeared with the usual cup of coffee. "I couldn't find any cream. Sorry," he said.

"That's okay." I picked up the morning newspaper. The headlines of the last several months passed before my mind's eye. One by one: April 27, 1959 - "Con flees Quentin, Gets Several Feet-Age Catches up." May 4, 1959 - "Bullets At Roadblock-Quentin Parolee Fights Cops, Dies." May 5, 1959 - "Life Term-Quentin Con Asks Transfer-Insane." May 15, 1959 - "San Quentin Fugitive Held In Virginia." May 23, 1959 - "Quentin Con Dies After Stabbing By Cell mate." May 26, 1959 - "Quentin Con Escapes—For Awhile." May 26, 1959 - "Convict Drowns In Sewer Pit At San Quentin." May 27, 1959 - "Another Quentin Con Escapes (Well Sort Of)." May 27, 1959 - Quentin Con Battles Cell mate—Badly Hurt. June 5, 1959 - Con Plans To Flee In Truck Foiled."

The joint managed to survive July 1959 without an execution. Meanwhile, my marriage stumbled along. It consisted of conquering the peaks of bliss while falling into the depths of despair on a weekly basis.

During the summer of 1959 the San Quentin Opera House, located in the middle of Bastille By The Bay, presented the musical "Guys and Dolls" to a captive audience of four thousand inmates and a few invited guests. Cassie declined to attend. I returned home that evening relaxed for the first time in days.

The following Monday, I began armed robbery interviews. As I was waiting for my next client, I read the jacket of Charles A. Behan, inmate assistant to the Catholic prison chaplain, Father Koburg. The job of Chaplains' assistant was considered a plum one among the brotherhood.

"Good morning, Mr. Sullivan." Behan smiled. He was a pleasant outgoing youth, serving ten to fifteen for armed robbery. An older brother had conned him into a hit on a Safeway store in Los Angeles.

"Good morning. Have a seat." Five minutes later I was his intellectual captive. Behan's vocabulary was more fitting a Ph.D. candidate in literature than a prison inmate. The tide of our conversation flowed back and forth. We settled on the topic of why America's prisons don't work.

"To the average person, the inner workings of our prisons are as much an enigma as the minds of the prisoners themselves. There isn't enough media exposure given the prison system in this country," he said. Behan glanced out at the pleasure boats drifting in the bay.

My office window, now a surrealistic view finder, became a looking glass through which my boys could see what they wanted to see. He continued. "Tough sentences, building more prisons, and the pitfalls of plea bargaining is barbershop talk in small towns as well as big."

"But there must be sociological solutions to the ills of society," I ventured.

"You call it corrections and rehabilitation. Inside the state legislature swims a plethora of controversy and conflicting attitudes. One fact that should be agreed upon by all is that prisons neither correct nor rehabilitate."

"Well, we're in agreement there," I said. "On the other hand our American system of imprisonment has been called more humane than that in most other countries."

"And in many ways that's true," my social issues debate partner said. "Socrates' sense of humanity to inmates may be reflected by the need for temporary relief from criminal acts. The state pays more attention to getting people into prisons than keeping them out."

Perhaps I could probe the depths of his soul, I thought. "What happens inside prison walls? What is expected of inmates? What kind of systems are in place to govern their lives." I tossed out all these questions.

"Everything that happens in the outside world happens inside the joint. Most correctional institutions are just miniature versions of the street. There is buying and selling, real estate and power struggle, love and hate, prostitution and drugs." Behan looked me in the eye, expecting to see shock.

"So what you're saying is that life on the inside is life on the street," I summed up.

"Yes, except that on the inside we cannot experience a most important concept - freedom. The only thing I have to struggle with is being away from my wife. And I miss going to restaurants and fishing."

"Are there any amenities provided inside the joint?" I asked.

"Sure. There are movies, exercise equipment, and radios. We also have access to typewriters and a library. There are art shows once a year and entertainers come over to entertain now and then."

"Anything else?" I asked.

"Many people are living better on the inside than they would on the street. Once you're here you can get almost anything you want. You want marijuana or cocaine, no big deal. They all look the other way."

I glanced at my watch. His time was up. "This has been quite a revelation to me," I said sincerely.

On his way out the door, he turned back. "I've been studying the sages. Solon said over two thousand years ago, 'Justice will only be served when those who are not injured by crime feel as indignant as those who are'."

"Great quote. Good luck," I responded.

After the interview I enjoyed a few moments of meditating on the billowy clouds and white capped waters of the bay. I picked up Behan's yellow jacket. Ramirez wanted to return the file. Giving yellow jackets to him is akin to handing Walter Mitty the keys to the TITANIC.

A letter fell out of the folder. It read:

Dear Warden,

I understand my son, Charles A. Behan, is to appear before the California Adult Authority on Tuesday, June 22, 1959 to be considered for Parole. I offer the following information not only as an apology, but perhaps as an explanation of Charlie's wrongdoing.

Charles and his younger brother were born and raised in Vancouver, British Columbia, where I practiced law. Their mother passed away when Charlie was five. I hired one governess after the other. The boys were not well disciplined.

In my desire to fill the void I gave them everything—money, cars, a beautiful home near Stanley Park in Vancouver with rivers and lakes nearby. They took their vacations in Europe and the States. I allowed my time to be consumed by political intrigue and a desire to succeed in the legal profession. In my selfishness I sent the boys to boarding schools as I climbed the ladder of success. Social functions, conferences, and elections ate me up alive.

A few years ago, unbeknownst to me, the boys drifted south to California. My appointment as Solicitor General of British Columbia took place a week before their arrest. The Scarlet Letter will belong not only to Charlie, but also to an unforgiving society,

244

whose collective heart has been hardened by decades of political rhetoric against what they know is an easy target. Politicians have convinced society that middle class felons are lurking around the corners waiting to trample their white picket fences. I know as an attorney I preached this sermon far and wide.

Charlie and his brother will be marked as sinners, outcasts, and offenders against the standards of decency in our society. Please give Charles another chance among the living.

I am, sincerely,

James H. Behan

Mr. Behan resigned as Solicitor General of British Columbia a month after his sons were convicted.

I started to pick up the next jacket when a cackle of conversation in Kinzer's office interrupted my thoughts. "Sullivan, you've got to see this." I elbowed my way to the window.

A large group of people were gathered below in front of the visiting center. Milling about were television crews, reporters, lawyers, prison personnel, and unidentified fringe fanatics waving hand painted signs lettered "Fry Baby Fry" in blood red. "We use gas, you idiots!" I yelled.

"I count forty-nine reporters," Fleming offered.

"I make it fifty-one," Kinzer said. "Looks like the press corps is in a feeding frenzy."

Mr. Mallachey joined us. "I don't know why all the fuss—the next date is late October. I think Chessman's latest book must have just been published."

"Yes, The Face of Justice," someone offered.

"Yeah. He likes attention," Barr added. "I think it's the second book he's smuggled out of the joint. Wonder how he does it?"

"Who knows? I hear Chessman's hard to handle," Fleming said. The staff believed Fleming had the most snitches in the joint. One by one we went back to work.

Kinzer walked with me back to my office. "I hear Judy Garland is coming to town. I'm a big fan of hers," he said.

"Me too. Where did you find out?" I asked.

"The morning newspaper. She's going to perform eleven nights at the opera house starting July first. Ginny and I are looking forward to an evening with Judy."

"Cassie would love to go. I'll mention it tonight." I was interested in socializing with Kinzer because I knew we had lots of interests in common—love of Jazz, San Francisco, and now Judy Garland.

"Maybe we'll see you there then." Kinzer returned to his office.

On the eve of Fourth of July, Cassie and I settled into our three dollar and seventy five cent seats in the upper balcony of the San Francisco War Memorial House. "Any higher and I'll get a nose bleed," I said.

Cassie leaned forward, "This is great." She grabbed my hand. The curtains slowly raised as an augmented orchestra began the opening prelude. After a few minutes of resounding overture, Alan King walked to center stage. He began a long monologue.

"I came home late the other night. My wife gave me a TV dinner as my punishment. 'How do I eat this?' I asked. 'Eat it like a popsicle,' she said. She forgot to defrost it." The first act ended.

"Swanee, Swanee, How I Love You My Dear Old Swanee" filled the auditorium. Judy Garland, shaped like a Toby Jug, sang and danced for a deliriously happy audience. We clapped and shouted throughout the entire performance. Never mind that she was overweight. Never mind that her costumes called attention to her figure rather than hid it. Never mind that many of her appearances were not only sad but somewhat embarrassing.

I leaned over to Cassie. "She can do no wrong."

"I love her," Cassie responded reverently. Her face shone with tears of happiness as she applauded until her hands hurt.

Dancer John W. Bubbles joined Judy in "We're A Couple Of Swells." Although many years her senior, he moved with a light and youthful grace. Judy picked up a microphone. A single blue light spotted her sitting on a high chair. All of her charms became apparent. She began, "Somewhere Over The Rainbow." The audience jumped to its feet.

"That's her song!" I yelled. Garland knew it would bring the house down and it did. All too soon the curtains closed and she disappeared into the wings. We started for home.

"I wish tonight would never end.," Cassie whispered.

"Ah, but it will. We can't live on memories," I responded.

"I'm so glad we came," she declared. Locked arm in arm, we stumbled to our car. Of all the memories I have accumulated over the past seventy years, our magical night with Judy Garland will stay with me forever.

The following afternoon we celebrated the Fourth of July by visiting the Jackson Street Irregulars. I felt at home in the second floor community kitchen. Nothing had changed.

Early in the evening, we all trooped down the hill to the Marina for the fireworks. "Oh, look!" Cassie pointed to a multi-colored starburst as brilliant patterns of light lit up the sky. We held hands and hugged. The pyrotechnical masterpieces were accompanied by choruses of oohs and aahs. That night we slept well.

AUGUST 1959. SAN QUENTIN CONTINUED TO MAKE the news. Headlines included, "Officer Interrupts A Quiet Drunk—In Quentin Prison Yard," "Escaped Con Nabbed After Short Spree," and, "A Warden's Wife Tells All About San Quentin."

The following Friday I stopped for gas on my way home from work. "Hi, Sean. How are you?" I looked over and saw Maggie, from Jackson Street, waiving at me from the next bay.

"Well, hi, Maggie. What are you doing here?"

"Same thing as you, Sean. Gassing up the bug."

"What's new?"

"Nothing. How's Cassie?"

"Still looking for a job. She's getting frustrated," I said.

"I don't blame her. Well, see ya'." Maggie walked away but stopped short of her car. Turning back to me, she called out, "I forgot to tell you. I saw your wife riding around North Beach in Walter McKeene's white Cadillac convertible this afternoon."

"Oh," I said. What else could I say? I forced what I hoped was a smile through clinched teeth.

"Say hello to her for me!" Maggie sped away in her 1950 yellow Studebaker.

I circled Steiner and Union streets several times before finding a parking spot. A caldron of suspicion boiled in my gut. An unsuspecting Cassie hugged me at the door.

"Guess what, Sean? I got a job! Bruce the bartender hired me as a cocktail waitress at the Vesuvio." She danced around me. "Now we can pay our bills."

I cupped her elbow and hurried down the ramp to the living room sofa. "Maggie tells me you've been driving around North Beach with Walter McKeane in his white convertible," I began.

"Oh, she did, did she? And have you been seeing Maggie?" I was taken aback by her counterattack.

"Hell, no!" I yelled. "I was gassing up in San Rafael on the way home when she drove into the station."

Cassie felt she had captured the high ground for the moment. She always believed the best defense is a good offense. "Don't change the subject," she demanded illogically.

I saw a tear trickle down her face. She's going to play it soft, I thought.

"Well, if you want to know the truth…" Her voice trailed off into a whisper.

I got right into her face, wailing, "Yes, tell me the truth."

"Okay. Well, after I left Bruce…"

"Oh. So now it's Bruce," I shot.

"Oh, shut up!" She pushed me back with both hands, then continued. "I went upstairs to Walter McKeane's gallery. Just out of curiosity." The blood drained from her face. "Maybe you'd like to know something," she ventured.

"What?" I moaned.

"Walter made a pass at me when we went into his art gallery."

"What kind of a pass?" I detonated.

She turned, looked over her shoulder in her best Betty Boop smile. "Wouldn't you like to know," she sneered.

I shifted the focus of my attack. "What's this about working at Vesuvio? Bruce is the best known womanizer in North Beach. More so than McKeane. If that's possible." Our tirade continued for another twenty minutes.

"I want to know what…" A knock at the door stopped me in mid sentence.

"There's someone at the door." Cassie walked up the ramp.

Two police officers stood in the doorway, blocking the fading light of summer. The older officer stepped forward and said, "We've had a complaint from your landlord, about a domestic quarrel."

"Sorry, Sir. My wife and I are having a little disagreement, that's all," I said. I tried to down play the situation. His partner huddled with Cassie in the kitchen.

My attempts to pacify the officer were met with, "You'll have to come with us."

"For what? Am I under arrest?"

"No, you're not under arrest. Let's just take a little ride to cool off." Both men stood beside me. Knowing retreat to be the better part of valor, I agreed. Cassie remained out of sight in the kitchen.

I sat silent in the "To Protect And Serve" black and white cruiser as we drove downtown. My love-hate relationship with Cassie boiled, then simmered, then slowly cooled. After a few minutes the car stopped.

"We're going to let you off here." The officer looked me in the eye, put his hand on my shoulder, and said, "Take it easy, Son. It ain't worth the effort." I headed for the nearest bus stop and home.

Cassie let me in the front door. She walked to the back of the living room and sat on the stage. Neither of us spoke for a few moments, each unwilling to shatter the silence. At length I mumbled, "I'm sorry."

"What?" she demanded.

"I said I'm sorry." I headed for the bathroom.

"Sean, we have to talk."

"Yes, you're right," I said wearily.

"Nothing happened between Walter and I. Nothing happened between Bruce and I," she asserted.

"I know. I guess I'm too possessive. Sometimes I feel I own you body and soul. Especially body."

"Sean, we've never discussed our problems. We've got to do something."

A tone of civility returned to our dialogue. The ripples of resentment and rejection slowly dissipated. Anger became peacemaking. We agreed to a truce.

"I'll try to be more patient and less possessive," I vowed.

"I'm not a bad girl, Sean. Try to remember that," she pleaded. We made love that night, reincarnating latent passions and desires. Our marriage was clearly in distress and badly in need of repair.

Thoughts of Cassie had been constantly on my mind when I reported for duty one foggy Thursday morning two weeks later. I like Thursdays. We interviewed white collar crimes. Nice and neat. None of the "my stepfather fondled my breasts," or the illiterate "he touched my virginia."

I'd begun the habit of bringing the morning newspaper from home. Ramirez' none too subtle ministrations had begun to me uncomfortable. But I still didn't see the storm warnings on the horizon.

"Killer Loses Pleas, Dies Tomorrow," I read. "Oh God. Another Black Friday," I said aloud. The next day I managed to survive another execution as I waded through the cesspool of depravity.

News Item, Friday August 21, 1959, "Slayer Nash Dies - With a Grin." I groaned aloud over the reflections of the day.

"Cheer up, Sullivan. It gets worse before it gets better," Fleming said. As if that would make me feel better.

"It's amazing what one human being can do to another, both psychologically and physically," I declared to one and all.

Mallachey placed his hand on my shoulder. "Welcome to the club, Sean. You need develop a tough hide."

I arrived home depressed. Cassie worked nights at the Vesuvio, seven p.m. until closing. Bruce drove her home after work. A thought which preyed upon me every waking moment.

The fragrance of sharp cheddar cheese and macaroni filled my nostrils as soon as I entered the house. "Your dinner is on the stove. Just heat the pot." Cassie stopped to give me a peck on my forehead on her way out the door.

"What time will you be home?" I demanded.

"Late. But don't worry, Bruce will bring me home."

That's what worries me, I thought. My eyes followed her across the room. "Your skirt is too short." Always the puritan, I had to say something. The door slammed shut behind her. I looked forward to another Friday night alone.

The following evening, we decided to stay home since we were broke. A quiet night might ease the stress and strain of our lifestyle. Smoke hung thick over the little theater turned living room. I had taken to a pipe years before. I preferred them to cigarettes.

Cassie and I were halfway through the "Gerry Moore Show" when the phone rang. Cassie got up to answer it. "Well, hi, Wally! How are you?" A muffled conversation continued while I enjoyed the antics of Carole Burnett on TV.

Cassie came back into the living room. "I'm going to meet Wally at Mels Drive-In. We have some business to discuss," she announced. Mels Drive-In, at the corner of Lombard and Steiner, would later serve as the locale for a successful TV series.

"What kind of business?" I demanded.

"He said he might have a job for me. I'll be back soon."

"Oh, that sounds interesting." Pleased at the possibility of Cassie quitting Vesuvio, I put my concerns aside and turned back to the television set.

One hour turned into two. The door opened. Cassie headed for the kitchen. "I think I got a job," she said.

"Great, doing what?" I asked. I barely heard the word "posing."

"What do you mean posing?"

"Life study."

"You mean in the nude?" I shot upright in my chair. She walked into the living room and stood some distance from me. "Wally has a friend who wants me to model for him," she declared somewhat defiantly.

"But you're my wife."

"He's willing to pay me fifty dollars."

"It's not the money. You're my wife." I couldn't let go of the phrase, as if it made a difference. "Why do you want to show your body to a stranger?"

"I'm not your personal property, you know. You don't have a monopoly on me. And you just don't understand art."

I tried to control my fury.

"Shhh. Remember what happened last time."

"To hell with the neighbors!" I roared.

"Wally is waiting for me in the car," she added.

"What kind of marriage is this?" I demanded. I couldn't hear Cassie's mumbled response. "What did you say?" I demanded. "I can't hear you".

"I said I regret having married you!" Cassie started for the door.

"Now you tell me."

Verbal retaliation flowed back and forth like the tide. She turned to me, her face sullen, and whispered the unthinkable. "You can't give me children," she challenged.

Deflated, I sank into my old recliner. Speech escaped me. I could not form the words to respond. I licked my dry lips.

"I'm leaving, Sean. And I'm not coming back." She ground out the words through clenched teeth.

Cassie opened the door and vanished into the dark of night. I lost my little girl that night. Forever.

17

"THE FINAL SEDUCTION"

EARLY THE NEXT MORNING, I HEARD A KEY turn in the front door. I opened it to see Cassie silhouetted against the morning sunshine. Bruce sat in his red pickup across the street.

"I need some of my things" she announced. She walked up the ramp and sat on the stage. Dressed in pleated khaki pants and a faded work shirt, probably belonging to Bruce the bartender, she appeared friendly and somewhat flirtatious. I even caught a wink or two. I put my arm around her waist in hopes of recapturing something which no longer existed. She stiffened.

I didn't know what I wanted. Finally I said, "There's an art show this weekend at San Quentin. Would you like to join me?"

"No."

I couldn't resist saying, "I see you brought your friend."

"Bruce has been very nice to me," she responded stiffly.

"I'll bet." Realizing I was on the wrong tack I changed course. "I'm sorry about last night. You don't have to move. We can still make a go of our marriage. Let's talk." I reached for her hand.

"No." She pulled away.

"What can I do to make you happy?" I demanded.

"Nothing, Sean. We can't go on pretending we have a marriage."

My pleadings were in vain. She hustled through the little theater apartment gathering her essentials, putting them into two large shopping bags. "I'll come back next week for the rest of my stuff," she said.

Then she turned and walked out. The hole in my heart opened wider. I began my self-inflicted martyrdom.

I headed for the office the following Friday, mentally preparing myself for another decent into a den of depravity. "Good morning, Mr. Sullivan. Coffee, cream, no sugar." Ramirez materialized before me, grinning his usual "I gotcha" grin. From behind his back he whipped out a brown bag and announced, "Fresh doughnuts, chocolate glazed. Just the way you like them."

"How did you get these?" I said. "And how did you know I liked chocolate?" Ramirez was the prison scrounger. I knew better than to ask any questions.

"Oh, a friend of mine works in the bakery," he said.

Increasing loneliness caused me to be more indiscreet at work. I mentioned my marriage problems to Ramirez on a daily basis. I saw him as someone to whom I could reveal my most intimate thoughts. Now I had broken Rule No. 6—never confide in an inmate.

During my orientation Mr. Mallachey had explained, "A convict is a prisoner with traditional values. One who has pride and respect, who maintains integrity. An inmate has no scruples."

"Mr. Sullivan, your first interview," Ramirez announced. I leafed through the folder of Inmate No. 90352, Burtowski. A Victim Impact Statement caught my eye. Steve Burtowski, Caucasian, age twenty-eight, married, one son, age three, auto mechanic, rape-sodomy, ten to twelve, stood at attention before me.

"Good morning. Have a seat." I tried to put Burtowski at ease. As usual San Pablo Bay caught his attention. He fantasized a moment of freedom. I had actually considered asking for an inside office due to the distraction power of the Bay, but I enjoyed its pacifying panoramas too much myself.

"Please, be comfortable." I motioned towards a chair.

A quiet young man with blue eyes accentuated by wavy blonde hair sat down in front on me. He had Nordic good looks. He looked good in prison blues. I silently offered a prayer on his behalf. "I hope the homosexuals haven't discovered you," I said to myself.

Much of the interview passed in silence. He was reluctant to speak. We weren't very interested in confessions which cleansed the soul, only "I did it." Burtowski answered my questions with a series of either, yes, no, or maybe. For my part, I added a few 'Uh, huh's" and "I see's" to the exchange. After twenty minutes I closed the interview, thanking him for coming in. As though he had a choice.

As he left I finished reading the victim's statement.

VICTIM IMPACT STATEMENT. Offender: <u>Steve Burtowski</u>. Sentencing: <u>May 15, 1959</u>. Cause Number: <u>92164</u>. Judge: <u>J. McKinney</u>. Defense Attorney: <u>John Davis</u>.

VICTIM IMPACT STATEMENT QUESTIONNAIRE. To be included with the Pre-Sentence Report and permanently included in the files and records accompanying an offender committed to the custody of a State agency or institution, in accordance with California Statute 234.1, subsection C. Victim's name: Bernice Burtowski. Person submitting impact statement: Me. Relationship to victim: I am the victim. Date statement prepared: n/a.

1. Please describe in your own words the physical, emotional, or psychological impact this crime has had upon you and your family. (If you are writing for someone else, who was the victim, describe the impact that you have directly observed.) Attach additional sheets if you need more space.

2. Describe any financial impact the crime has had on you and/ or your family. (This may be a general statement. Detailed information used to determine the amount of restitution will be obtained separately.)

3. Describe any permanent or long-lasting changes in your lifestyle, relationships, or career resulting from the crime that have not already been described.

And the answer read: *"I am devastated. My relationship with my family remains unstable. My friendships with my neighbors and acquaintances are non-existent. The lady next door makes remarks like, 'If you had better control over Steve, this would not have happened.' The lady across the street stopped me this morning and said that if I had been properly dressed my son would not have raped me. My sister remarked, 'How fortunate you have other children.' I am beginning to agree. If I had been a better parent this would not have happened. I stopped to chat with the mailman as I was leaving the house today and he said, 'Look at what you have allowed to happen in this nice neighborhood'."*

4. Describe anything about the crime which you believe the judge should especially consider in deciding what the sentence should be.

It ended with a signature line for the victim and the instruction to return the questionnaire in the enclosed pre-addressed metered envelope to the Victim/Witness Assistance Unit.

Ramirez walked into the office just as I finished this little narrative. I was attempting to digest the shock. "Now I've heard everything," I mused.

"Oh. That's the guy who raped his mother. Everybody in the joint knows him. I think he is still in isolation," Ramirez responded.

"My God!. What happened?" I asked.

"He got stoned and attached his mother." Ramirez went on in graphic detail.

Just after my last interview of the day, Mr. Mallachey appeared and announced, "Sorry, Sean. Another shakedown. This one may take some time."

"It doesn't matter. There's no one waiting at home now. Cassie left me."

"What!"

We sat in his office for the next forty-five minutes awaiting the all clear. I unloaded my tale of woe. Anyone who would listen to my story was a friend for life. Mr. Mallachey pulled out all the usual counseling techniques.

We were interrupted by the phone. A short muffled conversation took place. "All clear. They found him under the floor in the cotton mill. I don't know how he got there."

"There must be hundreds of hiding places in this joint," I ventured.

We stood up. Mallachey put his arm around me. "Sean, somebody once said, and I don't remember who, 'The exhaustion of passions is the beginning of wisdom'," he said gravely. I always get nervous when people put their arms around me and quote obscure proverbs.

"Well, I'm exhausted that's for sure. Thank you for your advice. I don't want to burden you," I said.

Life went on at San Quentin through August, September and October 1959. I missed Cassie and was beginning to realize the error of my ways. I drank more and began patronizing the local strip joints. I celebrated the ancient and honorable sport of quaffing the ale in the less notable saloons of San Francisco. The best of them served fifty cent drinks.

Despite the disapproval of Charles McCabe, Esquire, local San Francisco bon vivant and newspaper columnist, I enjoyed the Buena Vista Cafe.

San Quentin continued to make the news. Headlines buried in the first section from time to time included: "Killer Of Five Died In Quentin, Prison Discloses," "Two Quentin Cons Get Part-Way Out," "Rape-Killer Glatman Put to Death," "Killer Offers Eyes To Pastor," and "Robber Saved From Execution."

My newly acquired bachelor status led to an orgy of self-pity. Nobody would give me Cassie's new address or phone number. I became a part-time detective and a full-time stalker. My nondescript green 1951 Chevrolet faded into the scenery of the city.

After a weekend of searching, I discovered that she was working days at a baker and nights at the Vesuvio. I phoned her. "Hi, Cassie. How are you?"

"How did you get my phone number?" she groaned.

"Relax. Howard gave it to me. You're working at his bakery now?"

"Yes."

"Are you still working nights at the Vesuvio with Bruce the bartender?"

"Yes."

"Look, Cassie, I'm not your enemy. I miss you. Can't we get together some time soon?"

"Well, maybe, but not right now. I'm busy. Come over to the bakery in a little while and we'll talk."

I raced over to Union and Columbus, parked the car, and flung open the door of the bakery. Howard was standing behind Cassie. "Hi, Cassie. Hello, Howard," I said.

Howard Hessler was a long time friend of my old girlfriends, the three musketeers in Portland: Gloria, Eve and Lillian. Hoping to score with one or all of them in my college days, I would have coffee with them at Mannings Coffee Shop in downtown Portland.

I had met Howard in the early 1950's when he and Pete, as we called Lillian then, got married. The marriage didn't last long. Howard's left arm and side were paralyzed from a childhood illness, but that limitation hadn't prevented him from becoming a successful one-armed baker and a womanizer par excellence. He would eventually pass away of a stroke.

Cassie and I first engaged in trivial conversation. She smiled, revealing her Shirley Temple dimples. I dissolved into a puddle of penitence. After a few "I'm sorry's," I popped the question. "The cons are putting on a stage play at San Quentin next Friday and Saturday night, 'Stalag Seventeen.' Would you like to go with me?"

Cassie looked at the ceiling. One minute of my life ticked by as I held my breath waiting for her answer. "Okay, I guess so. How about Friday night? I can find someone to fill in for me at Vesuvio."

"Great. Six o'clock. What's your address?" I danced a little jig.

On Friday morning, I was wading through "man's immorality to man" when the next inmate appeared for an interview. As usual I had not read the file. He was a rotund, balding man, fortyish. He looked like he could be anybody's favorite uncle.

"Good Morning. Have a chair," I said. Of course, he headed for the window instead.

"Beautiful. Oh, to be on the water on a day like this," he mused. We began a pleasant conversation.

"How are you doing?" I asked.

"Fine. I've been taking classes and will soon have my GED. I also play the drums in the prison band."

"Sounds like you're keeping busy," I commented.

"Oh, I have everything but privacy. But I guess nothing is perfect."

Suddenly I began to relate to him. The psychiatrists call it transference. His easy manner, soothing voice and intense gray eyes held me in a spell.

"I enjoy music, don't you?" He leaned towards me.

"Oh yes." I rhapsodized for a few minutes on my love for the classics and San Francisco Jazz in particular. It was too late when I belatedly realized he was interviewing me.

"Do you have any children?" he asked midway into the session.

It was my turn to look out at the sailboats drifting by the joint. I revealed my most intimate thoughts on my inability to father a child. Since Cassie's leave taking, my sterility preyed upon my mind. We should have had children.

Forty five minutes into the conversation, the inmate got up to leave. "Well, Mr. Sullivan. I don't want to take any more of your time. Are you coming to the play tonight?"

"Yes. My wife and I will be there."

"See you then." He whistled his way out of my office.

Ramirez stuck his head in the door as Dave was leaving. "Coffee, Mr. Sullivan?"

"Yeah, okay." I began to read the drummer's file. A document titled "Diary of Death" in Dave's jacket caught my eye. I struggled through the twenty-four page journal and was transported far beyond my life experiences. Even in wet dreams, I could never conjure up such a fantasy. As I read the diary in its entirety, I alternately felt like gagging or gasping for breath. At one point I actually moved the wastepaper basket to my feet in case I had to vomit.

The diary had been found inside a briefcase Dave kept hidden beneath his bed along with a photo album. I read:

September. My problem was getting a kid to actually touch me and not scare him off. The answer came quickly. I found a group of six kids (three boys, three girls) in a school playground. I wanted to be touched badly. I wasn't worried about location, numbers or whether they were boys or not. I asked them if they wanted to play a game.

Saturday. Located a park. An ideal area. South and West sides are a wooded gully. Isolated areas especially in the East end. Within a half hour I saw three boys together. Good for rape and murder or kidnapping.

Sunday. Checked same area out. Intend to spend up to five hours this afternoon to obtain what I want. Depending on circumstances I will rape and murder at sight, or may kill from there and rape at home, or take to another area and rape again before murder.

Monday. Intend to have fun today as it is Labor Day Weekend. One boy about four was wandering away from teenagers playing ball or else I would have gotten him out of sight for rape or rape and murder.

6:00 p.m. Started walking away from car. After fifty yards three boys about seven years old passed me on bikes. I went back to my car for the knife. I intended to separate them to do two murders and then rape and murder but they rode off again. I will try again tomorrow. Three to three thirty seems to be the best time. I went back to the park that night. Found two boys. Nobody else around. About the proper age. I approached and said, "I want you two boys to come with me." The older one said, "Why?" "Because I told you to. You can bring your bikes if you want." I didn't want anyone to find the bikes and start looking for them. They both followed me to the most isolated part of the park.

Wednesday. I am trying to figure out a location for my next hunt. I must spend more time with boy or girl before killing and make sure the body is hidden better. I think I get more of a high out of killing than molesting.

Friday. Last night three sheriff's deputies pulled up in front of the house where I am renting a room. Landlady called them to evict another tenant because of a verbal fight. I hope they didn't realize I was the one in their sketch.

Tuesday. In surgery with live patients. They will have to be tied down regardless of whether they are conscious or not. I may do *surgery with or without pain relief or sedation.*

(Directly beneath this passage was a crudely drawn "torture rack" depicting bound children with the words "live kids" in parenthesis below it. The torture rack was found by the detective at the time of Dave's arrest.)

Murder Methods: Fastest - stabbing. Slicing throat - too messy! Slowest - starvation/thirst. Medium - Suffocation/drowning.

Murder victims will be asked, "I'm not going to do it, but if you had to die, do you want to choose how or have someone else do it?" They could choose stabbing, cut throat, strangling, suffocation, bleeding to death or starvation. Or they could roll dice, draw cards or pull straws from a hat. They could have surgeries with or without drugs. Do it quickly or make a ceremony out of it. With surgeries they could stay alive but undergo pain.

Wednesday. I now ask Satan that this boy be an easy target. I can't do much hunting for fear of being noticed by a witness. If certain conditions are met and I can remain sexually satisfied through physical contact, pictures or tapes, then I will gladly turn over my soul to Satan. If necessary I will meet with him or his aide to sign a contract. I hope I will not be frightened at my next meeting with him. I will exchange my soul for a long happy life as a pedophile, with plenty of action, and a possible contribution to the child pornography empire; with no danger of discovery by the authorities.

Sunday, 11.15 p.m. I went up to the little boy and asked him if he wanted to "have some fun and make some money." He seemed unsure but not scarred. I said, "Come on, this will be fun," and reached out my hand. He took it and walked to the end of the building with me. We got out of the sight of the other kids. I told him we were going to get into my car. He said "I don't want any money." I picked him up and said, "We're still going. Let's go ask your dad if you can go with me." As we drove along he said, "I live the other way." I said, "We're going to my house to play some games. Just do what I tell you and I promise I won't hurt you." He started crying. He said his dad and brother miss him. I was able to quickly quiet him.

Tuesday. Just saw a sketch of me on the news. I will be staying out of sight for about a month.

Friday. *I will tape his mouth shut with duct tape. Then I will use a clothespin to plug his nose. That way I can sit back, take pictures, and watch him die.*

Monday, *4.45 p.m. I now ask Satan to guide me and provide a boy for me tonight. Going to check out the local parks before going to a movie.*

The diary ended.

Dave was arrested that evening at a local theater as he was attempting to abduct a young boy. He coped a plea. The D.A. commuted the death sentence when Dave led police to several graves. He also cooperated in furnishing detailed information about his activities.

I managed to make it to the bathroom before throwing up in the toilet. When I got back, Fleming was standing in my office. He looked at me and said, "You look like death warmed over."

Then he added, "Good news, Sean. No shakedowns, no lock downs, no screw ups. We can leave on time tonight."

Cassie was waiting for me on the sidewalk when I pulled up in front of her apartment. We engaged in small talk on the way back to San Quentin. I made a conscious effort not to ask her any personal questions. Rumor had it she was having an affair with Bruce the bartender.

"Id please." The CO did a double take as we got to the gate. "Oh, it's you, Mr. Sullivan. Sorry." His gaze fixed on Cassie.

"This is my wife, Cassie," I said.

He waved us to the employee parking lot. The turnkeys passed us through the gates. Cassie remained wide eyed all the way to the dinning hall. A stage had been set up in front of the building. The prison band was assembled in a semicircle off to one side.

"Who are all those people in blue?" she asked.

"Inmates. Helpers, stage hands, gofers and many of the curious are convicts," I explained.

The band struck up the national anthem, followed by a short overture to "Stalag 17" as we seated ourselves. "This is the first time I've seen a play within a play. I remember the movie a few years ago," Cassie commented. She radiated happiness.

"William Holden won the Academy Award for best actor. And Robert Strauss was great as Animal," I said.

During intermission we mingled with the crowd. "There's nobody here from the office," I said.

"That's okay, Sean. I don't feel like meeting people. Just you and me." She squeezed my arm.

"Can I get you a coke or something?" If I was ever going to score points with Cassie, tonight was the night.

"No, thanks, not right now. I think they're about to start the next act." For the next hour we laughed, cried, ooh'd, and aah'd. We shared the gauntlet of emotions.

A major character in the play, called Animal, revealed himself by accepting special favors from the Germans. When he made his entrance, the building erupted with hissing, booing and foot stomping. "Why are they booing him?" Cassie asked.

"Because he's a snitch," I whispered. A minute or two passed.

"Now why are they hissing?" Cassie asked.

"He's the German commander."

The play ended to a standing ovation. As we walked out we were greeted with, "Good Evening, Mr. Sullivan." Startled, I turned to face David the child molester.

"Hello," I said. I steered Cassie out of the building.

"Somebody you know? Why didn't you introduce me?" she asked.

"Forget it."

"What's he in here for?" she persisted.

"Life without parole for child molestation and murder," I explained.

"Oh."

We drove to the North Beach area. Cassie's apartment was at the bottom of Telegraph Hill. I parked down the street and made a big production out of opening the door for her.

"Would you like to come in for coffee?" she purred.

"Sure." Expecting combat, I was taken aback by her cordiality.

She lived in a typical North Beach three-room flat with thrift shop furniture. Paint was peeling off the walls. Her rooms were habitable but not comfortable. I spotted the one easy chair in the room.

"How have you been? You don't look too well." She peered into my face.

I wasn't going to admit that memories don't keep one warm on a cold winter's night. I answered, "Oh, I'm okay. I keep busy."

"I made some chocolate chip cookies. Have some."

"Oh, great. I love chocolate chip cookies." We traded trivia back and forth like two prize fighters jockeying for position. Cassie went over to the green Salvation Army dresser.

"Bruce and I went to Carmel last weekend. It's really beautiful. Would you like to see some pictures?"

Oh, God. Here it comes, I thought. She sat at my feet and handed me photos of their two day soiree to Carmel By The Sea, narrating as she went along.

"This is Bruce and I together. A tourist took the picture for us. And here's Bruce pretending to jump over the cliff."

"That's an idea." I mumbled.

"This is Bruce looking for whales," she continued.

Another five minutes of this torture and I'm leaving, I said to myself. At last she put the pictures away. I cupped her breasts. She didn't resist, so I pulled her up savoring the sweet kiss of reconciliation. Or so I hoped.

"Follow me," she whispered. She led me to an alcove which passed for a bedroom. A squeaky roll away served as a bed.

She turned her back to me. "Will you undo me?" My hands shook as I fumbled with hooks and buttons. She stepped out of her dress and underclothes. I gawked. Staring at the thieves treasure, I became Ali Baba in a Thousand Nights. I pulled her down to the squeaky bed. She kissed me.

"Cassie, I want to..." I thought of Montaignes "An insatiate thirst of enjoying a greedily desired object."

"So do I, Sean."

I stroked her auburn hair. I fumbled with my trousers. She gave herself to me. Above the gasps for breath and squealing, I heard a key shoved into the front door and then the door slam open.

"Well, well, what's all this?" an unseen voiced sneered. Cassie froze. I moaned. Towering over us stood Bruce the bartender.

"What do you think this is, a cathouse?" he demanded.

I rolled off the bed preparing to do battle. Bruce stood before us smoking a black cigar. It stank. I covered Cassie with a bath towel.

"If you're finished here, old boy, I might have a go at her," he snickered. I dressed in record time as Bruce fumbled with his fly.

"Get out of here!" I yelled.

"Be a sport, old boy, she's only a chippy," he replied lightly.

Cassie sat frothing at the mouth, unable to speak, her lips bathed in spittle. Incoherent, guttural screams from her throat caused spasms of anger to ripple throughout her body.

"What should I do with this cripple?" Bruce the bartender asked. I hit him with all the force I could muster. He stumbled back with a face frozen in surprise. Grabbing my throat with both hands, he shook me like a rag doll.

"Bruce, stop it! You'll hurt him," Cassie screeched, finally finding her voice. Her towel fell to floor as she jumped, stark naked, off the bed and tried to grab the arms of my assailant.

We stumbled around the room, a fury of fists and legs. An eternity passed. Exhausted, Bruce and I stared at each other, gasping for air, like two bulls during mating season. Throwing Cassie a look of scorn, I walked out, tossing two dollars on the dresser as I walked by. "It was worth it!" I bellowed as I slowly closed the door.

The next morning, Mr. Mallachey was the picture of understanding when I asked for a few days vacation. I didn't go into detail regarding my recent encounter with Cassie's lover.

The drive North on 101 was a relaxing respite after the war of the Sullivans. I went on to Portland and visited Ma. As usual, she didn't ask questions but knew something was wrong.

After a particularly good dinner of chicken and dumplings one evening, I vented. "Ma, Cassie left me. We had a big fight and she moved out. I think she has taken up with somebody else."

Ma remained her stoic self. Thank God she didn't say, "I told you so." I knew she didn't like Cassie, but in the tradition of good mothers the world over, she remained silent.

Her only parting remark as I left her little apartment was, "Sean, you married her. You'll have to solve your own problems."

"Yeah. I know. Thanks for everything." I started to drive away.

"Sean, wait. Here." She pushed a twenty dollar bill into my hand. The return trip South on the coast highway cleansed my mind. I was greeted by the insistent clanging of the telephone as I opened the door to my apartment.

"Hi Cassie, how are you?" My spirits soared on hearing her melodious tones.

"Where have you been? I've been calling and calling," she said.

"I went up to Eureka and Portland to see the family."

She dropped the bomb. "I just wanted to tell you I filed for divorce," she said.

For a few heartbeats I couldn't think of anything to say. "Well, this a great welcome home. I looked forward to seeing you," I finally managed.

"I'm sorry, Sean, but it's over. Maybe we can be friends later, but not now." Her voice was wooden and distant. The word "friends" lit up my horizon. Cassie listened, less than patient, to my incoherent entreaties.

"I've got to go Sean," she finally said. "Bruce is at the door." The line went dead.

Thoroughly depressed, I headed for the kitchen. Ice cubes, a big glass and Chivas Regal rescued me. I put on a recording of "The 1812 Overture," sat down and held my drink in a death grip. My fingers turned white. I wanted to screech a primal howl.

Instead I drove downtown and parked near Mason and Taylor street. I set out for the nearest strip joint. A hustler spotted me staggering in his direction. "Welcome to the Pink Pussy cat, Sir. The show is about to begin." He held the door open for me, a courtesy I appreciated in my alcoholic haze.

Blurry-eyed, I lurched to a stool at the bar. I took note of the preponderance of males in the club. The smell of stale beer and cigarette smoke pervaded the premises. The only thing lacking was sawdust on the floor.

"Scotch and soda please."

"Yes, Sir. That'll be five dollars."

"What! I don't want to buy the joint." My aversion to bartenders increased by the drink. "Oh well. My wife has left me. What the hell…"

A drum roll interrupted my tale of woe. Hidden speakers blared forth, "And now here's Billee." The curtains parted. A pasty faced young man in his twenties pranced on stage. A g-string almost covered his genitalia.

"Let Me Entertain You And We'll Have a Real Good Time," rang throughout the room. Billee executed an accomplished pelvic thrust to the accompaniment of a strong bass beat. I froze. Several bumps and grinds later, I stumbled out to the sidewalk.

"Hey, your drink!. Dont'cha want your drink, fella?" The bartender called after my retreating form. Jaywalking across Mason Street, I spied another neon sign, this one blinking "Rumpus Room—Girls, Girls, Girls."

The doorman scrutinized me as I examined the posters of "Girls, Girls, Girls." I turned, weaving in his direction. "Sorry buddy. You can't come in here," he said.

"Why the hell not?" I roared. The force of my breath pushed him away. "And I'm not your buddy."

"Because you're drunk, that's why." He stood, arms akimbo.

"I'm not drunk. This is the way I walk. I was born this way." I wheezed like leaky bellows.

"You're not coming in here," he repeated. He sniffed the night air. The guardian of "Girls, Girls, Girls" gently pushed me away.

"Okay for you. I'll never favor this establishment with my presence again." Big threat. Mush-mouthed, I walked away. I returned five nights later to be admitted by another buddy.

Navigating my car through blurry eyes, I found Pacific Street, the fabled Barbary Coast of the gold rush days. Through eyes moistened by too much scotch and soda, I saw a scantily clad lady on top of a neon bucking horse. "The Purple Stallion" rocked back and forth. More 'Girls, Girls, Girls.' I walked stiff legged so I could pass inspection into this den of despair.

The major domo opened the door to paradise. The usual strip joint combo, led by an overeager drummer, pounded out "Night Train to Memphis." A tall, long-legged woman with almond eyes slithered through the curtains and performed a dance of delight which aroused my appetites. The dark-skinned beauty in the blue spotlight transported me on wings of desire to the Garden of Eden. Exotic suggestions punctuated by crashing cymbals blasted away the cares of the day and yesterday. At last I could see all of her. Well, all the San Francisco Police Department would allow.

The combo took a break in deference to the musician's union. Soon, a rustling sound shattered my thoughts. Turning sideways I saw her walking towards me through beaded curtains like jello on springs. Marilyn Monroe paled by comparison.

Standing over me with a smile that would seduce a stone statue stood my personal Salome. "May I join you?" Her voice was husky and sensuous.

"Of course," I croaked.

"My name is Jasmine," she murmured in my ear. In four words she oozed an invitation no man would forget.

"I'm, Sean," I managed to squeak out.

She sat down next to me. Her long fingernails, painted acorn, complimented the brown in her eyes. Jasmine slowly extracted a gold cigarette case from a pearl spangled purse. Her moist ruby red lips pulsated with each heartbeat.

"You got a match?" she whispered.

Affecting my best Bogart imitation, I flashed a Woolworth five and dime Bic lighter and lit her cigarette.

"Thank you." She kissed my fingertips. Smoke rings floated to the ceiling. So did I.

"What do you do, Sean?"

"I work for the State of California." Revealing my true occupation would probably empty the place.

"What kind of work?"

"Oh, I help people. Something like welfare."

Jasmine continued her gentle interrogation. I realized she was checking me out. I could be a liquor inspector.

All of a sudden I blurted, "How about a date?"

She smiled. "I have one more dance. Then we could have a little party at my place. Is twenty dollars okay?"

The mention of money rang the bell of reality. This isn't social. She doesn't like me for myself.

"Sure, why not?" I answered.

She wrote something on the back of a club matchbook and handed it to me. "This is my address. I'll be back soon." Jasmine slithered away into the smoke filled club and disappeared behind closed curtains.

"Okay." I looked forward to a carnal conquest of Olympic proportions. I waited outside on the street in wild anticipation.

"Follow me," she said. It was two fifteen in the morning when we headed West on Geary to the Sunset District of San Francisco. She signaled me to park behind her several blocks from her apartment. "The neighbors, you know."

"Good idea," I commented.

Jasmine opened the door to a thousand and one nights. Pushing aside strings of colored beads, I entered a large room decorated in a rainbow of colors. Oversized silk pillows adorned a queen size bed.

Simulated Persian tapestries covered the wall. A biblical oil of Salome, with the head of John The Baptist on a silver plate, adorned one wall.

"Make yourself at home," she whispered. "I'm going to change into something else." I sat on the bed as the pages of my life floated by one by one. I could not catch them.

Jasmine returned in a white silk peignoir which contrasted quite nicely with her dusky complexion. Her garment was transparent. "Would you like a glass of wine?" she asked.

"Sure." I fell back into the pillows.

"Let's light some candles." One by one she lit six tapers, appropriately placed around the bed. Captured by the light of the candles, I watched her peignoir hit the floor.

Daylight streaked across the Eastern horizon early the next morning, as I said good by to a prostitute who had a heart of fool's gold. A checker board of nights and days followed. Rejections by Cassie were followed by a lust for the flesh pots of San Francisco.

The holidays were approaching when I noticed an item in the entertainment section. "Return Of Witty Lowell High Alumna." Carol Channing was coming to town. Cassie would enjoy her antics. That evening I called her and found her phone had been disconnected. In a fury I raced to Howard's Bakery.

"Oh, she quit last week. She asked me not to give you her new address or phone number." I detected a slight smirk on Howard's face.

"Aw, come on, Howard. Be a good guy. What's her phone number?" I pleaded for the information. My arguments were in vain.

"Give her up, Sean. Women are a dime a dozen."

"But I love her. At least I think I do."

"Come into the back room. Let's have a drink. I have something to show you." We went into his living quarters.

"For a bachelor, you're doing pretty good," I commented.

"It's home. Is Vodka okay? It's all I have."

"At this stage of the game, who cares?" After several drinks, our speech became blurred.

"Want to see something interesting?" he finally asked.

"Sure." I had no idea what to expect. He laid some photos on the coffee table. I picked up the first one. My eyes slowly focused.

"My God! That's Cassie!" I sat stupefied.

"See what I mean? Find someone else, Sean."

I glanced at two or three more pictures. "These are all of Cassie in the nude!" I screeched. Pictures of Cassie with a naked Howard, and of a naked Howard with Cassie in a variety of playboy poses were placed before me one by one.

"Jesus! You son of a bitch, how could you?" I yelled. I huffed and I puffed but the photographs would not go away. Howard would not go away. I ran out the front door, wailing my pain in a world exploding before me.

"Why, Cassie? Why, for God's sake?" I implored the heavens above. Stalking her became a lifestyle. Sleepless nights were followed by days of "And then the gun went off," or the one to which I could personally relate, "I found her in bed with another man." I don't know who suffered the most—the inmates for their crimes of passion or me for considering deeds of revenge.

On a Saturday evening, I walked into the Vesuvio. Cassie was at the bar talking to Bruce. I forced a smile.

"Hi, Sean. How are you?" she said. Our conversation was cordial considering the circumstances.

"I've got two tickets to the Carol Channing show at the Curran. I think you'd enjoy it. What do you think?"

Her eyes darted to Bruce the bartender. I teetered on the precipice of a long pause. She looked back at me. "I don't think so, Sean. I have to work."

Now don't get mad, I said to myself. I shrugged. "Maybe some other time."

"Sure, Sean. Here, let me give you my new address and phone number."

"Howard said you had moved."

"Oh, you've been talking to Howard?" I saw not a flicker of remorse in her face. No explanation for her promiscuity was forthcoming.

"Yes," I said. I couldn't talk about the pictures. What could she say?

"I've been seeing the psychiatrist at the UC Medical Center," she offered.

"Good for you. What did he say?" I was pleased Cassie had been going to the doctor. That must mean she at least recognized that she had a problem.

"I took some psychological exams and scored high."

"Do you remember the names of the tests?" I asked. Always the counselor.

"No, but he said I have a high IQ. And that I have the body of a woman with the emotions of a child."

The tone of our conversation actually became pleasant. People were coming into the bar. I finished my drink and went home. I was never to forget the pictures.

I spent my weekends at Fisherman's Wharf listening to the old timers talk about the good old days when you could scoop up sardines by the buckets full. Fishing boats were powered by wind and muscle. The sardines disappeared in the 1940's but no one knows why.

After a particularly lonesome Sunday, I phoned my mother. "Ma, how are you?

"I'm fine, Sean. How about you? Have you seen Cassie?"

"Yeah, I have. I don't think she is coming back."

"Well, things will work out one way or another," she said soothingly.

"I don't suppose you would like to visit me?" I asked.

Ma laughed. "Are you tired of your own cooking already?"

"You'd like San Francisco. It's a beautiful town."

"Yes, it is. I was there during the war, remember? I'll think about it, Sean." She didn't want to reject me.

"Let me know soon." I didn't want to sound anxious.

"Okay, I will."

VARIOUS HEADLINES FOR OCTOBER AND NOVEMBER 1959 read: "Kennedy Here-Almost Running," "Brown Reprieves Rap Slayer-Mental Defective," "Prize Novel Analyzes Life Inside Prison," "Another Hit Group Is incubated At The Hungry I."

A few days later, Mr. Mallachey and Jack Barr came into my office.

"Where's Ramirez?" I asked. "I haven't seen him all morning."

After they had both seated themselves, Mr. Mallachey answered. "He won't be in for a few days. He got into an altercation with Clancy yesterday afternoon. He broke Clancy's nose. We don't know why. He's in isolation. Clancy is in the hospital."

"Probably a cigarette debt," Barr added.

"I didn't hear anything about it," I said.

"Well, now you know." Mr. Malachey lit his meerschaum as he sat at my desk.

"I know this a dumb question but what's it like being in prison?" I asked. Mr. Mallachey and Barr smiled at each other.

269

"Entering prison for the first time can be a frightening experience. It's the noise level that first strikes you," Mallachey said.

"Yeah, I know. I remember my little walk across the yard," I said.

"When you enter the joint you have entered a world all of its own. Each prison consists of administration, guards and security. I sometimes believe it's the inmates that run this joint, not the free personnel," Barr added.

"Rules in prison either antagonize or placate the inmates. Their main purpose is to control. Some of the CO's are real professional; others are the worst type of dirt poor and barely literate who exist in no man's land between welfare and prison themselves," Mr. Mallachey said. He could easily be taken for a Mr. Chips with his blue blazer and Weinstock slacks.

"Inmates deal in contraband and are capable of committing murder. They thrive on obtaining authority. Many are racist, homosexual, scheming and manipulative," Barr said.

"Sounds like they're negative people with psychological problems," I commented.

"The hard part is having contact with some prison administrators and CO's who have a preconceived set of notions concerning all prisoners." Mallachey drew on his pipe. Smoke rings floated to the ceiling.

"There are three classes of people in prison. First, those who are at home in prison. They have been conditioned from an early age. They are institutionalized and would rather be in prison than out. For the second class prison is a homeless shelter. A place where they are clothed, fed and told what to do." Barr paused in his analysis.

Mallachey jumped in. "These people aren't criminals in the real sense. They are usually unskilled, homeless and destitute and are forced by economics and social conditions to take the easy way out."

"What about the third kind?" I asked.

Barr explained. "For them crime is their vocation and they take prison in stride. A jolt in the joint is just an occupational hazard. On their release they intend to go back to gang banging, robbing, peddling dope, whatever is their crime of choice. Their time inside prison is an extension of their criminal lives on the outside."

"By the way, Sean. Ramirez spends much of his time with you," Mallachey interjected.

"He's a great story teller," I said. Still the alarms failed to ring.

"Yeah," Barr murmured.

Mr. Mallachey stood in the doorway. "How would you like to spend a few days in a work camp up in Mendocino County? It's a nice change from this place."

"Sure. Sounds great," I said. Administration wanted me out of San Quentin for a few days.

"I'll let you know the details." Mallachey left.

A few days later I met my mother at the Greyhound Bus Depot in San Francisco. "Hi, Sean. How are you?" she said.

"Hi, Ma. I'm fine. It's good to see you." We piled in the car and I took the scenic route back to my apartment. Down Market street to the Embarcadero. North to Bay. West to the Marina.

"Oh, what a nice little apartment. It's different," Ma said. She walked down the ramp surveying the flat.

"At one time it was a family theater. It's been converted into an apartment. I kinda like the place. It's near the bay and Fisherman's Wharf." Ma settled in and we caught up with the family gossip.

"I have to go to a camp near Wilits for a few days starting next Monday. Some prisoners are due for a parole hearing. Progress reports have to be prepared. You can fend for yourself?"

She smiled indulgently at me. "I think so. I've been doing it for many years."

"There is a Safeway nearby and we can stock up on groceries before I leave. The Marina is only a few blocks away. It's real nice to sit and watch the ships come in and out. Sail boats race on Saturdays and Sundays."

"Don't worry, Sean. I like to walk. I'll enjoy the bay."

Early Monday morning I began the four hour drive to the prison camp. Soon after my arrival I was shown to my quarters. The day passed quickly. My clients were up for parole. I fielded the usual "Do you think I'll make it this time?"

During the pre-dinner bull session with off duty personnel, an inmate walked into the hall. "Hi, Cookie. What do you need?" a CO asked.

"Good evening, Mr. Harris. We need some mace."

The Co started for a locked cabinet behind his desk. "How many?"

"Five."

"You know three is the limit."

"Sorry. You can't blame me for trying." He grinned.

"You'll just have to get by with two." A look of scorn rippled across the CO's face. The inmate smiled again and left.

"What's all this?" I asked. "Mace is nothing but a spice, isn't it?"

"True. But the inmates boil it into a concoction that gives them a high. So do inhalers," one of the CO's explained.

"I didn't know," I said. I returned home several days later. Working at the camp had been a nice change of pace.

Ma had learned the basics of the city bus system during my absence. She took number thirty one downtown and found a job at the Cliff Hotel on Geary Street. "I like to keep busy, Sean. And I can use the money," she explained.

"But it doesn't look good for my mother to be a chambermaid," I pleaded.

"It's honest work and the Cliff is a first-class hotel," she retorted. I could tell the conversation was over. To my relief, she seldom spoke of Cassie.

I began to ease off on my drinking sprees and nocturnal visits to the flesh pots of San Francisco. I became almost a homebody.

Early in November an article in the paper announced a forthcoming exhibit of Van Gogh at the De Young Museum. I thought of Cassie. "Hey, Ma. I bet Cassie would be interested in this."

"What's that, Sean?"

"A Van Gogh exhibit is coming to the De Young Museum next week."

"Why don't you call her?"

I had a tight grip on my emotions as I dialed her number. She answered right away. I jumped right in with, "Would you like to go to the Van Gogh exhibit with me next week?"

"No, I'm busy." My attempts at an "I don't care" tone failed.

"I'm going out, Ma," I called out as I fled the scene. I made another midweek foray into the Tenderloin District, staggering home in the wee hours of the morning. A series of nightmares brought out the demons who were beginning to take over my mind.

Occasionally Ma would ask, "Are you okay, Sean?"

"Yeah, I'm okay." I made feeble attempts to reassure her from time to time but she remained suspicious. Ma was my friend but not my confidante.

Ramirez continued to hold me under his Svengali influence. I thought him a fascinating story teller. I started to isolate myself from my co-workers. I had morning coffee and brown bag lunches, as well as afternoon breaks, all in my office, where I sat at the feet of my mentor.

One dreary Friday afternoon, I finished my reports early and contemplated another weekend without Cassie. Ramirez walked into the office. "Well, Mr. Sullivan—another day, another dollar."

"Yeah." I watched a Cal twenty-six footer breezing by with sails billowing in the wind. "Tell me something, Manual. How do I join the Mafia?"

"You can't. The real Mafia is Sicilian. In this joint we have the Mexican gang, the black gang and the white gang." He pulled a chair over to the window and sat down.

I wasn't having much success getting ahead in the world. Or so I thought. People, including friends and family, were not paying much attention to me.

"How did the Mafia begin? When and where did it all start?" I asked.

"It started in Sicily when Napoleon occupied Italy one-hundred and fifty years ago."

I nodded. "I read that in my history class," I said.

He went on. "A French soldier, stationed in a small town in Sicily, murdered and raped a local girl as she prayed in church. The news spread quickly through the town. Her mother rushed to the girl's side as she lay dying. Holding the daughter in her arms, she cried, "Ma Fia, Ma Fia.—My daughter, my daughter."

"Interesting," I said.

"Yes, but that's not all. The men in the village captured and killed the soldier. They formed an association which became known as the Black Hand to protect their families outside of the law. In effect, outlaws."

He continued. "One-hundred years later, immigrants from Sicily settled on the East Coast of America, usually in New York or New Jersey, and brought their association. Today it is called the Mafia or 'Casa Nostra,' meaning our family. Everything with them is family."

"How do I join?" I wanted desperately to be recognized but didn't know how in a socially acceptable manner.

Ramirez looked out the window and pondered the bay. "I'll talk to you tomorrow." He left my office.

That night I tried to slip away from Ma unnoticed. "Going out again, Sean?" she asked.

"Yes, just for a few minutes. I won't be long." I drove to the Vesuvio to confront Cassie for the last time. The patrons of the Vesuvio included the usual beatniks, dope peddlers and pimps. I feared for her.

"Sean, we're divorced. Can't you let it go?" She backed away from me.

Blind with fury and the need for revenge, I raged on. Four letter expletives exploded from my mouth, one after the other. Bruce the bartender grabbed me by the arm. "You'll have to leave," he said and firmly escorted me to the street. People stared at me as I fell into a gutter overflowing with recent rains. I crawled to the sidewalk. Grabbing on to a fire hydrant, I pulled myself upright and managed to walk to my car without further incident.

The following Monday, I waded through the never ending laments of, "I don't know why I was carrying a gun. I didn't mean to hurt anybody," and "my partner and I didn't plan to kill anyone. We just wanted the money. The manager wouldn't open the safe." At the end of the day, I confessed my adventures of the previous evening to Ramirez.

"She is the cause of all my problems," I muttered.

"Who?" he asked.

"My wife, or 'ex-wife,' I should say."

"Do you have a picture of her? We'll take care of it for you." It took a few seconds for his offer to penetrate my hate-filled thoughts. Then I realized I could have her murdered. A hit. A contract. A solution to my problems.

"I'm serious," he shot a knowing wink at me.

I thought, "I'm God! I determine who lives or dies." My body became an Atlas. No more slings and arrows. No more, "why don't you walk straight?" or "What's wrong with your legs?" or "I have a cousin with Infantile Paralysis."

"No, you idiot, not Cassie! Bruce the bartender. I love Cassie. I don't want anything to happen to her." I recoiled in horror. But the thought of putting a hit on Bruce appealed to me. I began to talk out of the side of my mouth a/k/a. James Cagney.

"Give us his picture," Ramirez said. As he got up to leave he handed me a stamped envelope addressed to his wife in Los Angeles. Quietly he said, "Would you mail this for me?"

"Sure." I didn't even feel the hook go into my short-lived career in penology. Ramirez had decoyed me into an untenable situation. He saw a great future in having a moral hostage. Thanks to indiscretions, my decent into hell had begun.

At noon, the next day, I unwrapped the inevitable tuna fish sandwich on rye. Ramirez came into my office. "Don't you ever eat?" I asked.

"Late lunch today." He settled down to enjoy his favorite view. I noticed his knuckles were bruised.

"What's the matter? You have a little disagreement with someone?"

"I had to make a Christian out of a new guy. Only way you get respect in this joint." I didn't ask for the details. He went on, "You gotta have respect otherwise you're either dead or on the shelf."

"What's the shelf?" I asked.

"The hole. Isolation. Here's a picture.." He laid a black and white photo before me.

"Looks depressing," I said.

"It is. Getting respect is how you do your time the easy way. Without it everybody and his grandmother would be on your back."

"Well, I'll remember that if ever I have to do time," I joked.

"When I got here four years ago the other cons told me to smash somebody. Anybody. Then I should act like I had changed. The secret is that everyone will fear you and respect you," he said.

"I guess survival is the name of the game," I said.

He pulled his chair closer, his brown eyes fixed on my face. "You have to make your bones. I've learned to never give in to the hacks. Never let them break your spirit. It's better to stand up for your beliefs than go out as a rat, a coward, or a snitch."

I left work that day, knowing I could not face another weekend sitting at Fisherman's Wharf feeding the pigeons. I phoned Cassie. "Hey, Cassie. This is Sean. How about coffee at Enrico's tonight?" I kept my fingers crossed.

She was so surprised she said yes before she could say no. At nine that evening, we met at Vesuvio and walked over to Enrico's sidewalk cafe. She looked cute in a blue blouse and checkered skirt. With her hair tied back in a pony tail, she looked like a cheerleader who could whip out pompoms at any minute to lead a hurrah for the home team.

"How have you been?" I asked. I put as much concern into my voice as I could.

"Fine, Sean. And you?" Her smile released all my frustrations of the last two months.

"Great. It's good to see you, Cassie." I said. We found a table near the sidewalk. The coffee au lait and croissants were great. The meeting was a disaster.

"Got a girl?" she asked.

"Nothing that's going anywhere. Got a guy?" I asked.

"Two at the moment," she answered. She volunteered nothing more concerning her love life. She studied the menu. "What do you recommend?"

"A divorce," I said.

"You've got to stop this, Sean. I'll file when I'm ready. Why don't you accept life the way it is rather than the way you want it to be?"

"Howard showed me the pictures. Stop sleeping with everybody in North Beach."

"Okay, that's it." She got up and walked off into the crowd. Clutching my coffee cup, I realized I had erased three years of marriage in less than one minute. A young man in a business suit approached me in the parking lot.

"May I bother you for a ride downtown, Sir?"

"Sure. Get in the car." My thoughts were all on Cassie.

"Can you drop by Mason and Taylor?" my passenger asked.

"Sure. My favorite spot." Maybe the strippers would take my mind away from the crisis of the moment. He wiggled closer to me, putting his hand inside my trousers. He squeezed the top of the rubberized urinal I wear. Jerking away from me, he grabbed for the door handle.

"My God, what's that?" he cried.

"A urinal. I was born with a birth defect. I have do not have control of my bowels or bladder," I explained as I pushed his hand away.

"Oh, you poor dear," he said. "Oh, let me out here." My friend disappeared into the Pink Stallion.

A few days later Ramirez and I spent another shakedown attempting to solve the crime problem. Gofers were excused from the security procedures if they remained in view.

"Prisoners need to take responsibility not only for themselves but for their environment. Especially on the outside," I declared.

Ramirez shifted in his chair. "Prisons won't be better places to live unless the free people make them that way. I know you like to be respected and you would like to respect others."

"You need to overcome the sanctity of the convict code and create a new one. The art of non-violence, according to Ghandi, is giving up self-righteousness, to be peaceful and relaxed," I went on.

"But everyone out there hates us. They think we're nothing but animals and monsters. We should make the public ashamed of prisons. We should stop fighting each other."

"Amen to the second part. I can't look at them with fondness, respect or compassion. People are relying on pills, drugs and alcohol to get by in life." I was on a roll.

"Over half the people in prison are there for non-violent crimes. We are in the grip of Nazism, this time towards the people who break the law."

"I don't understand what you mean by Nazism. I interviewed an inmate recently who expressed the same thought using the word Nazism. I live in the real world."

"No you don't," he shot back. "One hundred thousand men are raped in prison every year. Justice is punishment and pain."

"As far as I'm concerned, prison is the first response to all kinds of criminal behavior," I went on.

Jack Barr stuck his head in the door. "All clear you guys. We can go home now. Not you, Ramirez." Manual had the look of a wounded fawn. I have never seen such hurt on a man's face.

"I SEE IN THIS MORNING'S PAPER YOU HAD AN ESCAPE yesterday," Ma commented.

"Yeah. But we didn't have to stay overtime. No lock down." I replied.

"Are you going out tonight?"

"No." I knew Ma was suspicious of my wanderings into the various dens of Sodom and Gomorrah. She prepared fine meals every night while maintaining a well kept apartment at the same time. Home became a pleasant place to be, although Cassie was always on my mind.

Two weeks later Ma asked, "Did you know the convicts who escaped from the prison camp in Mendocino?"

"No. I was only there for three days."

"San Quentin made the front page today," she continued. "More coffee?"

"Yes, thanks."

"I made some peach cobbler."

"Oh, boy! Do we have any ice cream?"

She smiled at her little boy, "Yes." The gourmet delights and comforts of home were beginning to pacify me. Life became less stressful. I made fewer visits to the Purple Pussy Cat and the Buena Vista cafe.

The following Wednesday evening we finished a late dinner, thanks to another lockdown at the joint. I turned on "Victory at Sea," Channel Five. Ma and I had taken to sipping wine after dinner. She was not only my mother but my friend.

"How was your day Sean?" Ma asked. Never ask a counselor about his day if he is clutching, white knuckled, an alcoholic beverage.

"Oh, okay. I've been interviewing murderers all day long. Fascinating people."

"How can they be interesting if they have taken a human life? I think it disgusting," she said.

"I don't condone the crime. And they are first class story tellers. Of course they always pass out before the dastardly deed. The gun goes off by it self or a bloody knife is found in their hand."

"Sean, are you sure you want to stay in prison counseling? Have you thought of going back to teaching?" She was concerned about me.

"I need credits for a teaching certificate. Of course, I could get a temporary license while I take courses at the college."

She looked into my eyes. "That might be a good idea."

The next morning, Thursday, December 31, 1959, will forever remain foremost in the chronicles of my life.

"Where's Ramirez?" I asked Jack Barr as he passed by my office.

"I don't know. I haven't seen him."

Starting my day without the morning paper, Herb Caen's column, and a cup of coffee was unthinkable. One man's dank swamp is another man's teeming marsh. I was just starting to review the yellow jackets when Mr. Mallachey appeared.

"They want you down in administration. I'll escort you." He was not smiling.

"Yes, Sir."

We walked down to the conference room where parole hearings are held. Assembled in the room were Associate Warden Derek Nielson, Captain of the Guard, Vernon O'Reilly, the Warden's personal secretary, and two Marin County Deputy Sheriffs. Mr. Mallachey sat down and stared at the floor.

"Sit in that chair," Nielson ordered me. A chair was placed in the center of the room. Associate Warden Nielson studied some papers as he pointed his pencil at me. I considered it a threatening gesture.

"We have information that you have been smuggling mace and inhalers into San Quentin," he said.

18

"THE DARK NIGHT"

I REMAINED MUTE. THE FAMILY NAME WAS IN ruins. I would spend the rest of my days atoning for sins, real or imaginary.

The Associate Warden demanded, "Well Mr. Sullivan. Have you anything to say for yourself?"

"No." I clamped my jaw tight.

Nielson turned to Captain of the Guard O'Reilly and ordered, "Take this man into the next room and strip him. Now." O'Reilly had a tight grip on my elbow as he escorted me into a side office.

"Take off your clothes."

We had passed the time of day together whenever our paths crossed at San Quentin. O'Reilly was a pleasant fellow with a fixed smile. I complied by shucking my shirt and slacks. I stood in front of him in my shorts and socks.

"What's that thing?" He pointed to the rubber bag hanging down my leg.

"A urinal," I answered. I didn't offer any explanation. The Miranda warning did not exist at the time.

"Why?" he asked.

"I don't have control of my bladder." I ladled each word out as raw ore to an assayer.

He examined the four and a half feet of surgical scar tissue on my back, legs and feet. Eight surgeries and sixty-seven clinic visits to the Shriner's Hospital For Crippled Children during the 1930's had left more than scars. O'Reilly put his fingers inside my shorts.

"Why the wash cloth?"

"I don't have control of my bowels."

His faced flushed as he yanked his hand out of my underwear. "Get dressed," commanded. He left me alone with a deputy stationed at the door.

In the next room O'Reilly held the contraband high as he announced to all assembled my sins of recent days and nights. "I found these in his pants." He handed four packets of mace and three inhalers to Nielson. A smug-faced Associate Warden shot a side long glance at me.

Warden Dickey had quietly slipped into the room without saying a word. A wounded Mallachey continued to stare at the floor. Nielson stood up and proclaimed, "You are under arrest for the smuggling of contraband into San Quentin Prison." He turned to the Marin County deputies and ordered, "Take him to the county lock up."

A few days later, my attorney would inform me, "Mr. Neilson doesn't have the legal right to arrest you."

The warden walked out. Mr. Mallachey continued studying something unseen on the floor. Two deputies approached and stood on either side of me, each taking an arm and half walking, half carrying me to the patrol car. Once seated, I tried the door. It didn't have any handles. How could I escape from a police car inside a maximum prison. A cage within a cage. I don't recall the ride to the county slammer.

When we arrived at the jail, deputies started the booking process. Photographs were taken by a trustee, front view and side view. My fingerprints were smudged on the proper forms. I had taken my place in the Pantheon of crime beside the lessor gods of transgression.

Three hours later, Deputy Cunningham drove me back to the joint to retrieve my car. The thirty minute ride across the bridge filled me with conflicting thoughts. How could I possibly explain my actions of the last four months to my mother?

I opened the door to our flat and walked down the ramp.

"Are you hungry? I kept your dinner warm," Ma said. Her weathered face, lined with the woes of the world, silently asked the question, "why?" I sought salvation from Ma rather than God. Employing a stage voice, I began my apoligia.

"There are those in the human race who perceive, like hyenas, a presumed weakness in me. My soft spot may be real or imaginary to them. My seducer, Ramirez, seized the advantage and proceeded to mentally and morally dismantle me." I paused for effect. She didn't interrupt my soliloquy.

"Like a Jackal on the Serengeti Plains of Africa, he attacked my psyche, knowing I was unable to defend myself. My life long burden of physical disability coupled with a passive personality prevented me from being assertive. I was easily led down the garden path."

"Oh, Sean," she said. I choked back tears. She turned away.

I continued. "When I was young people were always doing things to me in the hospital and at home. I thought I had no control over these events. My attitude has always been they are going to stick it to me regardless of what I do. I got suckered, plain and simple."

The one light in the room flickered. Ma went into the kitchen and returned with a plate of corn beef and cabbage. "You'd better eat something," she said.

"I'm really not hungry." To please her I made a futile attempt to eat the meal but soon gagged. Uncontrollable weeping took over. Spasms of choking held me captive. Exhausted, I went to bed.

The next morning I asked, "Where is the morning newspaper?"

"I think the paper boy missed us again. I'll call him later." She had been advised by Tom Reade, our attorney, to hide the newspapers. There was some talk regarding suicidal tendencies but I had no intention of killing myself.

Thirty-one years later I read the news item about my arrest in both the <u>San Francisco Chronicle</u> and the <u>San Francisco Examiner</u>. The headline on page one of the <u>Chronicle</u> that day read, "Landlady Flees Thug. Plunges Out Window." On page three was, "Quentin Aide Held In Smuggling Case."

FIGHTS ON DEATH ROW FOLLOWED THE HOLIDAYS that year. The newspapers indicated the brawls were over a football game on television. I recognized many of the names in the paper. The battle over the tube did not concern a game. It was an undeclared war between the white and Mexican gangs.

I can't prove it, but a snitch by the name of Gus Mecouri was the object of Hispanic wrath. He was a "dead man," scheduled to be executed in April of 1960. A loner, he sought favor by naming people. Unfortunately, I was included on his list. Caryl Chessman was among the participants in the melee. He was executed four months later.

The following Monday, I appeared before Judge Joseph Bertaloni in Marin County Superior Court No. 1 for arraignment. I seldom used Lofstron crutches but this was an opportune time. The Canadian style devices gave me balance and stability.

My attorneys, Tom Reade and Fred Gaines, held both my arms at the elbow to stage the proper effect for the court. Tom said, "We waive reading of the charges, Your Honor."

Judge Bertaloni peered through his pince nez. "Mr. Sullivan, You are charged with four counts of smuggling contraband into San Quentin. Do you understand the indictment?"

"Yes, Your Honor, I do."

"How do you plead?" he asked.

Tom pinched me. I almost shouted, "Not Guilty!"

Judge Bertaloni smiled. I am sure he has seen plenty of nervous defendants in his career, but I became a whirling dervish that Monday morning. With palms sweating, knees shaking, and heart pumping, my adrenaline flowed through the spillways of my heart. I didn't know whether to feel silly, serious, or suicidal.

"Your next court appearance is set for Tuesday, January 12 at nine a.m. I will hear motions at that time." The judge started rise and leave the bench.

Tom Reade said, "Thank you, Your Honor. Mr. Sullivan has posted bail."

"Wait a minute!" Richard Hardesty, assistant district attorney, jumped up. His face flushed as he aimed his pen at me.

"Hope he doesn't shoot," I muttered.

"Shhh," Tom Reade said.

"This defendant knows better than to smuggle contraband into a prison. He received orientation and a copy of the rules. God only knows what other activities he might be involved in. I ask that bail be revoked." Mr. Hardesty sat down.

"Six points," I joked.

"Shut up," Fred Gaines advised.

"Objection, Your Honor." My attorneys leaped up at the same time. "Mr. Hardesty's personal asides are not germane to the issue," Tom said. He paused and placed his hand on my shoulder.

Reade spoke up. "This is a first offense You Honor. Mr. Sullivan has an impeccable history as a schoolteacher and counselor. He's not an escape risk. How far can he go on crutches?" I staged a cough, wheeze and gasp for air all at the same time.

"I agree. Bail is continued. Court is adjourned for fifteen minutes." Deputy D.A. Hardesty threw his pencil across the room. As he left court a pout creased his features and completely obliterated any sign of his normally affable Irish personality.

After dinner Ma asked, "How did it go this morning?"

"Oh. I pled 'not guilty' of course." I turned my face to the wall. I tried to keep panic at bay by struggling for air.

"Oh, Sean." Ma opened her arms to hug me.

I held up my hand to stop her. "I'm sorry. I can't stop." I gulped for more air. Uncontrollable fits of crying overcame me every night for a week. They always occurred at the same time. Ma tried to comfort me without touching me.

"Tom Reade is a good lawyer. Things will work out," she said reassuringly.

The following Saturday Fran and George Champion came over to visit. George and I had been friends since we went to the same high school in Portland. An attempt to concentrate on a game of pinochle proved futile. "Sorry folks, I usually don't make mistakes. What was trump?" I asked.

"Hearts. You're a good pinochle player, Sean. But not as good as me, of course." Fran smiled. They both tried to keep the conversation light. I hope I didn't embarrass them.

"Have you ever seen an execution, Sean?" George asked. I noticed Fran gently kicking his leg. We sometimes referred to her as 'Hurricane Fran.'

"No," I replied. "But Mr. Mallachey described one in graphic detail when I first started to work at the joint. The doctors claim the condemned is unconscious in thirty seconds. Their lips turn blue. Spittle drips out of their mouth. They tug at the straps. Their eyes bulge."

I turned to Fran and added, "One guy supposedly yelled, 'Warden, it smells like rotten eggs,' then he collapsed."

Ma interrupted, "I've made some cherry cobbler." She bustled into the kitchen with Fran in tow.

I looked at George. "I just happen to have a copy of the execution procedures for the gas chamber." I got up and found the folder, leafing through it for the procedures. "I brought this home from the joint." It read:

Execution Procedures for Gas Chamber

1. *Inmate received from County. Automatic appeal to the California Supreme Court started.*
2. *Social, psychological and psychiatric study completed 90 days after reception.*

3. Judgment affirmed or reversed by California supreme Court within one year or more.

4. Execution date is set by committing court if sentence is affirmed, 60 to 90 days before execution order is signed.

5. Procedures followed before execution: a) Three psychiatrists appointed 90 days before execution date; b) Psychiatric report, custodial, warden and religious evaluations submitted 30 days before execution; c) Psychiatric report submitted 7 days before execution; d) One day before execution inmate has last visit with family in the morning. Inmate is moved to holding cell around 5 p.m. Inmate requests last meal and is served about 6. p.m. Warden, Chaplain of choice, or officials may visit during the evening. Women are brought up from the California Institution for Women, Corona, and are housed in the holding cell on this day, under supervision of women matrons.

6. Execution day: 7:00 a.m. - Breakfast is served; 8:00 a.m. - Chamber is readied, Chaplain and medical officer arrive; 9:35 a.m. - Cyanide pellets are fastened in place; 9:45 a.m. - Warden and staff arrive; 10:00 a.m. - Warden signals, inmate is placed in chair, chamber is sealed, well under chair is filled with sulfuric acid, cyanide is lowered into acid; 10:06-10:14 a.m. - Doctors pronounce inmate dead; 10:15 a.m. - Witnesses leave the execution chamber, Warden leaves, acid and gas are neutralized and removed from chamber, Warden notifies Sacramento; 11:00 a.m. - Remains are removed to a local mortuary or to mortuary of family's choice.

There is no state executioner. A five man team, under a supervising officer, operate the chamber, transport the condemned, and carry out the overnight watch.

"I'll read this later tonight," George said. "Have they ever executed a woman?"

"Yes. Three since 1941 and one is awaiting execution now."

Fran and Ma returned from the kitchen. When we had finished our cherry cobbler the Champions bid us goodbye.

"They're good friends," Ma said.

"Yes, and about the only ones I have left. Everybody is abandoning the sinking ship, including members of my own family."

"Now, Sean, not everybody. This will show you who your true friends are." She made many attempts to console me during the long dark nights. My spirits climbed out of the hole little by little, day by day. I sought the absolution of my friends by retelling the San Quentin story.

For the next eleven months, I would repeat different versions of my story hoping confession would cleanse my soul. It didn't. Ma suggested

I talk to a minister. I agreed, but it was more to please her than to salvage my soul.

Standing in front of a large glass encased bulletin board the next morning I read:

"St. Marks Episcopalian Church—Sunday, March 13, 1960
Sermon "Repent Ye—Confess to God" Find out how the wicked may save their souls. Those who confess and forsake their sins shall have mercy. Ask and it shall be given to you.
The Right Reverend Arthur Cummings Howell, Pastor.
Come Worship, learn, serve, and grow with a dynamic Christian community. Holy Eucharist Sundays at 8 a.m. and 10 a.m. (with child care)"

I was met in the foyer of the rectory by a young minister in the process of attempting, unsuccessfully, to grow a beard. A large gold cross announced his faith. I felt reassured.

"Good morning, Sir." We shook hands. I didn't know if I should call him "Father," "Right Reverend," "Minister Howell," or what. I played it safe and stayed with Sir.

His office was appointed with a well stocked library, religious statues, paintings and other symbols of the calling. I had a gut feeling something was staring at me. I turned. On the opposite wall a painting glowed and in my mind I heard the clanking of an iron gate opening. It was Raphael's "Deliverance Of St. Peter." Shades of Vacaville. I stood captured by the splendor of the Angel.

The Right Reverend Howell looked to the heavens. "Beautiful. Don't you think?"

"Yes. I've seen it somewhere. I can't remember where," I said. I offered a silent prayer for the convict artist at the California Medical Facility in Vacaville. "God Bless you, Charlie, wherever you are." The pungent fragrance of unseen incense permeated my senses.

"Your mother tells me you have a problem. Perhaps I or my boss can help." He giggled.

I began a well rehearsed rendition of my sins, Rendition No. Five. As I talked, the minister stared as though I were an aberration materializing from the inferno. He managed to mumble a few controlled, "Oh My's." My monologue was interrupted more than once by, "I have never heard of such a thing."

My story concluded, he responded, "Shall we pray?" He fell to his knees clutching his iron cross. I joined him on the floor, knocking an ash tray off his desk in the process.

"Lead us not into temptation…" The entire prayer washed over me. "There now, don't you feel better?" he asked cheerfully. He helped me to my feet.

Choking back another crying session, I said, "Forgive me, Father, for I have sinned."

"I am not a Catholic priest." He articulated each word syllable by syllable through grinding teeth.

"I'm sorry, Sir. I graduated from the University of Portland. It's a Catholic college."

The now red-faced minister managed to spit out the question, "Are you Catholic.?"

"Oh no. But many of my friends went the University," I explained.

The Right Reverend Howell waved me out of his inner sanctum. "Join us for worship sometime," he said. Then he turned his back and walked out of the room. Thus ended another attempt at absolution.

A week later I noticed an ad in the newspaper. "Be your own Boss. Work in your spare time. Earn Extra money."

"Ma, I can earn some money delivering the morning newspaper. The San Francisco Chronicle is looking for carriers," I said.

"Do you think you can handle it, Sean?" she asked. "You'd have to get up early every morning."

"Well, I can't live off you until this thing is over. It's driving me nuts. I can give it try at least."

"Okay. If you think you can do the job." I hesitated. She asked, "What's wrong?"

"I need fifty dollars as a bond or deposit."

"We can manage that if you think it's worth the money. I got a big tip from the Swansons today." She was so diplomatic. It was always "we," never "I." The Swansons, of TV dinner fame, always requested my mother as their personal chambermaid whenever they stayed at the Cliff.

"Sorry," I muttered.

A few days later, the newspaper assigned me a morning route in the Pacific Heights area on Broadway. It included expensive town houses and high rent apartments. Every morning at four a.m. I got up and delivered the newspaper. My supervisor, an immigrant from Poland whose command of the English language left much to be desired, had the personality of a gorilla with a heart of gold.

"Get the paper out on time. Don't be late. Stay sober," he barked, crunching an unlit cigar between yellow stained teeth.

"Yes, Sir," I replied.

Two months later, I knocked on the door at Apartment 402 to collect for the paper. A loud argument could be heard through the walls. I waited. No response. I walked down the hall to Apartment 406.

"Good evening, Mrs. Schmidt. Collecting for the paper." I imitated a smile.

"Just a moment."

Just then the door to Apartment 402 banged opened. A short, unshaven man in a dirty t-shirt charged up to me and bellowed, "You've been seeing my wife, you son of a bitch!" I looked down the barrel of the largest handgun in San Francisco. Blue steel, glittering beneath the hall light, pointed first at the ceiling, then at the floor, and, finally, at me. The man, obviously drunk, began to wave his cannon back and forth.

"The bastard is going to shoot me!" I cried out.

At that moment Mrs. Schmidt reappeared, money in hand. In a blink of an eye, she saw the gun. "Oh God!" she cried as she slammed the door in my face. I flattened myself against the wall to escape the oncoming projectile.

"Hail Mary full of grace..." It was the only prayer I could remember from my Catholic education that would rescue me in the final moment. The door to Apartment 402 slowly opened. A lady in hair curlers, tied with ribbons of tissue paper, squinted at through tortoise shell glasses.

"That's the paper boy, you idiot!" she yelled. Stepping into the hallway, dressed in a torn nightgown, she grabbed my assailant's arm and dragged him back to their love nest. A few seconds later, the 406 lady popped out of the doorway again.

"Sorry." She handed me the money and padded back inside her digs.

Blood slowly began to recirculate throughout my body. I gave up trying to collect newspaper money that night. Ma stood in front of our apartment on my return home.

"The police called. Cassie's in emergency at the hospital. They said to phone the Mission District station. She tried to kill herself again."

"What else did they say?" I asked.

"They wanted to know if you were related to her. Apparently she said you were her husband. I told them she divorced you last October."

I didn't pursue the conversation. I was concerned about Cassie's latest suicide attempt, but embarrassed to talk about it with Ma. Instead, I changed the subject and told Ma the story of the blue nose gun.

"You? Her lover? Was the man is insane?" she said. I couldn't tell if this was a compliment or not.

The next morning I phoned Tom Reade to relate the latest adventures of a thirty-three year old newspaper boy. "I want to sue the so-and-so. He held a gun on me," I said.

Tom asked, "Did you call the police?"

"No. I didn't know what to do. I wanted to talk to you first."

"Good idea. Considering your present circumstances, I don't think you should file an action." We talked a few minutes before I agreed to follow his advice.

A few days later, I persuaded Ma to join me in a court appearances. We had just seated ourselves in the front row when a rhythmic clanking noise was heard behind us. Three desperadoes, all wanted for murder and mayhem, stumbled into the courtroom with chains around their waists and between their ankles. Escorted by four officers, they shuffled to the front row. Heads turned, stage whispers muttered, "What's that?" and "What's happening?"

I cast a glance at Ma. Her moist eyes sought God's mercy. I had led my mother into the arena of ultimate disgrace.

Tom Reade soon joined us. "Sean Sullivan. Case No. 542768. Four counts of smuggling contraband." The town crier, in the guise of a court clerk, announced my circumstance in loud clear tones to one and all.

The usual motions to dismiss were denied. Motions to postpone the pretrial hearing were granted. My next appearance was set.

Ma and I returned to San Francisco in silence. After the dinner dishes were cleared, we sat down in the living room. Ma turned and looked at me earnestly.

"Reverend Howell phoned this afternoon. He mentioned a doctor friend who has an office on Chestnut Street in the Marina. It's a few blocks from here," she said.

"Oh? What kind of doctor?" I started to play word games. I knew "doctor" meant "psychiatrist."

"Sean, you need help. Please! For me."

I could feel another crying fit coming on. I managed to hold back the rising tide of tears. I eventually called the psychiatrist, Dr. Licon, for an appointment—the first step in solving a problem.

"Hello, Dr. Licon? My name is Sean Sullivan. I was referred to you by The Right Reverend Howell of the Episcopalian Church on Union Street." So I began a six-month voyage through a world I had never known. The subconscious mind.

A few days later the doctor said "Please, be comfortable." Leonard Licon spoke in melodious tones soothing to my troubled mind. We agreed on a time for my weekly appointments, Thursdays at ten a.m.

"Would you mind if I recorded our sessions for my class at the University? I'll reduce my usual fee by half.

"I have no objection. Berkeley?" I asked.

"No, the University of California Medical Center. On Parnassus."

"I worked there as a night admissions clerk when I was going to grad school."

We chatted for a minute or two then got down to business. The balding man in his early forties sitting before me beamed confidence. He could be your next door Mr. Milquetoast.

"Should I lie down on the couch or may I sit in the chair?" I asked.

"Whatever will be more comfortable for you." Dr. Licon smiled. I sat in the recliner. Damned if I was going to look at the ceiling. I had endured too many trips on my back on the way to surgery at the Shriner's Hospital. Sometimes I felt like a two dollar whore on a fast Saturday night.

"I was a counselor at San Quentin. I've never been in therapy."

"You must let yourself go. Tell any story from cabbages to kings and back again."

"I understand," I said.

"Tell me anything passing through your mind, even if you think it's unimportant or nonsensical. Don't be embarrassed."

"Just being here embarrasses me. I never thought I would need therapy."

"You must free the pure metal of your repressed thoughts from the ore of unintentional ideas," he intoned. Every Thursday for the next six months, at precisely the stroke of ten a.m., we chipped away at my most innermost thoughts. Except on my sexual experiences, of course.

From time to time I conveniently forgot to keep appointments. "That is your subconscious throwing up defenses. A sort of call to arms against the unknown," the good doctor explained. After one grueling session in which I continued to demean myself, he questioned, "Do you want to keep punishing yourself for no reason?"

"If I wanted to torture myself I would look in a mirror," I answered. The sessions were boring although I did enjoy the verbal bowel movements. I started with day one and worked my way up to December 31, 1958. The day of the arrest.

Abruptly he said, "Tell me something about your father."

"He thinks I'm a biological mishap, that God punished him because I was born with a birth defect," I said. Dr. Licon continued his relentless probe with questions as answers to my questions. He soon struck a nerve.

"Tell me more about your father."

I exploded. I wanted to hit something, anything, anybody. I struggled to stay in my chair. Years of repression were released. Foul words spewed from my mouth like molten lava flowing from a volcano. I couldn't believe what I was saying. So called "talk therapy" is much maligned today, but I flushed out a mountain of hate, revenge and hysteria that morning.

I stuttered my favorite theme. "When I was young my father held a gun on my mother and me. My brother came in at the last second and knocked the pistol out of his hand."

I went on for another thirty minutes, pumping out years of accumulated mind garbage. Before his death in June of 1971, I would be able to finally accept my father and forgive him for not being what I wanted him to be.

"What's you opinion of therapy now, Sean?" Dr. Licon asked one morning.

"Well, I have a much better view of the moon now that you have burned my house down." A month later I walked away from my last session with Dr. Licon. I skipped down the stairs to Chestnut Street howling like the demons from hell.

"How did it go, Sean?" Ma asked when I returned home.

"You would never believe."

Two or three days a week, I spent my afternoons at San Francisco City Hall. I became a great people watcher. Sitting on a marble bench near the entrance one afternoon, I heard over the din of voices, "He's coming, he's coming. Make way."

"Bonjour monsieur le'president. Como tali vou?"

Charles DeGaul, accompanied by Mayor Christopher and entourage, walked into City Hall. I was immediately surrounded by the French colony of San Francisco. DeGaul looked straight at me as he headed in my direction.

"My God!" I thought. "He's going to shake my hand." I straightened up as best I could. At the last minute one of his countrymen elbowed me aside, grabbing DeGaule by the shoulders. Four security people made their presence known as they escorted the man off to one side.

I SAW CASSIE FROM TIME TO TIME. WE ATTEMPTED TO be nice to each other. I tried to hold my temper. Our conversations were light and airy.

"How are you?" I would ask.

"I'm fine. What's new?" she would invariably respond.

"Nothing much. If they convict me will you visit?" I ventured.

"No."

One day she invited me to her apartment. We viewed the usual pictures of "Bruce and I at Fishermen's Wharf, Bruce and I at the beach, etc., etc." After a few minutes Cassie became agitated. She was uncomfortable. "You'd better scoot," she finally said. "Bruce is picking me up for work."

The next day, May 3, 1960, my eye caught the headline, "Chessman Executed"

In July of 1960, Bertalucci ruled mace was not a drug and dropped all charges against me. I floated out of the courtroom in a state of bliss. As I turned into Steiner Street, Ma stood on the curb frantically waving at me. She rushed over and shoved a twenty dollar bill in my hand as I started to get out of the car.

"Here, take this and get lost. They're looking for you."

"Who?" I demanded.

"Tom Reade phoned. The D.A. resigned this morning and Haggerty has taken his place. He's going to have you arrested and re-indicted on the same charges. Go!" I got back in the car.

"No! Take the bus. They have your license number." Ma pointed to the No. 31 bus stop.

"Good idea!" I yelled.

A few minutes later, I jumped off the bus at Market Street and headed for the nearest movie house. Hunkering down in the darkest part of the house, I tried my best to become invisible. Three movies later, I rubbed my eyes as I walked into the daylight. I still can't remember the names of the films I saw that afternoon.

I donned the mask of a true San Franciscan. I didn't have a care in the world. I attempted whistling through a bone dry mouth. I sang a falsetto "Mother McCree" to anybody on Market Street. People stared, but then they usually do.

Eleven p.m. No. 31 was about to make its last run to the Marina. I phoned Ma.

"It's okay. I talked to Tom. They've re-indicted you on the same charges but you're free on the same bail. Come home."

The next day I talked to Cassie. "Why are they doing this to me? I feel like Jean Valjean in "Les Miserable.""

That night I came home from my paper collections and threw the receipt book down on the table. I announced, "I'm not making any money on this paper route. I think I'll quit." Pacing the room, I continued. "Hagerty has it in for me. He's out to get me no matter what. I'll never get back into the counseling or teaching business."

Ma spoke up. "Maybe you should think of something else."

"Like what?" I challenged.

"Remember your talk with Lloyd Astin the other day about rehabilitation?"

"Yeah. He suggested I apply to the state vocational rehabilitation office for assistance."

"Well?"

"Never!" I cried, startling Ma with my vehemence. "I worked with those people. I would be too embarrassed."

"Well, it's something to consider." She walked back into the kitchen.

My depression continued the next few days. I experienced a loss of appetite, feelings of worthlessness, isolation, uncontrollable crying, and lack of concentration. I exhibited all the classic signs of temporary insanity.

I told the boss I was quitting the paper route. He burst into a volley of expletives. I decided to take Ma's suggestion and apply for vocational rehabilitation. My former colleagues were obviously uncomfortable, but I thought I presented the perfect challenge.

The State of California placed me in an accounting program. I protested, citing my low grades in math. My yammerings fell on deaf ears. The next afternoon, the telephone rang as I returned from my first class.

A female voice I could not identify whispered, "Cassie is taking classes at San Francisco City College." Then the line went dead. After dinner I put into action "Plan C."

"Ma I don't think vocational rehabilitation will work for me. I am really not an accountant," I said.

"Why did they put you in that program?" she asked.

"They just insisted." I squirmed in my seat. "I think I might do well at court reporting. They have some good classes at City College."

"That's an idea, Sean."

"Remember, I started taking lessons in short hand at Father Delauney's suggestion when I was a student at the University of Portland?"

"Yes, I remember. How much would City College charge?"

"Well, I just happen to have their fee schedule. You can see the tuition is low."

My shameful ploy worked. I enrolled two weeks later in a shorthand course at San Francisco City College, in order to stalk Cassie. A day or two later, she spotted me getting into my car.

"What are you doing here?" she shouted.

"Taking a class in courtroom reporting. It's looking like I may not be able to get back into teaching or counseling."

"Let's talk," she said. We adjourned to the student union. Cassie bought a coke from the machine. I had coffee.

"I saw my doctor yesterday," she began. Her eyes followed an imaginary bug on the table.

"What did he say?" I gently probed.

"He said I have suicidal tendencies."

"He said that last year. Why?"

"Why what?"

"Why do you want to kill yourself?"

"I don't know." She suddenly sat straight up, a crazed stare on face. Her wild eyes took on a haunted look as she looked at me.

"You stay away from me. I'm going to see my lawyer." She got up, saucer eyed, and ran crying into the ladies room.

"I'm not following you. I'm taking a class here. What's wrong with you?" I called after her.

She returned a few minutes later. The verbal exchange continued with charges and counter charges until a horn honked. It was Bruce the bartender parked at the curb. Experience told me retreat was the better part of something, so I got into my car and drove home.

During the summer of 1960 Cassie was less able to work or to concentrate in any meaningful way. I made an appointment to see her doctor at UC Med Center.

"Some day she will end her life out of frustration and desperation. Who knows? I may try ECI but it's new." He continued to explain the medical options.

In the summer of 1960 I dropped out of my class at City College and enrolled at San Francisco State College. I took classes in psychology and sociology. My long suffering mother paid the tuition fees.

Half way through the summer term, Cassie attempted suicide once again. She always timed her attempts so someone would find her at the last second.

As for my legal problems, court appearance followed court appearance. A pre-trail hearing was held in November 1960. Two of the sweetest words I have ever heard were spoken by Judge Reading of Superior Court No. 2 on November 17, 1960: "Case dismissed."

In February of 1961, my mother and I moved to Portland. Ma had said, "I'm sorry, Sean, but there isn't any reason to stay in San Francisco. The Swansons sold their TV dinner business. And I'm not getting any younger."

"I understand. I'll try to get a job." I said.

"Portland is our home," Ma said, but she knew how much I loved San Francisco.

"This city means a lot to me. Someday I'll come back," I murmured.

We were driving over the Golden Gate Bridge on our way to Portland. To the city, the fog, the bay and Ma in particular, I eulogized the city where Cassie and I had been happy. "San Francisco is Saturday night at Bocce Ball listening to an aging Senior Melody sing a duet with a young opera singer; sipping Irish Coffee at the Yerba Buena cafe watching the tourists swing the Powell Street cable car around the turnstile; having your handwriting analyzed by Marie, the graphologist at Enrico's coffee house; snickering at Paddy O'Sullivan's attempts to best Jonathan Winters in an imaginary duel of duels; an enchanted evening with Cassie at The House That Jack Built with entertainment by Guissepi and Giovanna; watching the bartender at the First And Last Chance Saloon confusing the customers with his hidden PA system; having coffee and playing pinochle with George and Fran Champion; enchanted by Phyllis Diller and Tazzie Hamilton closing an evening of memories at the Purple Onion with everybody singing "Waltzing Matilda"; a night at the Hungry I listening to Ada Moore's soul rendering "Love For Sale"; and philosophical discussions about Jack Kerouac, the sweet prince of the Beat generation, and the meaning of life over a goat's eye in a pot luck dinner with the Jackson Street Irregulars. That's my San Francisco."

"Don't worry, Sean. You'll be back." Ma said.

"I can't live on memories," I replied. She started to put her hand on my back, but pulled back. A lifetime of undemonstrative conditioning was impossible to break.

Ma and I left the Golden Gate Bridge as Herb Caen's "Baghdad By The Bay" faded away like the tinkling of a camel's bell in the desert wind. No more. No more.

IN MAY OF 1961, CASSIE HAD CORRECTIVE HEART surgery. I wanted to be by her side. I sensed a reconciliation.

Good old Ma came through one more time, paying for my trip. I took the Greyhound bus in a feeble attempt to save money.

Benson Roe, MD, and his superb heart team performed the surgery at the University of California Medical Center where I had worked as a night admissions clerk. The evening before the surgery, Cassie's mother and I visited Cassie at the hospital. We left when loud speakers announced, "Visiting hours are now over."

"Goodbye, Mother. Goodbye, Sean" she said. Her voice had a tone of finality. She wanted to die in surgery.

The next day, after the surgery, I stayed with her a few hours. Her moans and groans filled the room. I suffered sympathy pains.

"Can't you do something," I begged the nurse. "She's in pain."

"Who are you?" she asked.

"I'm her husband, ex-husband," I added.

She squinted at me through horn rimmed glasses. "This is normal after a heart operation. Don't be alarmed." I was not pacified.

That was the last time I saw Cassie. The day before she died, I wrote her a poem.

April 15, 1964

Princeville, Oregon

Dear Cassie,

"Just a line to say I'm living,
That I'm not among the dead.
Tho' I'm getting more forgetful,
And mixed up in my head.
Sometimes I can't remember,
When I stand at the head of the stairs,
Was I going up for something,
Or did I just come from there.
And before the refrigerator,
My mind is so full of doubt,
Was I supposed to put the food away,
Or supposed to take it out.
And at times when it's dark,
With my nightcap on my head,
I don't know if I'm waking,
Or just getting into bed.
So if it's my turn to write you,
There's no need of getting sore,
I may think I've written,
And don't want to be a bore.
So remember that I love you,
And wish that you were here,
Now its nearly mail time,
So I must say goodbye, my dear.
As I stand beside the mailbox,
I can feel my face getting red,
Instead of mailing your letter,
I opened it instead."
Happy birthday, Cassie. I miss you.

Love, Sean

On April 16, 1964, her twenty-sixth birthday, Cassie stood before a mirror, exultant in her moment of self destruction. The glass projected an image of a deep unrippled pool matching the serenity of her thoughts. "What is beauty?" she asked her reflection.

The poet Tagore answered, "Beauty is truth's smile when you behold your own face in the perfect mirror."

Crying she begged, "Why can't they see I need help most of all?"

News item. Fairbanks Daily News-Miner, April 16, 1964

> A young typist apparently watched herself in the mirror today as she put a.38 caliber pistol to her head and pulled the trigger, according to her employer.
>
> Dead is Janet McKellar, about 26, who worked for Attorney Fred Crane of 126 Blanchfield Street in downtown Fairbanks.
>
> She apparently told some close friends, as she sat with them in a Fairbanks bar Wednesday night, that she was going to commit suicide Attorney Crane kept a few personal handguns and ammunition in a desk drawer in his office. Crane said he didn't think Miss McKellar knew where his guns were kept.
>
> According to Crane, Miss McKellar is a divorcee who has worked for him since December.

Cassie's trusting face will haunt me forever.

> *"Now my weary lips I close.*
> *Leave me, leave me to repose."*

Thomas Gray-The Bard, 1757.

"To write, is to sit in judgement of one's self." Ibsen.

298

ABOUT THE AUTHOR

Born in 1926, Robert McKellar underwent many surgeries to correct severe birth defects caused by spina bifida. Little was known about spina bifida in the twenties, and most children afflicted with it died. Despite the odds, McKellar not only survived, but also filled his life with meaning and adventure. He graduated from the University of Portland in 1949, then began a career in teaching that took him to Idaho, California, Hawaii, and Japan. When he wasn't teaching, he traveled the world, flew his plane, and wrote letters to his mother on which he based his memoir "An Accident of Birth." Published 1996.

www.ingramcontent.com/pod-product-compliance
Lightning Source LLC
Chambersburg PA
CBHW030250290526
45785CB00001B/39